The Critical Thinking Toolkit

The Critical Thinking Toolkit

Your Guide to Success in Learning, Thinking and Writing at University

Paula Beesley
Belinda Cooke
Laurence Morris
Louise Warwick-Booth

1 Oliver's Yard
55 City Road
London EC1Y 1SP

2455 Teller Road
Thousand Oaks
California 91320

Unit No 323-333, Third Floor, F-Block
International Trade Tower
Nehru Place, New Delhi 110 – 019

8 Marina View Suite 43-053
Asia Square Tower 1
Singapore 018960

© Paula Beesley, Belinda Cooke, Laurence Morris and Louise Warwick-Booth 2026

Apart from any fair dealing for the purposes of research, private study, or criticism or review, as permitted under the Copyright, Designs and Patents Act, 1988, this publication may not be reproduced, stored or transmitted in any form, or by any means, without the prior permission in writing of the publisher, or in the case of reprographic reproduction, in accordance with the terms of licences issued by the Copyright Licensing Agency. Enquiries concerning reproduction outside those terms should be sent to the publisher.

Editor: Kate Keers
Editorial assistant: Becky Oliver
Production editor: Sarah Sewell
Copyeditor: Neil Dowden
Proofreader: Bryan Campbell
Indexer: Judith Lavender
Marketing manager: Maria Omena
Cover design: Sheila Tong
Typeset by: C&M Digitals (P) Ltd, Chennai, India

Library of Congress Control Number: 2024953024

British Library Cataloguing in Publication data

A catalogue record for this book is available from the British Library

ISBN 978-1-5296-8319-6
ISBN 978-1-5296-8318-9 (pbk)

Contents

About the authors vii
Acknowledgements ix

Introduction 1

Part I Critical thinking for students 5

 1 What is critical thinking? 7

 2 Why critical thinking matters at university 21

 3 Becoming a critical thinker 33

Part II Critical thinking in lectures and seminars 51

 4 Critical thinking before lectures and seminars 55

 5 Critical thinking during lectures 73

 6 Critical thinking during seminars 85

 7 Critical thinking after lectures and seminars 99

Part III Critical thinking in assessed work **111**

 8 Critical thinking and assessments 113

 9 Critical thinking in essays and assignments 129

 10 Critical thinking in presentations 147

 11 Critical thinking in exams 163

 12 Critical thinking in practice learning and practical assessment: Skills practice, role plays, experiments, placements, volunteering hours, apprenticeships 179

 13 Critical thinking and responding to feedback 197

Conclusion 211
References 213
Index 221

About the authors

Dr **Paula Beesley** works as a Senior Lecturer in Social Work at Leeds Beckett University. She was a social care worker with adults with learning difficulties, a child protection social worker and practice educator, supporting social work students to critically think about their learning on placement. She has written books on communication skills development and practice placement learning in social work. Her teaching passions are supporting students to develop personal and professional skills through active and collaborative critical thinking on self.

Dr **Belinda Cooke** is an Educational Developer in the Centre for Learning and Teaching at Leeds Beckett University, where she supports colleagues to enhance inclusive practice in teaching in higher education (university education). She is a National Teacher Fellow and a Principal Fellow of the Higher Education Academy. She also mentors and assesses colleagues seeking professional accreditation via the HEA. Her most recent research interests include how staff in universities evidence excellent teaching, innovative, inclusive assessment in Physical Education in university, and developing assessment literacy with students.

Laurence Morris is the Academic Skills Development Manager of Leeds Beckett University and an Alumni Associate of Leeds Beckett's Centre for Learning and Teaching. He is a Senior Fellow of Advance HE, a Fellow of the Royal Geographical Society and an ILM-qualified coach. He has worked in academic skills development since 2010, including for the Ministry of Defence and as an academic librarian. Outside of work he is a keen mountaineer and published poet, living on a smallholding in the Yorkshire Dales.

Dr **Louise Warwick-Booth** is a Reader, working in the Leeds Beckett Centre for Health Promotion Research and the Centre for Learning and Teaching. She teaches on a range of modules within the UK, including, health policy, research methods and global health. She also leads a range of research and evaluation projects. Her research projects are diverse and include commissioned evaluation work within the voluntary and statutory sector. Her expertise relates to the evaluation of health promotion interventions with vulnerable populations, particularly women at risk of experiencing gender-based violence. She also leads pedagogical research into curriculum to improve the student experience. She is also the author of several textbooks, numerous journal articles and Sage Case Studies as well as films intended to enhance student learning.

Acknowledgements

As ever, my thanks go to Leeds Beckett University colleagues and students, without whom this book would not be as strong as it appears here, as I am stimulated to develop my critical thinking on a regular basis. Thank you to Ade, Lily, James and Alice, who are forever supportive of my love for writing.

Paula

As I approach retirement, my wild enthusiasm for all things pedagogical has not diminished, thanks to the inspiring staff and students at Leeds Beckett. The fact that my family share that enthusiasm is evidenced by the brilliant teaching they do: thank you Carlton, Michael, David and Mark.

Belinda

I would like to thank my colleagues in Leeds Beckett University Library and Leeds Beckett Centre for Learning and Teaching for all of their support and everything they have taught me in many thought-provoking and enlightening conversations. Equally, my contributions to this book reflect more than a decade's interactions with the student body of Leeds Beckett, for which I am also grateful. Thank you too to Victoria Morris.

Laurence

Thank you to all of my students, and colleagues who always challenge me to learn, and reflect especially those in the Leeds Beckett Centre for Learning and Teaching who continuously reignite my joy for all things educational. To my family – you always come first: Alex, Maia, Milana, Meadow and Race.

Louise

Finally, thank you to Sage and the publishing team, in particular to Kate Keers and Becky Oliver.

Introduction

This study guide focuses on developing students' ability to think critically and engage with teaching materials and learning opportunities to maximise learning and ultimately degree outcomes. The book provides an accessible theoretical understanding of the study skill of critical thinking and applies it to the practical demands of learning on any university degree. It is packed with practical instruction, learning activities, tips and hints, and examples of good academic practice to support the reader through their learning journey and development of critical thinking study skills.

In a world of fake news and fact checking, critical thinking and 'not accepting things at face value' is important. Being aware of our own biases and assumptions, and those of others, enables us to determine valuable insights from idle speculation.

This is no different at university. Critical thinking is important for students because it interrogates learning materials, students' own thinking and the thinking of others. By asking questions of *why* students are able to develop greater understanding of positionality. Whilst you can generally assume that teaching staff will not offer idle speculation and will be evidenced-based, you should not assume that they are offering definitive answers. Where they are right, it is beneficial to ask *why* to develop your own understanding. Where they are offering one opinion, you should ask *why* that opinion and *explore* other opinions to widen your understanding. You can ask why and agree; you can ask why and disagree. Put simply, critical thinking enables you to come to an informed decision for yourself.

Furthermore, every student at university is required to develop study skills, or they will struggle to engage with teaching materials, develop relevant knowledge and skills, and attain the desired degree/degree classification. Critical thinking is an essential academic skill that you will need to develop to succeed. However, developing critical thinking skills is not automatic for all students and can be challenging. Even for students with this skill, it can be developed further to facilitate deeper learning. This book aims to develop your critical thinking skills, irrespective of your starting point, to enrich your academic skills and studies.

Finally, developing your critical thinking skills has the added benefit that it will enhance your critical thinking in your personal life, so that you are able to evaluate tricky situations, and your future career, as employers value critical thinkers.

Chapter content

Part I introduces students to the concepts of critical thinking:

Chapter one will reflect on the foundations and value of critical thinking to give the reader context and understanding of the skill of critical thinking and develop your understanding of the benefits of critical thinking.

Chapter two will support you in developing your understanding of why critical thinking matters at university, supporting you to understand what critical thinking is, how it relates to deep learning, learning styles and educational objectives.

Chapter three will introduce models of reflective thinking and models of critical thinking in university and the impact of individual learning needs on critical thinking.

Part II supports the student through the experiential learning loop:

Chapter four will reflect on the importance of being prepared to enhance students' ability to engage with the coming teaching activity through active participation and critical thinking with preparatory materials.

Chapter five will reflect on the importance of active listening, lecture etiquette and note making to enable students to engage in critical thinking in lectures.

Chapter six will consider how to critically think in seminars and maximise your learning through effective interaction with others.

Chapter seven will first consider the ways in which you can maximise your understanding, knowledge and skills by critically thinking after both lectures and seminars.

Part III turns to critical thinking in assessed work:

Chapter eight will help the reader to engage effectively with written assessed work and consider a module's learning outcomes and marking criteria. It will also consider the use of artificial intelligence (AI) in critical writing.

Chapter nine will help the reader to think critically when writing academic essays and assignments, including formulating a plan, understanding structure and how to write a critical discussion.

Chapter ten will consider what a presentation is and how to approach it critically to enhance your engagement and performance. It will consider the importance of understanding marking criteria to maximise outcomes.

Chapter eleven will assist the reader in applying their critical thinking skills in the pressurised scenario of an academic examination through the process of preparing for an exam and working well in the exam itself.

Chapter twelve will discuss practical learning opportunities, consider critical thinking through experiential learning and collaborative experiential learning, and explore critical thinking in practical assessment.

Chapter thirteen will support you in developing your approach as a critical learner accessing and hearing feedback, enabling you to critically reflect upon your strengths as well as areas for development, in order for you to respond to feedback.

The book concludes with consideration of graduate attributes, the critical thinking skills that you will develop during your time at university to apply to post-education employment opportunities.

Learning features

The chapters will be interactive and learning features are included to guide the student through the development of their critical thinking in each chapter:

- Chapter objectives

These will set out what the chapter will cover and the critical thinking study skills that the reader will develop by engaging with the chapter.

- Which student is critically thinking

This will present two students and the reader is asked to reflect on where critical thinking is evident in the example. This should prompt critical thinking on your own critical thinking skills and if they can be developed.

- Top tips

Top tips to facilitate good academic practice will be highlighted throughout each chapter for ease of access.

- Case studies

Brief case studies of academic practice will be used in chapters to require the student to critically reflect on their own critical thinking study skills. Answers will be provided to further stimulate critical thinking.

- Individual learning needs

This will focus on students' individual learning needs, how they can impact on your ability to become a critical thinker and provide targeted advice. It is important to recognise that we are all unique. Whilst studying at university and engaging in the complex task of critical thinking to enhance understanding and deep learning, for students where they have disability or health issues that impact on their ability to study, or for students where English is not their first language, studying and critical thinking can be even more challenging.

- Critical thinking action plan

Readers will be asked to critically think about their critical thinking skills and identify strengths and areas for development. There will be an action plan in each chapter that asks readers to identify goals for development and asks them to review the goals after six weeks.

- Further reading

Each chapter will conclude with a summary and further reading. Working through each of these features will support the development of your critical thinking skills.

Ultimately, the increased emphasis on critical thinking in higher education compared to your previous studies reflects the potentially inspiring stage of your academic journey you now have reached. Previously you might largely have been a relatively passive recipient of information and knowledge, simply repeating it as required in exams or assignments. At university level, you will generally be expected to go beyond this, applying your understanding of what you have learned to specific scenarios, questions or academic problems. It is this higher level of applied academic understanding that critical thinking supports. We hope that you enjoy this book. We see it is a stepping stone, part of a journey towards a lifetime of critical thinking that enhances your personal, academic and professional life as you are able to engage with a curious approach to life that enables you to question yourself and the world around you to learn more. Even as technology continues to develop, and artificial intelligence tools change both the nature of academic assignments and the way we work, critical thinking skills remain a core foundation for how to successfully engage with a rapidly evolving world.

PART I

CRITICAL THINKING FOR STUDENTS

Part I introduces students to the concepts of critical thinking (Chapter one), critical thinking in university (Chapter two), and models of critical thinking (Chapter three) and individual learning needs that may require additional time, approach or coping strategies in relation to critical thinking (Chapter three).

Critical thinking should be an everyday part of our lives: we make decisions throughout each and every day that require us to weigh up our options, filter our preferences and decide what is the best option for ourselves and/or others in any given situation. However, we often make decisions with unconscious competence (Burch): *without thinking*. You might not consider in too much depth where and when to have which coffee on the way to university, but the decision will be dependent on multiple permutations including:

- an assessment of your need for coffee (so do you take the first available vendor);
- your previous experiences of the available vendors (so you may be prepared to walk further for one you prefer);
- if you are late for a lecture so are rushing or dislike the lecturer's style so are in avoidance (so may grab the nearest, or furthest, vendor to your lecture theatre);
- you may require oat milk (so need to go to the one that uses your brand); or
- the one where your friends are (so need to consider time and location instead).

Unless, of course, you always go to the same vendor for the same order because it is 'what you do'. However, you may ultimately limit your coffee enjoyment by not applying a curious approach to a new vendor. Here you are processing multiple different pieces of information and critically thinking to make an informed decision.

- Will you try a new coffee shop that appears?
- Will you take a new recommendation?
- Will you vary your order depending on weather, season and what you feel like on the day?

Critical thinking in university is similar. When presented with a lecture you may:

- consider multiple information sources and weigh up their reliability, validity, context and purpose;
- reflect on the course and module learning objectives to consider relevance of materials and prioritise;
- be impacted by peers' and teaching staff's needs and perspectives.

Critical thinking enables you to *challenge*. This means that you challenge your own thinking, challenge other people's opinion rather than accepting it, challenge what influences you and why, and challenge your basic assumptions. Critical thinking also allows you to *defend* your opinion. This means that you know the basis for your opinion and are able to justify your thinking, which can be helpful when wanting to repeat successes or explain poor outcomes. It is the *informed* decision-making that is important here: often it is not what you conclude about the lecture contents that matters but the process that you go through to facilitate your understanding that is critical.

This part of the book is the foundation of developing your critical thinking skills. By understanding what critical thinking is (Chapter one) and why critical thinking is important in university (Chapter two), you will be enabled to become a critical thinker through the introduction of models of reflective thinking and models of critical thinking (Chapter three). You will then be able to move into the more practical chapters of the book where these principles are applied to academic practice.

1
What is critical thinking?

CHAPTER OBJECTIVES

- Be introduced to the concepts of critical thinking
- Develop understanding of what is critical thinking
- Develop understanding of the benefits of critical thinking
- Develop awareness of the barriers to critical thinking and how to address them

Introduction

This chapter will reflect on the foundations and value of critical thinking to give the reader context and understanding of the skill of critical thinking.

> The logic of the critique is important: it challenges the legitimacy of an account not in terms of its content, but by questioning or illuminating the interests it serves. (Gergen, 2023, p. 20)

The chapter will develop your understanding of the benefit of critical thinking as moving beyond accepting what you hear, read or are told. In short, critical thinking asks you to engage from an *inquisitive* perspective that enhances your understanding, knowledge and skills.

What is critical thinking?

Critical thinking is an important academic skill. Without it your learning will be superficial as it will impact on your ability to prepare for and participate in lectures, seminars and practise learning activities and effectively engage with and complete academic assessments. It is that fundamental to your academic success.

It is not a new idea

Critical thinking asks you to consider your education with a questioning perspective. That is not to say that heckling your lecturer with inflammatory arguments is the right approach, but instead that you move beyond taking the lecturer's wisdom at face value to engage in an understanding of their teaching and opinion to develop these ideas into your own knowledge base. Perhaps the most iconic image of critical thinking is portrayed by Rodin's *The Thinker* statue, where a naked man is sat on a plinth arguably contemplating life. Here, you are not asked to replicate his pose, but instead to replicate his implied philosophy that time spent critically thinking is both of value and productive. A modern equivalent is the thinking emoji.

The godfather of critical thinking can be considered to be Socrates. He identified that the people in power, the Greek men of his generation and before them, were entirely influential in how people thought and behaved. They created laws and dictated what was right and wrong, with the general population assuming that they were knowledgeable and correct. The parallels with contemporary society's fact checking of social media and news stories are not lost on us, where critical thinking has been resurrected as an important facet of challenging influencers, politicians and news outlets alike.

WHICH STUDENT IS CRITICALLY THINKING?

Ken and Lisa are politics students. Both read an article on a social media outlet which claims that all politicians are corrupt.

Ken reads the article and accepts it at face value. He takes this as knowledge that is factually correct and absorbs it into his belief system: all politicians are corrupt.

Indeed, when chatting about the subject with friends after a lecture he cites it as an absolute fact and bases his argument on it. The writer's opinion has become absolute.

Lisa reads the article and asks herself what the foundation for it is: what are the writer's views, what was the aim of the article and what is the basis of the claims. She recognises that it was the writer's opinion and when chatting about the subject with friends after a lecture she initiates an interesting debate about the merits of the opinion. As a group they explore the idea and develop their understanding and own thoughts and opinions in relation to what corrupt means, consider how 'corrupt' is measured, wonder if there are there exceptions to the rule and reflect on the impact of a corrupt politician.

Socrates argued that position and power did not equate to absolute knowledge and that it should not be assumed that leaders were consistently correct. The term 'sheep' springs to mind here, often used in a derogatory context to indicate a lack of thought about a presented position. Put simply: do you want to follow the crowd or be an independent thinker? Gergen (2023) argued that leaders, and here we apply academic teaching staff as your leaders, have an ethical duty to ensure that their position is factually correct. It can be assumed that teaching staff spend time accessing and assessing teaching materials to recommend the most relevant, appropriate and reliable sources for your learning: an ethical approach to education. However, that assumption must not be taken as an absolute. Consider if a lecturer has a rival book that they do not want to promote, has a fixed opinion on the topic so does not promote all perspectives or misses a helpful text. That is not to say that they will, but critical thinking means that you are examining the teaching materials from an objective manner to consider if they are as good as the teaching staff member claims them to be.

Socrates suggested that leaders and their views should be questioned to enable criticality and an exploration for the basis of their views. 'Critical' is based on the Greek work *kriticos*, but it is important to be aware that this *does not mean criticism*. A better interpretation of 'critical' when applied to thinking would be *discerning judgement*. A discerning judgement is one determined by the exploration of evidence rather than simply taken from an individual's, societal or commonly agreed opinion. Cottrell (2023) suggests that critical thinking is being able to:

- stand up for and support your own opinion;
- challenge your own opinion;
- be aware of the influences on your opinions;
- hear all perspectives;
- thoughtfully challenge other people's opinions.

It is helpful here to use these points. Critical thinking is an *active* skill. Critical thinking will require you to make an informed decision that considers both your own opinion and that of others to weigh up a range of different perspectives to make a discerning judgement.

Social construction would argue that the commonly agreed norms and values change as society changes (Gergen, 2023), which needs to happen through critical thinking about ongoing appropriateness and relevance. If students did not conform to the social constructed norm that they attend lectures on time, and an alternative constructed norm was that whenever a student arrived that the class paused whilst the student arrived, settled by unpacking of equipment and a recap provided of missed discussion, it is unlikely that much teaching would happen. However, with the advent of recordings of lectures and online teaching facilities, does this norm remain relevant in contemporary society? That is not to say that it should change, but that discussion should be undertaken to review if it remains a relevant norm and if it needs to shift to include a more flexible approach.

Top tip !.!

> To put it simply: if you surround yourself by like-minded people, how do you know that your opinion is right or wrong?
>
> Weighing up the pros and cons, the thinking behind the opinion and why you all agree will enable you to challenge and develop your opinion.
>
> That is not to say that you will challenge your thinking and come to the conclusion that it is wrong. Indeed, it may strengthen your opinion and give you an evidence base to locate your opinion on. In contrast, it may challenge the opinion and develop your thinking such that your opinion shifts a little or even radically.
>
> It does not matter if it reinforces or changes your opinion. The aim of critical thinking is not to come to a predetermined outcome. The aim of critical thinking is to enhance your understanding so that you are making an informed decision about the like-minded opinion.

Critical thinking is not easy

It is not unusual for you to find it tiring, frustrating and sometimes confusing. But that is often a very good sign because it means you are recognising the complexities of the issues you are exploring. Not only is critical thinking a key skill but it also means you are much better able to have more nuanced discussions and therefore are less likely to over-simplify your explanations.

How to critically think

First, we need to consider how to critically think: it is an academic skill and like any practical skill requires you to understand how to undertake the skill so that you can practice to develop it. Chapter three provides models of critical thinking to develop this skill, but at this stage it is helpful to consider that critical thinking comes from being aware of you bias, being curious and drawing conclusions.

Be aware of your bias

Critical thinking is the concept of not taking things at face value. Let's go back to the social media post that Ken and Lisa read that all politicians are corrupt and consider this from a range of perspectives. If you believe politicians are fundamentally trying to do good, then you are likely to disagree with the statement, whilst if you believe that politicians are more likely to take a backhander or exaggerate their expenses then you are more likely to agree with the statement. This is *bias*. Bias can be conscious, so that you are actively thinking this through and identifying your own position and agreeing with it, or it can be unconscious bias, where you are not aware of your own thought process, but it still impacts on your position on the statement. Many people will have a confirmation bias: see I told you that they are all corrupt and now someone I respect says the same, so we are both right. Chatfield (2022) suggests that you slow your thinking down to reflect if your thinking is biased, and if reading an article similar to the one Ken and Lisa read you could consider:

What was my original view and how am I applying it to the article?

> Top tip 1.2
>
> If the idea of critical thinking feels overwhelming, consider these synonyms that may feel more accessible:
>
> analyse, appraise, ask, assess, audit, clarify, cogitate, compare, conclude, consider, contrast, contemplate, critique, defend, deliberate, dissect, enquire, evaluate, examine, explain, explore, justify, inspect, interpret, interrogate, investigate, judge, mull over, ponder, probe, question, reflect, review, ruminate, scrutinise, speculate, study, wonder
>
> The commonality of this list is the expectation that you will think and consider, rather than accept at face value.

Be curious

By asking this question it can slow you down and enable you to see the bias, which you can then address through critical thinking. Indeed, Cottrell (2019) advises students to query surface appearances. A critical thinker has a *curiosity* that enables them to ask questions, consider the same point from a variety of different perspectives, weigh them up and come to a conclusion. Chatfield (2022) argues that critical thinkers should be sceptical and objective. Approaching the social media article with scepticism enables you to be open minded as you are open to doubt and uncertainty, whilst objectivity enables a neutral and non-judgemental approach, both of which prevent assumptions being made about the factual basis of the article.

In addition, critical thinking is about *considering all perspectives*. It is important to recognise that this may require additional time investigating alternative views to enable you to consider all perspectives. As such, the ability to research topics will also be enhanced. Continuing to consider the social media article that argued all politicians are corrupt, you might ask yourself:

- Can I find evidence to support the position that all politicians are corrupt?
- What do I define as corrupt?
- Is there an ethical code for politicians?
- If investigations into politicians corruption is reported:
    - how is this reported and by whom?
    - what is the purpose of the reporting?
    - how are the statistics constructed? Are they designed to minimise or maximise the impact of the statistics?
- Can I find evidence to suggest that some politicians are corrupt, but that others abide by the ethical code?
- Are there some sources that I feel are more trustworthy than others? What do I base that position on?
- Am I open to be persuasion? Can I change my original position?

Draw conclusions

Finally, critical thinking is about drawing your *own informed conclusion*. Having identified any bias and applied a curiosity to consider all perspectives, the final task is to balance competing views and take account of facts in order to determine your own position. In many ways, we don't mind if you decide all politicians are corrupt or not, so long as you have critically thought about the issues, weighed up the arguments and come to an informed opinion. It is the process that is important here.

Baron (2019) reflects on the importance of *open-minded thinking* in politics, reflecting that politics is inherently corrupt as those in power often prioritise their own needs and the needs of those in society with whom they identify or will gain

CASE STUDY 1.1

Ken is a politics student. He is asked to critically think about the following statement:

> The Tory party were in power from 2010 to 2024. As their MPs were elected by the public, this lengthy holding of power demonstrates that they were representing and meeting the voters' needs and were a trusted and reliable government for fourteen years.

If Ken approaches this without critical thinking, he would accept at face value that this statement is correct. It seems a reasonable assumption that if voters saw the Tory policies and practice and the majority of the population chose to vote them back in across general elections in 2015 and 2019, then they must have been doing a good job.

However, if a critical thinking approach is taken, Ken may take a more analytical approach to this statement.

First, Ken identifies his own political *bias*. Whilst this should not impact on his analysis of the statement, the fact that he himself supports the Tory party may lead him to a biased analysis that the statement is in fact correct.

This makes Ken *curious*. The statement is correct that the Tory party was in power for 14 years. However, his political knowledge is likely to extend beyond this simple factual basis. He should know that there have been criticisms made of the government during that time for the handling of austerity measures, Brexit, Covid and immigration to name but a few contentious subjects, which have resulted in leadership challenges and a reduced majority.

Developing this further, Ken takes his knowledge and understanding about a mixed experience of the Tory policies and practice and applies this to the issue of poverty. His knowledge informs him that poverty (bar during the Covid pandemic) has increased steadily during this time (JRT, 2024).

He *concludes* that not all voters' needs were met or of the same opinion that the Tory party were trusted and reliable and is able to see the faults in the statement despite his personal political views. By recognising his bias and taking a curious approach he has been able to see different perspectives on the statement.

With critical thinking he is able to adapt his initial response to the statement that it was correct to a more nuanced and informed response. He now perceives that, although some of the population's needs were undoubtedly being met, not all voters' needs have been met by the Tory party. Furthermore, whilst he perceives the Tory party as reliable and trustworthy, not all voters agree with that statement.

benefit from. Baron argues that *open-minded thinking* enables the judgement of the thinking of others, so that where political students critically think about the decision-making by politicians, it should be interrogated for bias.

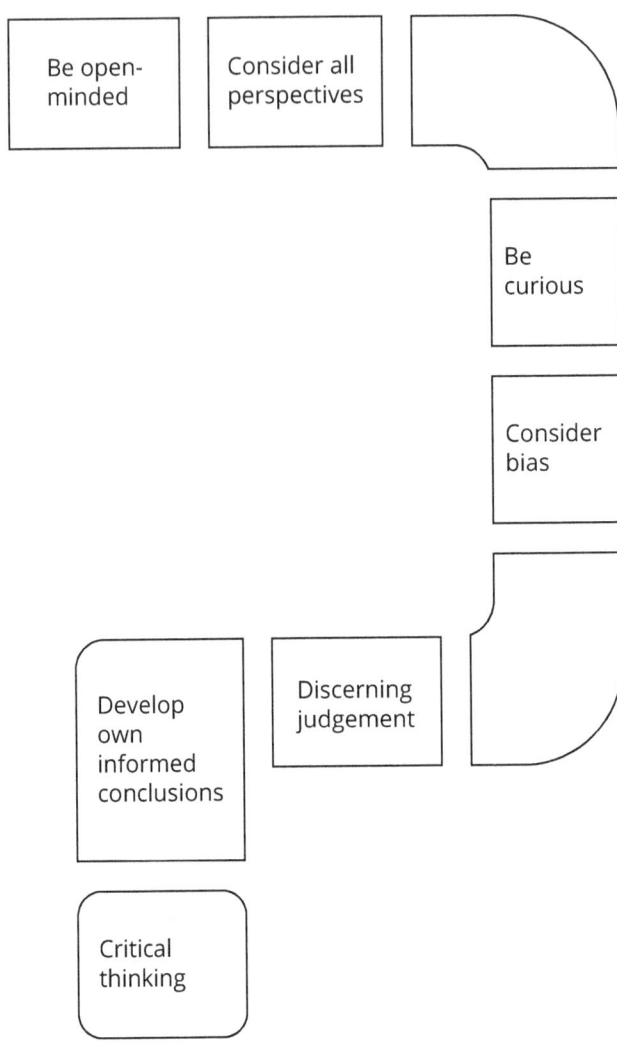

Figure 1.1 Critical thinking means asking questions

It can be helpful to consider critical thinking as the ability to ask yourself questions, as Figure 1.1 shows.

Benefits of critical thinking

The benefits of critical thinking are numerous. First are two professional advantages:

- You are likely to get a better grade on each assessment and overall degree classification.
- Employers value graduates who are able to think critically, so you are likely to develop your career well.

However, this is because you are likely to have developed more skills than critically thinking which include:

- problem-solving skills, which will support you personally and professionally;
- enhanced and informed decision-making skills, as you are able to evaluate a range of information to determine pros and cons and establish a best course of action;
- research skills, as you have developed the ability to identify and engage with a variety of sources;
- emotional intelligence, as if you are able to understand different perspectives you are more likely to be aware of your own and other people's feelings which enables you to respond more appropriately;
- self-reflection skills, as if you are able to analyse situations you are more likely to be able to transfer these skills to yourself;
- leadership skills, as you apply all of the skills above.

The more that you practise critical thinking, the more proficient that you will get and the more all of these other skills will develop too. Indeed Cottrell (2023) suggests that critical thinking sharpens your mind, indicating that it is beneficial for you holistically not just academically. It can assist you to analyse information on social media, in relationships and in jobs. As such, critical thinking in academic situations can support your ability to avoid manipulation and reduce the likelihood of making mistakes.

Finally, a benefit of critical thinking is developing the ability to transfer learning from one situation to another. Critical thinking requires taking your current knowledge and applying it to a new situation, the transferring of knowledge and skills. This is a priceless skill as you move into your career. Whilst this may seem a long way away as you start your academic studies, the conclusion will reflect on the importance of critical thinking in your lifetime. Equally, it should not be forgotten that many students will need, or choose, to work alongside their academic studies to gain finances and experience: practice critical thinking can be applied in any work environment you may engage in now or in the future once the skill is developed.

Barriers to critical thinking

It is important to recognise that there are many barriers that can prevent us from critically thinking regularly or effectively.

The first and most obvious barrier to critical thinking is not thinking. If you accept everything at face value, then you limit yourself and your development of knowledge and skills. It should be recognised that it is perfectly possible to get through life in this way and no critique is made here if that is your choice.

However, the theme of the book is critically thinking and we urge you to think to enrich your life and enhance your knowledge and skills.

The second barrier is undoubtedly being closed to new ideas. A closed-minded student is one who will not consider different perspectives, so does not think *critically*. This can be because they have an egotistical approach to their thinking, and consider that they are already right, so no further interrogation of the facts is required. They will often surround themselves by like-minded and similarly closed-minded people who reinforce that they are correct. Whilst students remain entrenched in their position, personal growth is often limited, as social conditioning and social construction of opinions prevails to support their position.

A further barrier to thinking can be cognitive fatigue. Here, students are exhausted by their studies, often experienced at the end of a semester where multiple assessments are due. However, it can also occur where students are studying the wrong subject or at the wrong time, creating a demotivational factor. Smith (2018) found that where students are tired of studying they experienced reduced emotional wellbeing and lower academic grades. This brings us to another barrier: emotional intelligence. Where students have low mental health, poor coping strategies and are not aware of the impact this is having on them, they may struggle to engage with critical thinking.

Top tip 1.3

To overcome barriers to critical thinking, there are a number of actions that you can take:

- Set aside time to reflect on a daily basis to develop the habit of reflecting. This can be:
    - Thinking
    - A written diary
    - Notes
    - Mind map
    - Discussions with others
- Avoid distractions. This will provide the space we need to process and reflect.
- Consider the space in which you can best reflect:
    - Is this in your home?
    - Is this when you are walking?
    - Is this at university?

- Experiment with different environments to find out what works best for you.
- Ask questions:
  - At first start by doing this in your daily life, imagine you are a child who constantly asks 'why?'. This will develop your inquisitive muscle.
  - Apply this to self
  - Apply to your values
  - Apply this to your discussions
  - Apply to your reading
  - Apply this to your critical thinking
- Look after yourself:
  - Take breaks when you need them
  - Set yourself SMART (specific, measurable, achievable, realistic and time-bound) targets
  - Give yourself rewards for achievements
- Develop self-awareness:
  - Be aware of times when study is more productive for you.
  - Be aware of what you find hard and what triggers you.
  - Don't avoid these but develop coping strategies to support you where these occur.
- Access support and advice:
  - Books and study guides provide excellent advice.
  - Tutors, academic advisors and library staff are equipped to offer you knowledgeable support
  - University guidance: designed to support different learning styles and needs.

Finally, Cottrell (2023) reflects on where students feel ambiguity and doubt, and here we recognise this as a barrier to critical thinking. Where, despite having practised and developed your critical thinking skills, you will inevitably identify situations where you remain unclear of your position. This is fine to experience, and we would urge you not to be avoidant of critical thinking because you feel doubt or a lack of clarity. The joy of critical thinking is that you can weigh up and present different perspectives' strengths, areas for development and further discussion and come to the informed conclusion that you cannot make a clear recommendation. Life is not simple and critical thinking is not simple: don't be afraid to say that, having weighed everything, you can see both sides but on balance here is your discerning judgement.

When to critically think

Schon (1983) argued that reflection can be undertaken in action and on action, and in 1991, he added reflection for action. If we replace reflection with critical thinking, we can see that critical thinking can be undertaken for action (preparation for lectures and seminars), in action (lectures and seminars) and on action (after lectures and seminars). This demonstrates the importance of continual critical thinking. It is not an isolated or silo-ed activity, but instead critical thinking should be undertaken before, during and after learning activities. It should be integrated as a core element of your learning to enhance development of knowledge and skills.

Top tip 1.4

> Critical thinking can be done anytime and anywhere.
>
> To develop the skill of critical thinking, practise in your daily life. When you watch a TV programme, read a book, chat with friends, before, during or afterwards stop and critically think about what may happen and why and what happened and why.
>
> Your commute to and from university is a great time to critically think about the lecture content. On the way reflect on what might be covered, what you already know and what you might learn. On the way back, mull it over in your mind as to what was said, how you feel about the content, and how it will enhance your learning. Consider if there was anything that you disagreed with, and if so why.

Critical thinking action plan

Please reflect on your critical thinking skills and where you need to develop a skill develop your critical thinking action plan.

Worksheet 1.1 Critical thinking action plan

Critical thinking skill	Action to be taken	Review after six weeks
Ability to see beyond an initial statement		
Ability to see own bias		
Consideration of different perspectives		
Ability to draw your own conclusion		

Conclusion

In summary, critical thinking is the skill of identifying and neutralising bias, taking a curious approach that enables you to consider all perspectives before coming to an informed decision on your own opinion. Critical thinking can help you to engage with deeper thinking, develop greater understanding and tackle complex topics. It can also help you to avoid making assumptions that lead to errors that cause you at best embarrassment and at worst can influence decisions and events that have an impact on yourself and/or others.

Further reading

Chatfield, T. (2022) *Critical Thinking: Your essential guide*. London: Sage.
Cottrell, S. (2023) *Critical Thinking Skills*. London: Bloomsbury.
Williams, K. (2022) *Getting Critical*. Basingstoke: Red Globe Press.

Each of these books provide a clear and accessible introduction to critical thinking that can be applied to the later chapters.

2
Why critical thinking matters at university

CHAPTER OBJECTIVES

- Develop an understanding of why critical thinking matters at university
- Develop an understanding of how you learn as an adult learner
- Develop an understanding of educational objectives and deep learning
- Develop an understanding of individual learning needs

Introduction

This chapter will support you in developing your understanding of why critical thinking matters at university, enabling you to understand what critical thinking is, how it relates to deep learning, learning styles and educational objectives. The chapter outlines how critical thinking is important in universities, in relation to performance outcomes such as degree classifications for students. It will introduce ideas about how students learn, learning styles and link these to educational objectives, as well as introducing Bloom et al.'s (1956) taxonomy and deep learning.

Why critical thinking matters at university

Chapter one defined what critical thinking is and provided you with a range of examples of what it involves. A key goal of university (or higher) education is to support you as a student to develop critical thinking skills (Pascarella and Terenzini, 1991). You will therefore often be asked to think deeply about something and to make judgements through how you critically think and analyse specific to your subject as well as each assessment task. As already discussed in Chapter one, developing your critical thinking involves developing curiosity, questioning, reflecting and being aware of bias held by yourself and others, to support you in making your own informed decisions. In practice, it is important to be able to judge information, theories and arguments (Price, 2024). Critical thinking matters at university because those students who demonstrate it achieve higher grades and better degree classifications. Critical thinking is highly valued as a learning outcome at all levels of university study, so as a student who demonstrates effective critical thinking, you are more likely to achieve educational success (O'Hare and McGuinness, 2015). In addition, achieving a good degree classification can make a difference to your lifetime earnings as a graduate (Britton et al., 2022). Time spent developing the skill of critical thinking can impact on your academic success and beyond as you develop the skills of decision-making, research and evaluation, emotional intelligence, self-reflection and leadership, as Chapter one has already discussed. Critical thinking is also important in practice; for example, students who are studying nursing need to learn to apply critical thinking in a range of areas including when analysing concepts (Franco-Tantuico, 2022), when learning on placements (Bellaera et al., 2021), when working with patients (Price, 2024) and when developing their research skills.

WHICH STUDENT IS CRITICALLY THINKING?

Dominic and Jane are first-year nursing students who attend a seminar on critical thinking.

Dominic is new to critical thinking as a concept. He listens to the tutor's tips about critical thinking and makes some notes. He saves them for later use.

Jane makes notes and then follows up with some further reading about the importance of critical thinking in nursing. She finds it helps her to develop her understanding of how to use critical thinking by knowing more about what it involves, and why it is important to her own practice. She takes some time to reflect on her own biases before she begins to work with patients.

Both students have listened to the content provided by their tutor, but Jane has engaged with more learning materials to further enhance her understanding (see Chapter seven for more on how to develop your critical thinking after lectures and seminars).

In educational terms, critical thinking is the ability to engage with the learning of new topics and development of existing knowledge and skills. It is important that you approach new learning materials with an open mind, putting aside your own personal opinions and biases so that you are able to identify relevant and reliable information sources that support and stretch your learning needs (as discussed in Chapter one). Vygotsky (1978) reflects that students have a *zone of proximal development*, which is the gap between current knowledge and skills and their potential ability to learn. Critical thinking enables you to develop that potential ability by moving beyond the obvious and what you currently think that you know.

Critical thinking in university requires you to access a range of learning materials that enables you to compare and contrast what different authors say about a topic, whilst also analysing and evaluating each author's position. By questioning information on a topic and challenging both your own and experts' pre-existing ideas you will develop your own clear, logical arguments based on sound reasoning and evidence. Career success is about navigating practical as well as desirable ideas (Price, 2024). Cottrell (2019) notes that critical thinking is complex, as it starts with critical reading and then ends with critical writing (see Chapters four and eight for more on this) in which you find and articulate your own voice. Moon (2009: 11) calls this *academic assertiveness*, defined as 'a mix of self-awareness, the development of capacities, some new ideas and specific techniques, and a willingness to apply this to yourself, to learn from it and change'. Moon (2009) suggests that academic assertiveness involves you as a student finding an appropriate way to engage in critical thinking or debate, whilst working independently to develop your own capabilities. Being academically assertive includes the following behaviours:

- finding an appropriate 'voice' – a way to express yourself, and your ideas, whilst engaging in critical thinking and debate;
- the willingness to engage in challenges, accept challenges and to disagree;
- the ability to be able to deal with not being 'right' sometimes; making mistakes, failing and then recovering from these experiences;
- the ability to be open to feedback on your performance (at university and beyond);
- the willingness to listen to and hear the views of others;
- the ability to understand that other people can also make mistakes, and fail;
- the ability to be proactive, to make judgements and to take action based upon the judgements;
- the ability to develop an appropriate level of academic self-esteem.

How you learn

Before turning to critical thinking, it is first helpful to consider *how* you learn. This will enable you to understand both the importance of taking responsibility for your own learning as an adult learner and reflecting on your preferred learning style.

Top tip 2.1

> You will need to invest in developing your academic voice, during your time at university. Your academic voice should be more formal than everyday speech, avoid the use of 'I' unless instructed to and provide an evidence-based argument that weighs all perspectives of a discussion.
>
> This is an ongoing process that will take both time and practice. Consider a range of strategies to help you to develop your voice, starting with paying attention to academic language in your own discipline, the ways in which opinions and evidence are used, and how assessments are expected to be structured.

Adult learning principles

First, it is good to reflect now on your attitude to learning. Do you feel that it is the lecturer's job to *teach* you?

Top tip 2.2

> At university you are expected to take responsibility for your own learning.
>
> This means that you will need to be actively engaged with your course, proactive and enthusiastic in that engagement, and take the initiative to ask for support where necessary.
>
> It also means that you will need to own your actions. You will be accountable for the level of academic effort and rigour that you put in and accept the glory or consequences where this impacts on academic achievement.

New-to-university students often find that they have to adapt to a different way of learning, as university learning is orientated to the andrological (adult learning) principles (Knowles, 1973; Knowles et al., 2020). Adult learner principles assume:

- **Self-concept.** Adult learners will be autonomous, independent and self-directed.
- **Readiness to Learn.** Adult learners naturally want to learn 'for its own sake' (Sennett, 2008, p. 9) so are ready to do so. However, there needs to be a motivational factor, a reason, for them to engage in learning.

This is developed through the other andrological principles:

- **Motivation to learn.** Adult learners are more likely to engage with a task if they want to than if they are told to. Internal motivation comes from engaging with a purpose and value to the learning, which can include personal educational or developmental targets; peer or family pressure to succeed, or financial gain (increased graduate career options).
- **Orientated to learning.** Adult learners are more likely to engage if they see a purpose in the learning. This can include being motivated to undertake preparation as it will enhance ability to contribute in lectures or seminars, complete assessed tasks or contribute to post-university life.

It can be helpful to reflect if you feel ready, orientated and motivated to learn. Critical thinking is primarily a self-directed task and requires the andrological principles to be evident for it to be effective. If you are not yet ready to undertake autonomous critical thinking, then it may be that you first need to reflect on whether you are on the right course or even if studying is right for you at this time, and we would direct you to your tutor for support on critical thinking into careers choice. However, this book takes an assumptive approach that you are ready, orientated and motivated to learn through critical thinking.

Despite the need to take responsibility for your own learning, you will not be undertaking this alone. Adult learning in university will be scaffolded by teaching staff to support you to develop in a stepped way, in line with Vygotsky's (1978) notion of moving through your *zone of proximal development*. Academic courses are mapped to develop your learning so that it is graduated across the course duration: the learning you will acquire progresses in a planned manner. Conversely, the level of support you receive will reduce as the course progresses and you become more competent at being an independent learner. Scaffolding can be seen as support provided through module specifications, the learning materials supplied before a lecture or seminar (Chapter four), lectures and seminars (Chapters five and six), tasks set with lectures and seminars to undertake after teaching (Chapter seven), individual tutor support, the support services that the university provides, peer support, and modelling, observation, experiential learning (Kolb, 1984) and collaborative experiential learning (Beesley, 2024) in practice learning settings (Chapter twelve). Scaffolding of learning is a teaching technique in which your tutors deliver content in distinct segments, with higher levels of support at the start of your learning journey, and then less and less support as your develop your understanding of new concepts and subject material. Returning, then, to how adults learn, it is engaging with all these support provisions that will maximise your learning and the development of your knowledge and skills.

Learning style

Adult learning is best when it is practical, builds on existing knowledge and is goal-orientated (Knowles, 1973). If we also apply Lewin's (1936) dedication to the integration of theory to practice and an understanding that nothing happens in isolation we can conclude that development and learning is best taken holistically from a mixture of doing, feeling, watching, reflecting, thinking and applying theory to learning. However, we know that some students engage with some types of learning more easily and enthusiastically than others. We call these learning styles. Kolb (1976) suggested that students tend to favour four learning styles:

1. **Diverging:** Students who are divergent learn best through concrete experience (doing and feeling) and reflective observation (watching and thinking), which means that they will learn best by doing something themselves or observing other people and critically thinking about what happened. They may struggle with critical thinking in preparation for learning activities.
2. **Assimilating:** Students who assimilate learn best through reasoning, abstract conceptualisation (understanding why and application of theory) and reflective observation (watching and thinking), which means that they will learn best by critically thinking before a lecture or seminar and then observing to apply their learning. They often like to be organised and understand what is expected of them, making critical thinking in preparation for lectures and seminars particularly relevant for them. They may struggle with critical thinking in practice learning environments.
3. **Converging:** Students who are convergent learn best through being able to solve problems which means that they will engage with critical thinking as preparation and prefer practical learning tasks and interactive approaches to learning so enjoy presentations, practice learning and seminars. They may struggle with critical thinking in taught sections of lectures as prefer interaction.
4. **Accommodating:** Students who are accommodating learn best through using trial and error and enjoying discovering for themselves. Students with this learning style can adapt, but they prefer to learn through active engagement. They much prefer seminars, practice learning and presentations, but will struggle to apply critical thinking. They prefer to be given feedback than identify it for themselves and prefer to be told what peers learnt than undertaking critical thinking before or after a learning activity.

In Chapter five we will discuss the visual, auditory, read/write and kinaesthetic (VARK) (Fleming, 1987) learning styles and in Chapter twelve we will discuss the Honey and Mumford (1982) learning styles which are activist, reflector, theorist or pragmatist. It can be helpful to understand how you learn best, but it is important that you do not become so entrenched in one learning style that you forget to ensure rounded learning through application of all four strategies.

Top tip 2.3:

> If you know that you are an active learner or pragmatist, you will need to work much harder to develop your critical thinking skills as they will not come naturally to you. There is limited value in always doing if you do not learn from your successes and mistakes.
>
> However, if you are a reflector or theorist you will need to focus your development on moving beyond critical thinking into the doing. There is limited value in understanding of self and others and knowledge if you do not apply it to life.

This returns us to the point that in order to be a holistic, well-rounded learner you need to develop skills in doing, feeling, thinking, understanding and applying theory. The rest of this book focuses primarily on the critical thinking element of learning, but we know that critical thinking requires doing, feeling, thinking, understanding and applying theory, but also requires a level of interrogation.

Educational objectives

Critical thinking at university can be seen to be linked to educational objectives. These develop as your course progresses and the academic demands increase each year.

Bloom et al. (1956) developed a taxonomy of educational objectives (illustrated in Figure 2.1) that indicated the increasing complexity expected of students in relation to engaging with learning. It can be argued that education at primary school relates to the development of knowledge, for example the learning of times tables or phonics rules as facts that need to be known, and education at secondary school continues to develop knowledge whilst developing an understanding of the topic, for example the use of the times tables in wider maths skills such as algebra or Pythagoras. Next must come the application of learning so that it can be transferred from one situation to another, which requires an understanding of the knowledge to enable effective transferability of knowledge and skills.

However, at university level the education comes at a higher level, where analysis starts to take place. A key goal of university programmes is to teach students to think critically (Dekker, 2020). It is here that higher level or *deeper thinking* occurs, which Bloom et al. (1956, p. 144) called 'fuller comprehension'. They

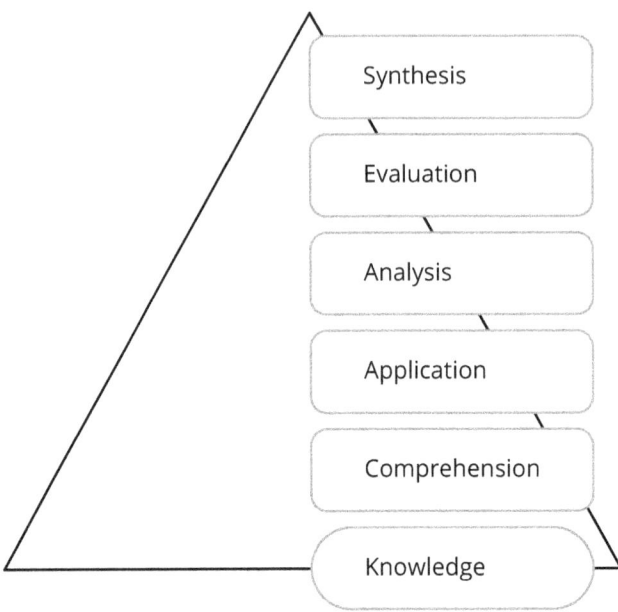

Figure 2.1 Experiential learning loop

Adapted from Bloom's taxonomy of educational objectives (Bloom et al., 1956).

argued that a student is required to identify the key points, explore the relationship between each of the key points and identify the structure that combines the key points. Analysis is followed by evaluation, where tasks are undertaken 'appraising the extent to which particulars are accurate, effective, economical, or satisfying. The judgments may be either quantitative or qualitative, and the criteria may be either those determined by the student or those which are given to him' (Bloom et al., 1956, p. 185).

Finally, synthesis is the last educational achievement, which is the creation of your own perspective. Where a student is undertaking a doctoral study, they may strive to create new theory, knowledge or wisdom to inform existing knowledge in the field of study. It can be argued that critical thinking is the combination of Bloom et al.'s (1956) educational objectives that require knowledge, understanding, analysis and evaluation of a topic or point to enable the synthesis, or creation, of your own opinions, values and views.

Demonstrating that you can make sense of a topic, and express this in an analytical way verbally, as well as in written form, illustrates that you are learning more deeply.

Top tip 2.4

> The words used in this taxonomy will be expressed by your tutors when they provide you with details of learning outcomes and objectives (see Chapter eight for more on this). Therefore, these words can also be seen in assessment tasks as well as marking criteria.
>
> Pay attention to the words being used before you start to complete assignment tasks because these are indicating the type of learning that you need to demonstrate in your submission.
>
> For example, the tutor has provided an outline of grades to be allocated according to this component of a written assignment for nursing students. The tutor has indicated that 30% of the overall marks are allocated to 'analysis of the problem'. A student who offers 'outstanding argument and/or analysis. Independent thinking. Highly competent, rigorous and impressive application of evidence and theory to solve the problem' will be awarded a higher mark. In comparison, a student who submits their work with an absence of analysis and/or argument. 'No evidence of attempt to solve the problem or provide an answer' will be given a lower mark.

Deep learning

Craik and Lockhart (1972) introduced the concept of surface and deep learning. When students surface learn, they tend to regurgitate material without fully understanding it. They may focus on goals such as achieving high grades and impressing others. In deeper learning, students immerse themselves more in the subject material, and are motivated by learning more, rather than simply focusing on assessment requirements, although often achieve this as a result anyway. Critical thinking is seen to develop deep learning as it enables the student to make sense of the topic. Deep learning leads to better educational outcomes and longer-term understanding and use of your learning materials (Cerbin, 2018), it moves you beyond just repeating and describing knowledge.

To develop your own critical thinking skills, you could apply Bloom et al.'s (1956) lens to your own subject area, looking at a specific practice skill, or exploring a specific topic as a starting point.

> **CASE STUDY 2.1**
>
> Sarah is a student nurse who is learning about different medical conditions including asthma. Applying the taxonomy to her learning, you can see that her learning moves along the stages of the taxonomy (adapted from Seibert, 2023).
>
> *Knowledge* – Sarah can define asthma as a medical condition.
>
> *Comprehension* – Sarah can describe the pathology and physiology of what happens to the body when a patient has asthma.
>
> *Application* – Sarah can outline the signs and symptoms of what she expects to see when a patient experiences an asthma attack.
>
> *Analysis* – Sarah, when treating a patient who has experienced an asthma attack, can compare what she expected to see (signs and symptoms) to what she observed by analysing the data that she gathered from patient observations.
>
> *Evaluation* – Sarah can evaluate the health status of her patient, using the data that she has gathered from her observations: e.g. is their attack subsiding, or is the medication that she has administered working effectively?
>
> *Synthesis* – Sarah can now decide what the next steps are that she needs to take for her patient, having synthesised all of her previous learning.

It will be important to think about the many ways in which you can develop your own deep learning, at every point of your course. Engage in problem-solving tasks that are set for you by your tutors, take part in classroom discussions, practise how you approach analysis, work on self-assessment techniques where you assess your own progress and take opportunities to access university training to support you in building your critical thinking skills over time. Many universities now offer critical thinking courses designed to support you in developing your skills in this area.

Finally, each subject has *threshold concepts*, core ideas that once you understand enable you as a student to transform your own understanding of your subject, facilitating you to move on in your learning (Meyer and Land, 2003). They highlight three important areas:

1. As a student, you need to engage with *troublesome* ideas and concepts by critically thinking around it to explain subject specific knowledge and present it in your own words. By understanding the difficult areas, you will engage with the easier areas more easily.

2. Learners need to use *recursive* approaches. This means taking different perspectives on the same material available to enable deeper learning.
3. Learners need to use *excursive* approaches, in which your learning journey also includes diversions as new ideas can come from doing this.

By embracing these deep learning ideas, your critical thinking will enable you to develop your engagement with and understanding of your chosen subject.

Critical thinking action plan

Please reflect on your critical thinking skills and where you need to develop a skill note this in your critical thinking action plan.

Worksheet 2.1   Critical thinking action plan

Critical thinking skill	Action to be taken	Review after six weeks
Ability to understand why critical thinking matters at university		
Ability to communicate judgements, being academically assertive		
Ability to learn as an adult		
Ability to understand educational objectives		
Ability to learn deeply		
Ability to identify and develop coping strategies for individual learning needs		

Conclusion

This chapter has outlined why critical thinking matters at university, supporting you to understand what critical thinking is, and explaining how it relates to deep learning, learning styles and educational objectives. Time spent developing the skill of critical thinking, and academic assertiveness (Moon, 2009), can impact positively upon your academic success. Critical thinking skills also stand you in good stead for after your time as a student, in your graduate career.

Further reading

Chatfield, T. (2022) *Critical Thinking*. London: Sage. This book covers all areas of critical thinking in university, with the introductory chapter about what is critical thinking and why does it matter most useful as a starting point.

Cottrell, S. (2023) *Critical Thinking Skills*. London: Bloomsbury. This book is very useful for outlining critical thinking skills and contains activities and exercises to support your own self-assessment.

Price, B. (2024) *Critical Thinking and Writing in Nursing*. London: Learning Matters. Your own institution will have resources for critical thinking, which are worth accessing.

3
Becoming a critical thinker

> **CHAPTER OBJECTIVES**
>
> - Develop an understanding of models of reflective thinking
> - Develop an understanding of models of critical thinking

This chapter will introduce models of reflective thinking and models of critical thinking in university. It will discuss the impact of individual learning needs on critical thinking for students with a Reasonable Adjustment Plan and ethnically diverse students where English is not their first language.

Becoming a critical thinker

In the previous chapter we have discussed what critical thinking is; here we lay the foundation of how to critically think that will support your engagement with the other chapters in the book. We recommend that you try all of the different models and exercises provided in this chapter to critically think about and establish the style of critical thinking that works for you. This is as important an element of critical thinking as the task itself: understanding you.

> **WHICH STUDENT IS CRITICALLY THINKING?**
>
> Ted and Henry are both criminology students who have submitted their first academic assignment and received grade and feedback.
>
> Ted starts his course feeling that he is able to present all competing positions well, as he has been taught to at college.
>
> He is proud of his first assignment that he submits. However, he is upset when the feedback is that, whilst he describes the different perspectives on the topic well, to enhance future assignments he needs to meet the learning outcomes in more depth by *applying* the knowledge.
>
> Henry starts his course feeling that he is able to present all competing positions well, as he has been taught to at college. However, he has attended an academic skills tutorial and recognises that his critical thinking needs to continue to develop, and he engages with the recommended learning activities.
>
> He is proud of his first assignment that he submits. He is delighted when he achieves a high grade for his submission. The feedback praises that he has presented the different perspectives on the topic and applied them to the topic analytically.

As discussed in Chapters two and eight, the learning outcomes are related to Bloom's taxonomy of educational objectives (Bloom et al., 1956). Whilst Ted was able to demonstrate his comprehension of the knowledge, Henry enhanced his grade by also applying and analysing his knowledge. In short, he applied critical thinking to his knowledge so that he was able to provide a discerning judgement and demonstrate deeper learning within his academic work.

When learning, you need to revisit learning materials at times that suit you, so that your learning process continues. In your own learning process, you should allow room for mistakes to be made and lessons to be learned.

Top tip 3.1

> Share learning, discuss difficulties and work with peers and teaching staff to enhance your critical thinking and understanding.
>
> It is important to know that you are not alone in your learning challenges.

Reflective thinking

Reflection is a key component of critical thinking, and reflective assessment tasks are a prerequisite of many university courses. Reflection is a skill that is also required in workplaces, as it supports us in thinking about our experiences, attitudes and practices – why did I work in that way, and what might I need to change?

Top tip 3.2

> Reflection is about more than describing your experiences; it involves critically thinking about them in a number of ways. It involves questioning – what happened, and why it happened. It should also involve questioning ourselves – if the same experience happened again, would you change how you reacted and what you did? So, use language to help you to reflect; for example:
>
> I felt that ...
>
> I learned that ...
>
> If this happened again, I would ...

We start by relating the *reflective practitioner* model (Schon, 1983) to academic studies. First, Schon identified that you make reflective decisions in the actual moment that weigh up your knowledge base, skill set, and needs of the individual situation, arguably the basis of critical thinking. He called this *reflection-in-action*, and you might do this during a lecture or seminar (Chapters five and six): hear and react to information to come to an opinion at that moment. However, he identified a second reflective point, where afterwards you reflect on the activity and to inform future practice. He called this *reflection-on-action*, and you would do this when you critically think after lectures and seminars (Chapter seven). He latterly added a third reflective point (Schon, 1991 that was *reflection-for-action*, which is the critical thinking in preparation for lectures and seminars (Chapter four).

Reflective thinking can be applied to all your academic studies. The reflective practitioner model can be seen to apply to lectures, seminars, assessed academic work, presentations and practical learning activities. Shortly after the publication of Schon's book came Kolb's (1984) experiential learning cycle, which has subsequently been modified in a variety of ways, but all have the same underpinning principles that provide a way to reflect on action.

> **Top tip 3.3**
>
> **Critical thinking is not always linear**
>
> When writing an academic assignment, you might reflect for action by making an assignment plan, reflect in action by reading and reflect on action by critically thinking about how you will use the materials, reflect in action by writing the assignment and reflect on action to enhance your first draft assignment and review it again using reflecting in action. Finally, you might reflect on action when you get feedback so that you can enhance your future academic work, using reflection for action.

The experiential learning cycle requires you to undertake an activity, having *concrete experience*, which you are asked then to reflect upon to consider what you felt went well and what did not go as expected, using *reflective observation*. This is followed by a period of *abstract conceptualisation*, where you apply theory and knowledge to the situation to develop an understanding of why the result was as it was and consider different theories to inform future practice. This is followed by a planning stage to enable *active experimentation*, where different options are considered to enable consideration of the most appropriate way to undertake the activity again, the principle being that students learn from both their successes and mistakes and apply them to future interventions. Kolb (1984) argued that one of these stages alone is insufficient to develop knowledge and skills, but that all should be undertaken to optimise experiential learning.

Relating this to an academic process can at first glance be unrealistic. Experiential learning? I am not doing, I am being taught. So why would I want to reflect on my experience? Well to put it simply, learning at university is not about being provided with information, absorbing and regurgitating it in an exam or academic assessment in the form of an essay or assignment. University is called higher education as it requires you to be ready, orientated and motivated to learn, as well as autonomous, independent and self-directed (Knowles, 1973) as an adult learner, which enables deep learning, concepts that are discussed in Chapter two.

Instead, it is helpful to consider each lecture you sit in, each seminar you contribute to, each book you read, each article you access, each exam you sit, each essay or assignment your write, each practical learning activity you undertake – in short all academic activities – as an experience to reflect on. It is only by taking this approach that you begin to become a critical thinker. There are several models of reflection that you can use to support your critical thinking.

Jasper (2013) outlines a simple model of reflection which uses the ERA cycle:

- Experience
- Reflection
- Action

Experiences can be both positive and negative; what matters here is how you develop your thinking in response to these, and how you think about what happened, examining your feelings, and response to it. You can then decide if next steps are needed, leading into a cycle where you then start to analyse your next experience.

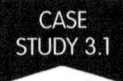

CASE STUDY 3.1

When applying this to Ted and Henry in the first example of the chapter, it can be seen that Henry attended the *Experience* of a study skills tutorial. He *Reflected* that he needed to continue to develop his critical thinking skills and took *Action* by engaging in the recommended learning activities.

Another model that is easy to apply and use was developed by Driscoll (2007), using Borton's (1970) key questions:

- What?
- So what?
- Now what?

If you ask yourself these questions, you are beginning to critically analyse your experiences. The 'what' question, is suggesting that you describe the experience that you had and consider it in context. Then, 'so what' is telling you to consider your learning from this experience. The final 'now what' is encouraging you to critically think about what you might (or might not) change as a result of your thinking.

Finally, there is Gibbs' (1988) learning by doing model, which is more complex than the reflective models that have already been described and is closer to Kolb's original experiential learning cycle. Gibbs' (1988) model contains six stages:

- Description
- Feelings
- Evaluation
- Analysis
- Conclusion
- Action plan

Gibbs encourages you to start with considering an experience to reflect upon, briefly describing the event. You can then focus on how you felt before, during and after the experience, mirroring Schon's (1983) reflection for-, in- and on-action model. Then to develop your critical thinking, you should evaluate the experience by considering what was good or bad about it, so that you try to make sense of it. This is a form of analysis and should encourage you to once again decide if other actions should have been taken. The final stage of this model involves building an action plan of steps to take if you find yourself in a similar situation. Each of the models outlined here provides you with a structure to follow.

Top tip 3.4

> Attend a lecture or seminar and apply your critical thinking using each of these models of reflection.
>
> Which model works better for you?
>
> Try them all, and feel free to be flexible and adapt them to develop a reflective system that works for you.

Critical thinking

Developing this further, whilst reflective thinking asks you to consider an experience and develop knowledge and skills by learning from your strengths and areas for development, in addition to what went wrong and what could be done differently to transfer learning to a future similar activity, critical thinking asks you to take a *critical* approach to the academic activity. As discussed in Chapter one, critical thinking is the skill of identifying and neutralising bias, taking a curious approach that enables you to consider all perspectives before coming to an informed decision on your own opinion to enable a discerning judgement.

In order for you to get started with critical thinking, there are a range of strategies available for you to apply in your own learning. Chatfield (2022) outlines *ten commandments* for you to use when developing your critical thinking, which are a useful starting point for all students starting out in university education.

Table 3.1 Ten commandments for critical thinking (adapted from Chatfield, 2022)

Commandment	Explanation
1. Slow	Pause to think more deeply about content, materials, questions. If you choose to get on with it, you are missing the opportunity to consider it reflectively.
2. Save mental energy	None of us have unlimited concentration power, so work out the best place (environment for you to study in) and avoid distractions (emails, social media, friends, etc.)
3. Wait	Allow yourself time to pause – time is a useful filter. It can help with concentration and decision-making.
4. Be self-aware	It is okay to say that you don't know, and to need to do more reading, writing and research. No one person can be an expert in all areas, including your tutors.
5. Think of lost costs	If you have put lots of time and effort into something (an essay for example) it feels easier to keep going, rather than to consider if this is the right approach. You may need to be brutal if things are not working out. Learning always takes place, even when you make mistakes.
6. Use strategy	Don't be tempted to focus on short-term success, for example one good grade; you need to build strategy to learn more deeply, so keep working.
7. Averages	An amazing result, e.g. one very high mark, is just that – amazing! A failure is equally very disappointing. However, you need to focus on trends and averages, rather than outliers – if you are generally achieving marks in the 50% category, working on your critical thinking will improve your average.
8. Look for disproof	We can all confirm our own ideas constantly by looking for proof of them, so seek out challenges, contradictions and disproof to challenge your own views. This will help you to learn to test your thoughts, ideas and opinions.
9. Pay attention to frames of reference	Be aware of the power of perception. Perceptions are not truth and are always relative and embedded in what you both see and experience.
10. Consider all options	Are you really being offered a choice? Is there a different view, opinion or way of thinking outside of what is being suggested?

Like reflective thinking, there are a number of models that can be used to assist and develop your critical thinking. The use of a model gives you structure and ensures that your organised approach covers a range of aspects.

Top tip 3.5

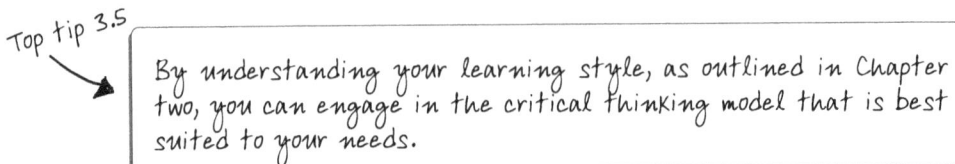

By understanding your learning style, as outlined in Chapter two, you can engage in the critical thinking model that is best suited to your needs.

Tripp (1993) introduced critical incident analysis to bridge the gap between reflective thinking and critical thinking. Here, we term a lecture, seminar, feedback or reading in preparation for completing an assignment, or a practical learning activity as the critical incident.

- Account of the learning activity
- Initial responses to the learning activity
- Issues and dilemmas highlighted from the learning activity
- Learning from the learning activity
- Outcomes for future learning activities

You will easily identify the similarity to Gibbs' (1988) learning by doing reflective model. An argument against Gibbs' model is that it enables a superficial reflection as it does not ask the reflector to challenge their assumptions. The critical incident analysis (CIA) adds that layer of criticality to each stage to ensure that deeper thing occurs.

However, models of critical thinking require you to integrate information presented to you. First the RED model (Pearson Education and TalentLens, 2021) asks you to:

- Recognize assumptions
- Evaluate arguments
- Draw conclusions

Critical thinking starts by not taking information at face value and being able to recognise the assumptions of your lecturers and the authors of the work you are reading, as well as your own. The RED model advocates that gathering of information should be undertaken from a range of sources to facilitate engaging with a variety of perspectives. This enables you to evaluate a range of different perspectives objectively and analytically weigh them up based on their merits. Finally, it directs you to ensure that you have an understanding of all perspectives before you draw your own conclusions, arguing that this makes for informed decision-making and problem-solving.

CASE STUDY 3.2

When applying this to Ted and Henry in the first example of the chapter, it can be seen that Ted did not *Recognise* the assumption he made that college and university academic assignments are identical whilst Henry engaged with the teaching and learning outcomes to enable him to *Evaluate* what was required of him and *Drew* the conclusion that he needed to apply and analyse the knowledge of the topics required.

Providing more depth to critical thinking are the Toulmin model (Toulmin, 1958) and the FRISCO model (Ennis, 1996).

Toulmin model	FRISCO model
Ground	Focus
Claim	Reason
Warrant	Inference
Back	Situation
Rebuttal	Clarity
Qualifier	Overview

These critical thinking models support you to identify the strengths and weaknesses of the learning materials which subsequently enhances your own academic argument. First, the Toulmin model asks you to determine the grounds (basis) for the argument and consider what the claim is based on and if it is warranted to understand the foundations of the discussion and identify bias. Secondly, it asks you to test and evaluate the discussion by considering what backs (supports) the argument and what a rebuttal (difference in perspective) could be to come to a qualifying statement, or informed conclusion, to your critical thinking. Similarly, the Frisco model asks you to consider the reason for the discussion and what it tells you before seeking context and clarification to provide an overview of the work.

A different approach that may appeal to the less process-driven students is a questioning approach. Nosich (2009) suggests that there are three parts to critical thinking:

1. Ask the question.
2. Answer the question.
3. Accept your reasoning.

Similarly, the five whys critical thinking model can be used. This is similar to Driscoll's (2007) 'what?' reflective model, but instead prompts you to ask 'why?' five times.

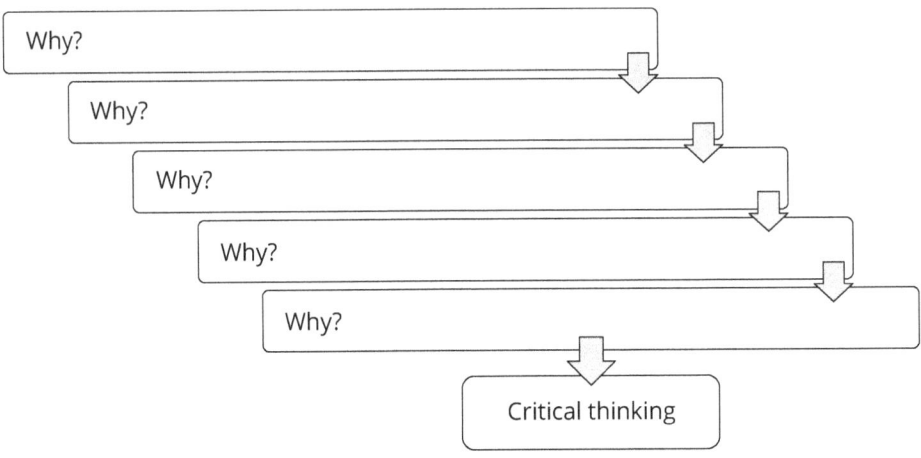

Figure 3.1 Driscoll's (2007) 'What?' reflective model

This model is based on the principle that not accepting things at face value and by resilient question asking you will achieve deeper learning as your understanding grows.

CASE STUDY 3.3

Henry attends a lecture on criminology. In the lecture, feminist criminology is introduced which is a new subject to him, although he understands the basic issues of feminism. He decides to critically think about a feminist perspective and uses the five whys critical thinking model.

Why is a feminist lens applied since aren't all criminals the same?

No, men and women should not be considered as homogeneous. They have different needs and different experiences of the world.

Why do women experience life differently than men?

Gender stereotypes remain prevalent. Women often have to both conform within a male-controlled society and take on male attributes to succeed. Yet they also have to remain 'feminine'.

Why don't women just break the narrative and act like men do?

Because we live in a white patriarchal society where men continue to control the narrative. When a man is a criminal he only breaks laws, when a woman is a criminal, she breaks laws and societal expectations. Going to prison is a bigger deterrent for women than men.

Why is prison more of a deterrent for women than men?

Perhaps because they are seen as the carers and family-orientated, perhaps because society expects them to take a more hands-on approach to parenting that distance from children is a greater deterrent.

Why do women feel the loss of the parenting role greater?

Because social construction has taught them to be the mother, carer and nurturer, so they feel it more. We need to go back to the social construction of women's roles as advocated by feminism.

Whilst this is simplified thinking it shows how Henry developed his understanding and deeper learning on the topic.

In contrast, the six thinking hats (De Bono, 1985) is excellent for visual learners:

- white for facts and data;
- red for emotions and feelings;
- black for risks and drawbacks;
- yellow for benefits and opportunities;
- green for alternatives and possibilities; and
- blue for process and control.

The idea here is that you 'change hats' so that you are conscious of moving between different stages of critical thinking, which inevitably enhances it. Equally you can have some fun and make different images represent each stage.

When critically thinking using the six thinking hats, you should first apply facts and data: what do you know about the event, activity or situation, is there further information that you need to gather to enable you to understand, what academic knowledge can you apply? This would be followed by reflecting on your emotions and feelings: what did you feel and why; but this needs critical analysis of why you felt this way, which can be challenging as you will need to be open and honest with yourself, sometimes about difficult or hidden topics. It is important to weigh both the risks and opportunities to develop possibilities, but this must again be done with an open and critical approach that considers all perspectives and allows you to be open to different outcomes. However, this needs to be undertaken within boundaries, which can be procedural, ethical and value-based, societal and course expectations and norms, or the knowledge that you would reasonably be able to apply at this stage in your academic

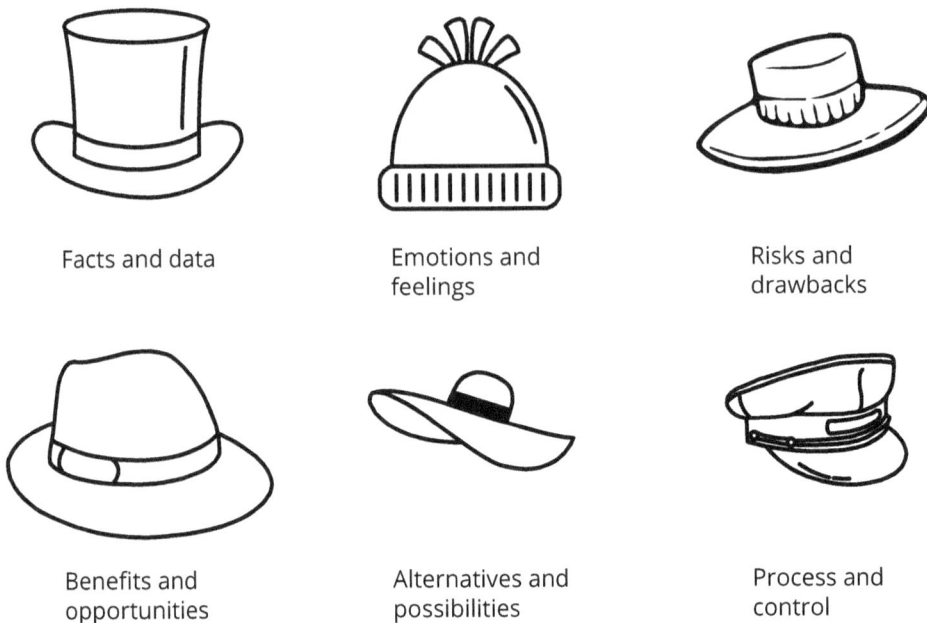

Figure 3.2 The six thinking hats illustrated (adapted from De Bono, 1985)

career. By wearing each hat you will understand the incident from a variety of perspectives. It is helpful to acknowledge here that when critically thinking in practice learning (Chapter twelve) the wearing of different people's metaphorical hats can develop empathy and understanding for everyone's situation and is a great critical thinking tool with different hat labels.

Irrespective of the critical thinking model that you chose to use, it is beneficial to be aware of the need to reflect, identify bias and recognise assumptions, be curious by asking questions, and weighing up strengths and areas for development, evaluate and analyse all perspectives, and come to your own informed conclusions by considering alternatives and possibilities and applying your understanding and knowledge. Critical thinking can help you to engage with deeper thinking, develop greater understanding and tackle complex topics.

Individual learning needs

Students with individual learning needs may have to develop their own coping strategies to enable them to engage with coping strategies.

Students with a health issue or disability

First, it is helpful to consider what we mean by students with a Reasonable Adjustment Plan (RAP). This is used throughout the book to denote a student with a physical disability, learning disability, health or mental health issue that they have discussed with the university. A plan is then formulated to support their academic studies through a reasonable adjustment such as support from a disability support worker, longer time for assignments and/or exams, or adaptions including assistive technology. In the academic year 2021/2022 in the United Kingdom (UK), 19% of home students declared that they had a reasonable adjustment (HESA, 2023) yet completion rates and degree classifications for these students were lower primarily than students without a disability health issue (OfS, 2024). The social model of disability (Oliver, 1983) would argue that this is because university learning is designed for healthy and non-disabled people and does not allow for variation of need. Although Beck (2022) argued that inclusive course design should be considered where possible, it is here that the reasonable adjustment is required to address this lack of equity.

> **Top tip 3.6**
>
> Your university will have a disability support service: use it!
>
> They are experts in supporting students with a disability or health issue and will be able to offer practical support and advice that will enable you to engage with your course in a more productive manner.

However, it is clear that you will need to do more than some other students on your course. It is common that students with a health issue or disability may take longer to engage with critical thinking. This is not a criticism, just a sad fact of life. This can be due to a range of factors:

- if you suffer from chronic fatigue you may need to engage in shorter and more frequent critical thinking sessions and may need to determine priorities from self-directed studying versus travel to and engagement with lectures;
- if you have a learning disability it may take longer to process information and therefore your ability to critically think may be slowed down;
- if you have a physical disability you may need to use audio books which take reading longer to access;
- if you experience anxiety or depression, motivation to critically think may be more difficult for you at times.

This is by no means an exhaustive list and you should reflect on how your disability or health issues impacts on your ability to study. However, this should then lead to the development of coping strategies to enable you to manage both your individual learning needs and critical thinking.

Top tip 3.7

> Ask for clarity: ensure that you fully understand the academic expectations on you so that you can fulfil the course requirements.
>
> Develop coping strategies that you know work for you: these will enable you to engage with critical thinking.
>
> This book has many ideas and tips for all students that you should engage with, but also provides tips and advice specifically for students with individual learning needs.

The most important thing that you can do is to be *proactive*. By taking control of your own education, asking for help when you need it, engaging with learning materials as soon as they are available so that you are organised and ready, and taking account of how you learn to maximise your engagement, you will set yourself up well for critical thinking. McNicholas (2020) suggests a *success attitude*, effectively suggesting that you can train your brain to think critically where it does not come naturally to you: through practice makes perfect. However, it is not quite that simple. Beesley and Walkden (2024) found that societal stigma created a sense of shame for students with a reasonable adjustment plan, both where they needed to use it and where they needed to ask or remind teaching staff for support that they were entitled to.

Ethnically diverse students

This can cover international students who are studying abroad and resident students who may not have been born in the resident country. 34.4% of students starting a undergraduate degree in England were ethnically diverse yet their completion rates and degree classifications were lower than white British students (OfS, 2024). It is clear that ethnically diverse students are disadvantaged during their time at university. Critical Race Theory would suggest that the experiences of ethnically diverse students in a white, middle-class constructed environment of a university disadvantages those students as they are not prepared to engage in this framework.

Going to university can be daunting, but if you are an ethnically diverse student this can be particularly overwhelming. If you have moved from a diverse school or a country of origin to a predominantly white-British university, this can be your first experience of being 'different' (Osbourne et al., 2021) and Bunce et al. (2021) found that an inability to relate to peers impacted BGM students' learning experiences and outcomes. For example, if the majority of the course 'goes for a pint' after lectures but you do not drink this can be very excluding and it is often where social relationships are formed that are then taken into lectures and seminars, so you are likely to feel even more separate and unable to engage in critical thinking in groups.

Undoubtedly, teaching staff and white peers should engage with change through their own critical thinking, but until then sadly the need to adapt within a white society remains a requirement for most Black and Global Minority heritage students. This is not to say that ethnically diverse students lack the skills to participate well within university and engage with critical thinking. Instead, you may have to develop a new set of cultural norms to adapt to the situation whilst also holding on to yourself and your identity, no mean feat. However, it has been identified that both your own and others' critical thinking will develop more productively in interactional diverse groups (Karpacheva, 2023) and that students will be open to challenge and addressing social injustice as a result (Álvarez-Huerta et al., 2022).

Many universities operate a Eurocentric curriculum, which means that they require students to understand the requirements and expectations of a white educational system. However, Elhinnawy (2022) in researching the experiences of criminology students, found that motivation and engagement by ethnically diverse students dropped where student identity was not recognised. The research recognised that where students developed a sense of course and university identity that engagement in the course, and by default critical thinking, increased. Examples of an inclusive curriculum include:

- Learning materials by ethnically diverse academics and authors.
- Ensuring that lectures and seminars discuss the needs of a diverse population.

This will also enhance the social and cultural learning of all students, by enabling critical thinking of all perspectives. Whilst this chapter's example has provided a feminist consideration, Critical Race Theory could alternatively be inserted to stimulate wider thinking. However, it is recognised that academics need to embrace this proactively and an inherent power differential often deters students from raising or suggesting such ideas, yet you can search for your own ethnically diverse authored materials and use them within your lectures, seminars and assessment to model good practice.

If your educational experiences have been different than the white, British, middle-class norms, you may find it difficult to adjust to university expectations. The challenges that you face here may be feeling incompetent through lack of transition support and the lack of the ability to act autonomously due to different educational experiences impacting on cultural competence (Bunce et al., 2021). Respect for a teacher is an excellent cultural trait, but if it prevents you from asking what to do or from taking the initiative to develop your own learning, it may restrict your learning.

As such, it may be that you do not have the same basic critical thinking skills that your peers may start university with. An awareness of this is essential as it will enable you to spend additional time familiarising yourself with these first three chapters that explore what critical thinking is, why critical thinking matters and university and on becoming a critical thinker.

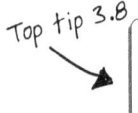

Top tip 3.8

> Don't be afraid to express your opinion.
>
> Ask other students questions:
>
> > why do you have that opinion?
> >
> > what do you think of this perspective?
>
> Remember your worth: you bring a different perspective that can only enrich and develop everyone's knowledge and skills through critical thinking and discussion.

Critical thinking action plan

Please reflect on your critical thinking skills and where you need to develop a skill develop your critical thinking action plan.

Worksheet 3.1   Critical thinking action plan

Critical thinking skill	Action to be taken	Review after six weeks
Ability to reflectively think		
Ability to critically think		
Identify a model that works for you		
Identify any individual learning needs		

Conclusion

In this chapter we have focused on how to become a critical thinker. First, a range of models of reflective thinking were provided to support your understanding of how to think and reflect on everyday matters. Secondly, models of critical thinking were introduced that enabled you to move to a critical perspective academically. The chapter ended by considering individual learning needs, where it was recognised that some students will need to put more time and effort into critical thinking to enable them to engage as effectively as other students. This section will reappear throughout the book.

Further reading

Chatfield, T. (2022) *Critical Thinking: Your essential guide*. London: Sage.
Cottrell, S. (2023) *Critical Thinking Skills*. London: Bloomsbury.
McNicholas, A. M. (2020) *The Dyslexia, ADHD and DCD-friendly Study Skills Guide: Tips and strategies for exam success*. London: Jessica Kingsley. Whilst this book is focused on exam strategies for students with a learning disability, it provides excellent resources and ideas.
Williams, K. (2022) *Getting Critical*. Basingstoke: Red Globe Press.

Each of these books provides a clear and accessible introduction to critical thinking that can be applied to the later chapters.

PART II

CRITICAL THINKING IN LECTURES AND SEMINARS

In order to maximise your learning in taught activities, here including lectures and seminars but taking account that you may experience other taught activities, you will need to critically think before, during and after them. Part II introduces the experiential learning loop, where you see the importance of viewing taught activities as interactive.

The experiential learning loop

University will provide *scaffolding* for your learning in the form of preparatory tasks and/or reading materials, learning activities including lectures and seminars, and directed tasks for after-learning activities. Whilst your tutors will create opportunities for you to foster your critical thinking, it is important to note that their activities alone are not enough. All classroom interactions will require your critical thinking before, during and after the learning activity to maximise your development of knowledge and skills: an *experiential learning loop*. This combines Kolb's (1984) experiential learning cycle and Schon's (1983, 1991) reflection for, in and on action model, both discussed in Chapter three, to demonstrate the importance of your proactive critical thinking in your development of knowledge and skills.

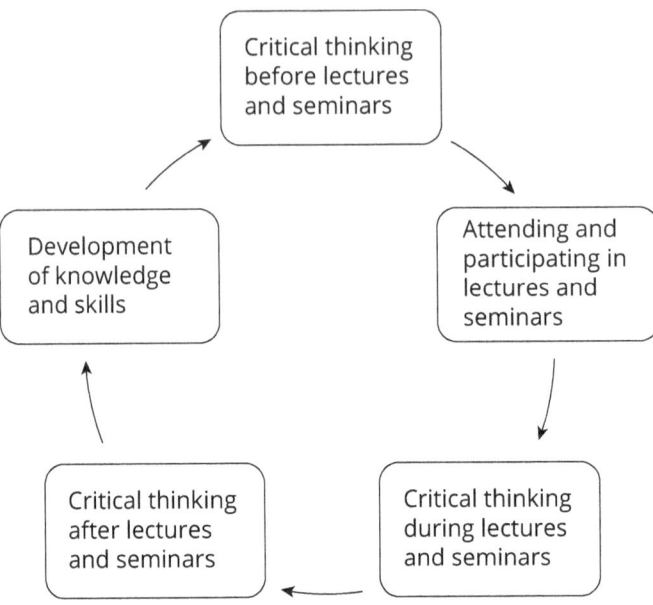

Figure Part 2.1 Experiential learning loop

As can be seen from Figure Part 2.1 which illustrates the experiential learning loop, students learn not just from attending lectures and seminars, although that is important to the development of knowledge and skills at university. In the first stage, students engage with critical thinking *before* lectures and seminars (Chapter four) to plan and facilitate their engagement with the lecture or seminar, and support them in reflecting to take action. In the second stage it is imperative that students attend and participate in the active experimentation, which facilitates the third stage, which is critical thinking during lectures (Chapter five) and seminars (Chapter six), effectively reflecting in action. In the fourth stage, students critically think *after* lectures and seminars (Chapter seven) effectively reflecting on action, by using evaluation or reflective observation and application of existing knowledge or abstract conceptualisation to the learning activity. Finally, stage five enables the student to identify that they have developed knowledge and skills, which they are able to apply when returning to stage one of preparing for another lecture or seminar. 'For learning to occur, there has to be some kind of change in the learner. No change, no learning. Significant learning requires that there be some kind of lasting change that is important in terms of the learner's life' (Fink, 2013, p. 34).

Engaging in and developing your skills in critical thinking is not easy, therefore it requires investment – in both time and practice to develop your thinking. It is important to know that the type of learning required to develop critical thinking, can and does feel uncomfortable. Knowledge can feel *troublesome* (Meyer and

Land, 2003) when we are trying to develop our understanding, and we may respond emotionally as a result.

Top tip Part 2.1

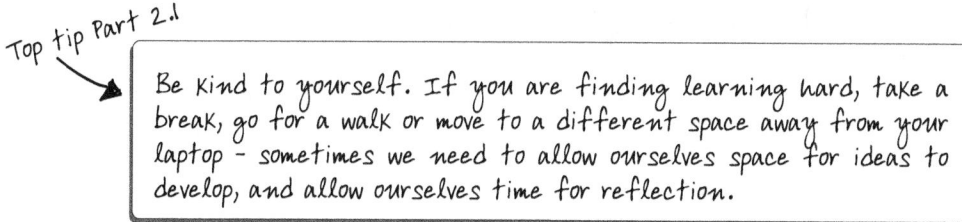

Be kind to yourself. If you are finding learning hard, take a break, go for a walk or move to a different space away from your laptop — sometimes we need to allow ourselves space for ideas to develop, and allow ourselves time for reflection.

This section supports the student through the experiential learning loop considering critical thinking before, during and after lectures and seminars, which ultimately is learning that is then applied to assessment tasks outlined in Part III.

4

Critical thinking before lectures and seminars

> **CHAPTER OBJECTIVES**

- Understand the importance of active preparation for lectures and seminars
- Develop critical thinking skills when considering preparatory
    - Reading materials
    - PowerPoints
    - Activities

Introduction

Critical thinking before lectures and seminars is the first stage of the experiential learning loop, by preparation will facilitate your effective engagement with the lecture or seminar as you are preparing for action (Schon, 1991). This chapter will begin by reflecting on the importance of being prepared to enhance students' ability to engage with the coming teaching activity. It will then support the reader to consider active participation and critical thinking with preparatory materials. It will ask the reader to consider accessing reading materials with a critical eye and practical ways to engage with PowerPoints and learning activities.

Starting the experiential learning loop: active preparation

There is a popular adage that 'if you fail to prepare, you are preparing to fail' (attributed to Benjamin Franklyn, n.d.), which has been paraphrased by sportspeople, business gurus and politicians alike to demonstrate the benefit of planning and preparation towards a successful outcome. A similar common saying is 'you only get out what you put in'. These two sayings indicate that you cannot be a passive participant in *your* education. Godfrey (2023) argues that the point of university education is to build on existing understanding to develop knowledge and skills through active learning. Indeed, Cerbin (2018) identifies that deep learning is achieved through critical thinking before, during and after a lecture, indicating the importance of active preparation.

WHICH STUDENT IS CRITICALLY THINKING?

Abbie and Angela are geography students who attend a lecture.

Abbie attends the lecture on time every week and feels committed to the course.	Angela allocates two hours to undertake preparation before each lecture.
In the lecture she struggles to engage with the materials because the lecturer seems to be assuming a knowledge she does not have. Yet other students seem to understand and are able to engage in the discussions.	She knows that it doesn't always take her two hours to work through the materials, but she likes to make notes and to reflect on the materials before attending the lecture.
She feels lost in the lecture.	In the lecture, she is able to confidently engage in discussions based on the pre-lecture materials.

Obviously, we are hoping that you are aiming to be the later, as this chapter is designed to support you develop active preparation for lectures and seminars. Lecturers will have spent time identifying the most appropriate reading and preparatory materials to complement the lecture or seminar, so they are worth engaging with. It is worth remembering that two hours is the maximum length of time that reading is effective and that you should take regular breaks in that time (Kneale, 2019).

Preparation enables you to begin the critical thinking process to understand the topic for delivery and/or discussion. Indeed, Snead et al. (2023) undertook comparative research with American financial management students and found a clear indication that engagement with preparatory materials had a positive impact on students' understanding of the lecture materials. Where you have pre-existing knowledge and understanding of a topic developed through preparation, you are better placed to engage with the materials as you understand the foundations which you are able to build upon as more complex concepts are discussed within the lecture or seminar.

When considering the andrological (adult learning) principles (Knowles, 1973; Knowles et al., 2020) discussed in Chapter two, if you are motivated, ready to learn and see value in the learning materials you will be actively participating in your own learning. When you ask yourself 'why bother?' or 'could I be doing something better with my time?' it is likely that you have lost motivation to engage with preparation for a lecture or seminar. If you cannot understand how they enhance your learning, it can be worth talking to the module leader to develop your understanding of their purpose and therefore your motivation to engage with them.

In contrast, where you can see a link between preparatory materials and the lecture, if you perceive a link between the topic and your module assessment, or just have a keen interest in a topic, you are more likely to engage with the preparatory materials as you will be more motivated to engage where you see the value in doing so beyond the lecture or seminar you are preparing for. This is achieved by being independent, self-motivated, able to work things out for yourself, able to set goals to improve your work, able to organise your time, able to work out when and how you learn best (Cottrell, 2019). Reflect and consider which of those skills you have strengths in and which you need to develop.

Top tip 4.1

Don't confuse preparation with planning.

Planning is organising yourself to do the preparation.

Preparation is actively engaging with the reading materials and reflecting on the PowerPoint materials that will be presented to you in the lecture or seminar. It enables you to move to critical thinking before lectures and seminars, which in turn ensures that you are ready and able to learn.

Preparation is associated with confidence, making you feel more able to participate in critical thinking in lectures and seminars. In contrast a lack of preparation can induce anxiety, which is known to reduce concentration and ability to actively listen and engage with learning, further impacting on your participation with the lecture or seminar and development. Returning to the adage at the start of this section, are you 'preparing to fail' or are you preparing to succeed?

Critically thinking before lectures and seminars

Good practice dictates that lecturers will upload preparatory materials before lectures and seminars. First, it is helpful to be aware of the learning objectives for the teaching session when reading preparatory materials. This will be for the actual session (located in the PowerPoint), the module (located in the module handbook) and the course (located in the course handbook). This will enable you to understand why a topic is on the curriculum, how it fits into the course and why it is of value to you as a learner to motivate you to engage with the preparation and learning (Knowles, 1973; Knowles et al., 2020). For students on professional courses, your lectures or seminars may also be linked to professional learning and assessment criteria and for apprentices to Knowledge, Skills and Behaviours (KSBs).

The chapter will now consider the preparation and critical thinking required before lectures and seminars. Broadly speaking, this falls into three categories: reading materials, PowerPoint presentations and activities.

Reading materials

It can be helpful to think about *how* to access preparatory reading materials. Hopkins and Reid (2018) argue that an effective active reader is strategic, selective and systematic, which is a helpful starting point.

The first is to be strategic, where it is helpful to consider what you need to read (Chatfield, 2022). It can be helpful to look at abstracts and chapter summaries to determine in which order you want to read them to ensure that you build your understanding as you progress through your preparation for lecture or seminar.

Top tip 4.2

Do not mix up unengaged with strategic learning. Strategic means putting in the most effective use of your time for the maximum learning.

Where there is choice of preparatory materials, it is likely that they cover a range of complexity and presentation styles, so ensure that you read the option that most suits your reading style. If you are academically minded, a journal article may be a good starting point, whilst if you learn in a more practical way, a chapter from an interactive textbook is more likely to engage you. Each will enhance your understanding and development of knowledge. By approaching preparatory materials strategically, you will be able to identify through a first skim read that you do not need to access a more straightforward text or that trying to read a complex article may be beyond you. It is important to be aware of *your* learning needs rather than try to compete with your peers, as everyone is on their own learning journey. Reading the wrong preparatory materials can impact on your confidence and enthusiasm. That said, it is important that you don't 'give up' just because you do not understand it at a glance (Cottrell, 2019).

A further strategic consideration is *when* to engage with preparatory materials. It is likely that you will have a busy life, with social, work and/or family commitments competing with study requirements and a set lecture and seminar timetable. Consider *where* you best read and what lighting works best for you (Cottrell, 2019). It is helpful to schedule preparatory reading time to avoid prevarication and avoidance.

> **Top tip 4.3**
>
> Consider when you are most able to read effectively.
>
> If you are a night owl schedule your time to engage with preparatory reading for later in the day.
>
> If you are exhausted by early evening, earlier in the day will be a better time to read.

As such, it is important to use your time strategically to engage with the preparatory reading materials to maximise learning. The second point is to be selective. Here, Hopkins and Reid (2018) suggest that you do not assume that you need to read from cover to cover but instead read the relevant sections. Finally, be systematic and organised. It is unlikely that a 'quick read' will enable you to engage with preparatory reading materials in any depth. In order to engage in critical thinking in relation to preparatory materials it can be helpful to work through the chapter or article a number of times, as illustrated in Figure 4.1.

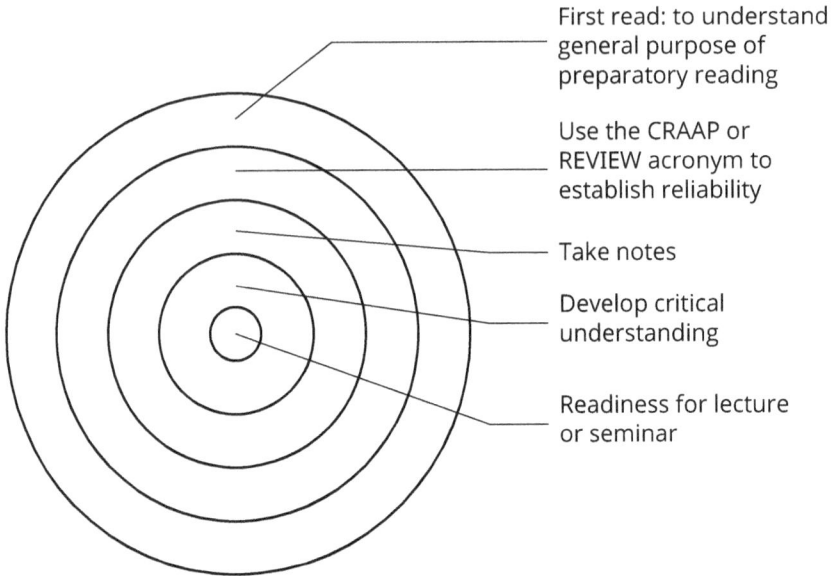

Figure 4.1 Multiple reading of an article or chapter develops critical thinking

First Read

Initially, it can be helpful to read the preparatory material without making any notes or undertaking critically thinking about the content. This enables you to read the chapter or article as a whole and gain an understanding of the purpose of the reading (Redman and Maples, 2017). You may begin to identify key themes in this first read, which can be helpful to jot down, and will begin to engage you in critical reading (Chatfield, 2022).

Establish reliability

It can be helpful to critically think about the reliability of the preparatory materials. This is not to say that one source is better than another, but to say that their purpose and therefore academic reliability would be different and inform your use of them. The acronyms CRAAP and REVIEW have been adapted from Leeds Beckett University materials to support you in your critical thinking before lectures and seminars.

> Currency: is this a contemporary reference? If not, is it a 'classic' that underpins current understanding of the topic?

Relevance: why are you being asked to read the article? Seeing value in your preparatory reading will enhance your ability to engage in the topic.

Authority: do you feel that the author has credibility within your field? Does the reading demonstrate academic knowledge of the topic?

Accuracy: do you feel that the source is reliable and truthful?

Purpose: is the preparatory reading objective? Is there any political, professional or personal bias?

A similar mnemonic is REVIEW, which covers the same points in a different order:

Relevance

Expertise of the author (authority)

Viewpoint (purpose)

Intended audience (purpose)

Evidence (accuracy)

When published (currency)

Use of either acronym can support your understanding of academic reliability and stimulate your critical thinking about reliability of preparatory materials.

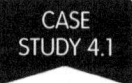

CASE STUDY 4.1

In order to assist you in the development of your critical thinking, it can be helpful to compare two sources and evaluate them using the CRAAP or REVIEW mnemonics (outlined below to try).

Angela, a first-year geography student on a module on renewable energy, has been given two preparatory reading items to engage with. They have been asked to critically think about each of them for discussion in a lecture about solar energy.

1. National Grid (2023) How does solar power work? www.nationalgrid.com/stories/energy-explained/how-does-solar-power-work
2. Sareen, S. (2022) Legitimating Power: Solar energy rollout, sustainability metrics and transition politics. Environment and Planning E: Nature and Space, 5(3), 1014–1034. https://journals.sagepub.com/doi/full/10.1177/25148486211024903

Critical thinking in lectures and seminars

C	R
R	E
A	V
A	I
P	E
	W

Figure 4.2 Evaluate 'How does solar power work' using CRAAP and/or REVIEW

C	R
R	E
A	V
A	I
P	E
	W

Figure 4.3 Evaluate 'Legitimating Power' using CRAAP and/or REVIEW

It is likely that you began by identifying that both have *Currency* being written in 2022 and 2023 in relation to the publication date of the book. Similarly, you could argue that both have *Relevancy* if the lecture topic is solar energy as both address this topic. Thus far you would potentially argue that they are equal in their reliability as a source. You may feel that they have equal *Authority*, as Sareen is an academic expert in the field and the National Grid is an expert in energy production. However, here you may start to feel that the academic reliability begins to diverge. You may feel that Sareen's article 'Legitimating Power' has an academic foundation and builds on previous researcher's work to develop an argument giving it *Authority*. In contrast, you may feel that whilst National Grid may have a foundation of knowledge, it is not evidenced and referenced in 'How does solar power work?', reducing its *Authority*.

Moving to *Accuracy*, it can be difficult as a student to determine if a source is reliable and truthful. However, what we can say is that where a journal article has been peer-reviewed by an expert in the field that it has been verified by a second (and often third) source, giving it reliability and therefore assumption of *Accuracy* through the reputation of the journal. In contrast, it can be argued that a website, particularly for a national organisation such as National Grid, has its own reputation to uphold. Whilst we would hope that it has been fact checked before uploading to the internet, this cannot be verified so reduces the *Accuracy* that we can attribute to 'How does solar power work?'. As such, we might also consider *representativeness* (Chatfield, 2022). In considering *Accuracy*, it is helpful to critically reflect if the source represents the social or cultural norm.

Finally, in considering *Purpose*, arguably the greatest critical thinking must be applied. Firstly, you should consider the basis on which they are written. Arguably, the National Grid receives funding from the UK government and is required to abide by national policies on renewable energy, so may lack objectivity. In addition, there is an element within this webpage of self-promotion that will inevitably bias its presentation to align with the organisation's objectives. Indeed, if you access www.nationalgrid.com/about-us this page sets out the organisation's value and mission statement, does re-reading 'How does solar power work?' now have a subjective approach that aligns with their 'strategic priority' for 'clean ... energy'? You could argue that the *Purpose* of 'How does solar power work?' is information provision rather than academic reliability, so why then has the lecturer asked you to read this as part of the preparatory materials? Critically think about this question. It may be that you feel that the lecturer wanted to give you an easy week; that they are anxious that your cohort know nothing about solar panels so what is their opinion of you all; or that they are trying to provide varied resources that require you to critically examine their positionality in the wider context of green energy.

In contrast, when considering the *Purpose* of 'Legitimating Power', it is important to remember that whilst research should be carried out in a non-judgemental manner, that personal and professional bias is inevitable in any research. Research bias can come through researcher subject interest, funding criteria, choice of methodology, availability of and identity of research participants, and choice of data collection and data analysis methods (Patton, 2015). It is important to acknowledge that where the researcher is reflective on their positionality, they can minimise unconscious bias and enhance the validity of the research outcomes (Mason-Bish, 2019). Nevertheless, a critical thinking approach to reading a journal article should take account of these factors.

You might consider that Sareen's interviewing of a range of industry experts gave the article a clear reliability and credibility, but it is important to remember that the interview questions would have a *Purpose* as they would have been designed to elicit opinion in specific areas. This does not negate the research, but highlights that all research is undertaken through a lens of the research objectives, which sets out the *Purpose* of the research.

It can be seen that both provide reliability, but that critical thinking undertaken to compare the two could arguably conclude that 'Legitimating Power' provides a greater depth of academic reliability due to its *Accuracy* and *Purpose*.

Note Making

Hopkins and Reid (2018) advocate the importance of being organised and making good notes through identifying and recording description, analysis and evaluation of the preparatory materials.

Top tip 4.4

> It is helpful to have a notebook or electronic folder per module.
>
> It will enable you to organise notes from preparatory materials, lectures, seminars and reflective notes after teaching.
>
> Some students like to print an article or chapter to enable them to highlight with different colours different themes.

When making notes it can be helpful to have a system so that you can distinguish when you are paraphrasing or summarising the author(s)'s ideas or when you are lifting a quote directly. In addition, page numbers can help you locate the areas you are referring to when you revisit your notes.

It can be a helpful student activity to access an article or chapter recommended to you from your course and try both of the note-making methods below to determine which works most effectively for your ability to be systematic.

The first is simply an approach where you read the chapter or journal and make notes chronologically as you read them. This can be considered passive, but when combined with the adaptation of a Cornell template illustrated in Table 4.1 it can incorporate critical thinking.

Worksheet 4.1 Critical thinking Cornell note-making proforma

Preparatory materials full reference

	Description	Analysis	Evaluation
Introduction			
Literature review			
Methodology			
Findings			
Conclusion			
Overall thoughts			
Further reading			

Worksheet 4.1 can be adapted to suit your needs. This example is to be used with a journal article, but the headings in the left-hand column can be changed to [introduction, main theme 1, main theme 2, main theme 3, conclusion, overall thoughts, further reading] for a book or webpage.

In contrast, pattern notes are organised thematically. You may think of these as a spider diagram or a mind map. In pattern notes, you are building visual connections and have the freedom to make these as creative as you wish.

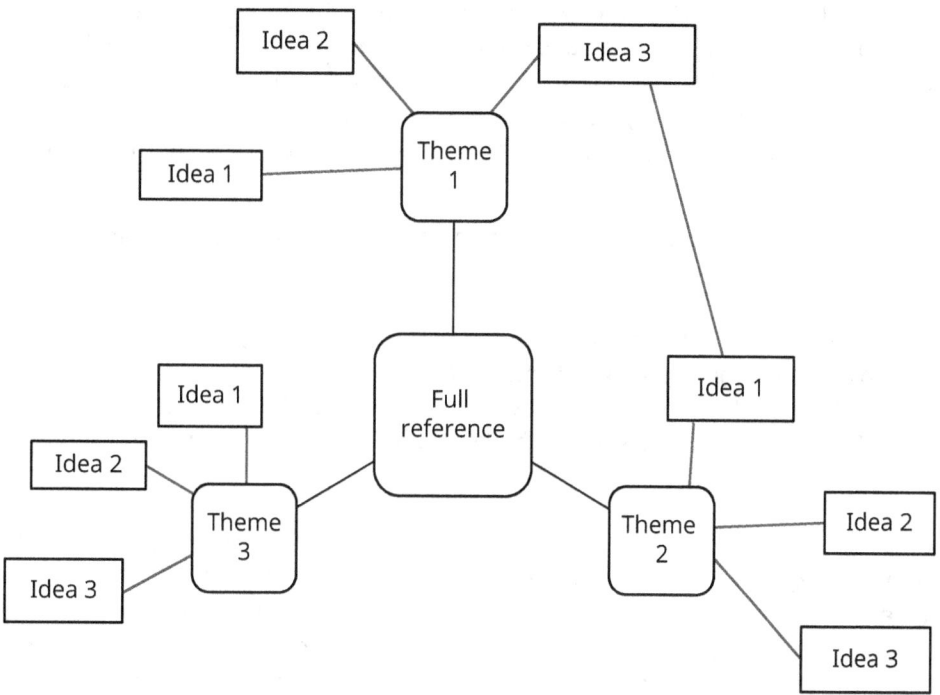

Figure 4.4 Pattern notes

Figure 4.4 illustrates how a spider diagram, mind map or pattern notes can be developed, again being as creative as you wish. The 'theme' could be each learning outcome or those identified from reading the chapter or article, as identified in the *developing critical thinking* stage.

The important part here is that you make notes. Writing things down can aid memory and understanding. It has the benefit that you are able to return to them when you need to, avoiding the need to re-read the whole chapter or article. Finally, time spent making notes of preparatory materials can be useful when it comes to assignment writing or revising for an exam, as will be discussed in Part III, as you have already started the process of critical thinking about appropriate materials. You may even want to add an extra line to Table 4.1 stating 'things to add to my assessment'.

These are your notes, make them work for you.

Develop Critical Understanding

The close, or deep, read of the chapter or article should be undertaken to develop critical understanding of the preparatory materials (Redman and Maples, 2017). In order to learn from a deep read, it is helpful to read a section and allow yourself time to critically think and understand the topic, which will facilitate learning (Kneale, 2019). 'Close reading means carefully and closely reading a text, giving yourself enough time and space to understand and engage with its meaning, and to re-read elements as needed in order to fully grasp them' (Chatfield, 2022, p. 162).

It can be helpful to have questions in mind when reading a chapter or article critically:

- What are the key themes that the author(s) is/are trying to establish?
- What do they base these key themes on?
- Do I feel that these key themes hold up to CRAAP or REVIEW scrutiny?
- How do the key themes link to the lecture/seminar that the preparatory reading is linked to?

Cottrell (2023, p. 75) suggests that the reader should 'read between the lines' when reading preparatory materials, as it can be helpful to identify assumptions that are made within the text. In some chapters and articles, you may find an assumed knowledge, where common understanding or language is used to unite identity. For example, in Sareen's (2022) Legitimating Power, sustainability metrics are discussed, which are meaningless to the uninitiated student but clear to the geography student. This does not invalidate the article but makes it harder to follow at times. Much assumed knowledge it used to facilitate a concise writing style and expedite reading, so is very helpful (Cottrell, 2023).

In contrast, there may be information that is assumed that does not assist the development of the chapter or article discussion. This can be where a conclusion is drawn without clear foundation, evidence or academic proof as the author(s) assumed that you would make the inferred leap with them. Alternatively, the conclusion may be drawn from 'false premises' (Cottrell, 2023, p. 82), therefore calling into question both the authority of the author and the accuracy of the chapter or article. Similarly, where the author(s)'s conclusion seems incongruent with the discussion posited, this should be identified. Put simply, where 2 + 2 = 5, you will need to critically think whether the question was wrong, if the numbers were presented incorrectly, and where the answer came from. It is here that critical thinking is essential: spotting a lack of or inaccurate information to base conclusions on should be part of your analysis of a text.

PowerPoint presentations

Most lectures or seminars are based, be it loosely or strictly, on a PowerPoint presentation that outlines what will be covered in the session. Provision of this at least a day before the lecture or seminar supports students' preparation and critical thinking.

> Top tip 4.5
>
> It is helpful to convert the PowerPoint into a document that you can write on, electronically or print and hand write on.
>
> This enables you to note down ideas, thoughts or questions you have whilst critically thinking about their content. This can be taken to the lecture or seminar as a memory prompt and added to with notes in the lecture.
>
> To do this electronically, go to View on the top tab and then use Notes Page.
>
> To print, either print with Notes Page or determine how many pages per slide you want at the point of printing.

Work through each slide and ensure that you understand content. The first slide is often a learning objective and it will be helpful for you to reflect on your existing knowledge and what you want to learn as part of your critical thinking before lectures. By measuring pre-existing knowledge, you can then assess your learning after the lecture.

It is helpful to be aware that PowerPoint slides are often designed as starting points for discussions or teaching so will be expanded upon by the lecturer to develop your understanding. Do you have questions that the slides raise for you? If so, you will want to listen to the lecture and if they are not answered having prepared enables you to ask for clarification within the lecture and ensure your understanding of the topic. Critically thinking about the slides prior to a seminar discussion enables you to question and consider what the lecturer is asking you to contemplate with the information provided. Furthermore, it enables you to start to formulate some responses so that you feel able to contribute effectively to a discussion.

Activities

Some preparatory materials will request you to undertake an activity prior to a lecture or seminar. This could be a learning activity from a specific book, website or an attachment for you to complete.

An excellent example of this can be found in relation to engineering students and teaching of how to write a lab report. The preparatory activity might be to read the example lab report found at https://study.sagepub.com/sites/default/files/annotated_lab_report.pdf, construct a lab report based on a recent lab experiment undertaken by the cohort and come to a seminar ready to present and discuss your lab report.

This involves multiple layers of critical thinking. Firstly, you must read the example and critically reflect on if this meets the criteria set out by your own module and lecturer. What would you change, what would you use as good practice, how will you construct your own report to ensure that it clearly communicates the experiment to the reader? Secondly, you will be required to critically reflect on the experiment itself. What went well, what did not go as expected, what can you learn from the experiment? You may need to undertake reading to assist you in this which should also be taken through a critical lens, as discussed above. Finally, you will need to write the lab report itself. Is the lab report accurate, is it clear, is it concise? By writing it and then critically reviewing your work you will enhance the finished product and your understanding of how to write a lab report and be prepared for the seminar discussion.

It is important to recognise that in order to learn from the activity in a discussion, you will need to have completed the activity for the good of the cohort. Lack of preparation reduces the efficacy as time is spent on doing the activity instead of discussing and learning from it (Beesley, 2024). As such, you will need to understand the value of the activity to ensure that you are motivated to complete it, so do seek lecturer support if the guidance is unclear.

Individual learning needs

The importance of organisational skills and allowing time for critical thinking before lectures and seminars is never more the case than for students with a learning disability, where reading, understanding and internalising learning can take longer. For students with a learning disability, for example dyslexia, concentrating and focusing on preparatory reading materials can be particularly challenging. Here a strategic approach is very important. First, we advocate that if you have a reasonable adjustment plan that requires the provision of learning materials before the lecture or seminar to facilitate your learning, but it is not custom and practice that you share this with your tutor or module leader. For example, common practice can include learning materials provision prior to the lecture, but if you needed the PowerPoint to be on white background for your ability to engage with it, let them know. We know that that can be challenging as labelling yourself as needing additional time to prepare is difficult (Beesley and Walkden, 2024). However, without preparatory materials supplied early enough for robust preparation, deep learning is impossible.

The advice throughout this chapter remains highly relevant, but further strategies to engage with preparatory reading can be setting shorter periods of time or set sections of a book or article. Little and often can enable reading and reflection times to maximise understanding. In addition, consider if your written or aural language skills are better and read or listen to materials depending on which works more effectively for you. Most importantly, do not leave preparatory reading until the last minute, as it can often take longer to engage with and may leave you emotionally and/or physically tired, which may impact on your ability to engage effectively in lecture or seminar (Beesley and Walkden, 2024). It can be helpful for people with a learning disability to:

Read aloud.

Identify if audio books are available or use assistive technology to read aloud for you.

Use a coloured overlay, increase word font size.

Use a ruler to follow lines on a written text.

Consider what the text is about before you start reading so that you have a firm foundation to build from.

Ask questions: how, why, where, when, what? Use the five whys or the 'What?' models of reflective and critical thinking outlined in Chapter three.

Use visual aids. Draw, use mind maps, use the six hats model of critical thinking, etc.

Use coloured highlighters on books (that you own) or on your notes.

Create summaries: short summaries in your own words will help you to access notes in the future.

(Adapted from McNicholas, 2020)

Finally, actively reflecting on discussion questions before lectures and seminars is particularly helpful for students with a learning disability to enable them to participate proactively.

For students where English is not their first language, it is equally important to allow yourself time to engage with the preparatory materials. In addition, technology advances such as Google Translate enable you to be strategic in your reading of books and articles. However, a word of caution is that translation services are not always effective in picking up the nuances so use them with that understanding.

Critical thinking action plan

Please reflect on your preparatory skills and where you need to develop a skill to develop your critical thinking action plan.

Worksheet 4.2   Critical thinking action plan

Critical thinking skill	Action to be taken	Review after six weeks
Motivation to engage with preparatory materials		
Engagement with reading materials		
Engagement with powerpoints		
Engagement with preparatory activities		

Conclusion

This chapter has set out the value of critical thinking in preparing for lectures and seminars in enhancing your learning, the first stage of the experiential learning loop. We advocate a robust and multi-layered approach to engaging with preparatory materials to maximise your strategic development.

Of course, if you fail to engage with preparatory materials your engagement in the lecture or seminar will be significantly impacted. If you have read a chapter or article, glanced at the PowerPoint, or written the answers to an activity quickly on the bus on the way to university, it is unlikely that you will have had time to engage in critical thinking and reflection, so it will not have been a learning exercise for you. It is only with time allocated to preparatory activities and critical thinking that you will engage in deep learning.

Instead, preparation through active participation and engagement with preparatory materials enables participation in lectures and seminars, which further enables your learning.

Further reading

Chatfield, T. (2022) *Critical Thinking: Your essential guide*. London: Sage. Chapter six considers *assessing evidence and planning your reading strategy*.

Cottrell, S. (2023) *Critical Thinking Skills*. London: Bloomsbury. Chapter six supports the reader to *read between the lines* and Chapter seven supports the reader to consider *does it add up*.

Godfrey, J. (2023) *Reading and Making Notes*. London: Bloomsbury. The book guides you through the art of reading and note making.

Redman, P. and Maples, W. (2017) *Good Essay Writing*. London: Sage. This book provides useful sections in Chapter five on *reading* and *note taking* and in Chapter six on *thinking critically*.

5
Critical thinking during lectures

CHAPTER OBJECTIVES

- Understand the importance of critical thinking in lectures
- Develop critical thinking skills when:
- Listening to lecture information
- Actively participating in lectures
- Note making

Introduction

The chapter will reflect that students participate in lectures in different ways, the second stage of the experiential learning loop. It will reflect on the importance of active listening and lecture etiquette. This will be supplemented with discussion on active participation and the importance of asking thoughtful and relevant questions in lectures, where critical thinking during lectures is the third stage of the experiential learning loop.

The chapter will reflect on the dilemma of note making versus listening in class and the value of recorded lectures to enable students to engage in critical thinking in lectures. It will outline different note-making strategies. This chapter will consider the difficulties that students with a RAP or where English is not the first language may face in live note making.

Of course, the first achievement towards critical thinking in lectures is to actively attend lectures, and this chapter is written from an assumption that this will happen.

Critical thinking in lectures: the doing and reflecting in action part of the experiential learning loop

The first question to critically reflect on is: what is a lecture? A lecture can be imagined as an often-dry sharing of subject information by a lecturer stood at front of the classroom working through PowerPoint information. Add to this little interaction with the students who are often bored, asleep or on their phones. This image is portrayed in movies and media as the traditional form of lecturing. It is important to ask if either the lecturer or student has undertaken any critical thinking before the lecture or indeed will do any during the lecture.

WHICH STUDENT IS CRITICALLY THINKING?

Dina and Isa are History students. Consider if you can identify their behaviour patterns in yourself or course mates.

Dina attends all lectures where she can but recognises that her health can impact on her ability to attend lectures.

Isa attends all lectures where she can but recognises that her part-time job can impact on her ability to attend lectures.

Dina has a support worker as part of her Reasonable Adjustment Plan (RAP) who makes notes for her. Dina sits attentively in lectures and actively listens throughout. However, she does not actively contribute within lectures, as she feels that lectures are for learning not talking.

Isa listens in lectures and makes copious notes of what is said. When it comes to the opportunity to ask questions in lectures, she often asks for repetition of points that the lecturer has already covered, as she is too busy making notes to think about what is said.

However, a lecture should be more than an information-delivery system. 'Good lectures are viewed as well-organized presentations that stimulate student interest and learning' (Cerbin, 2018, p. 151). Students learn best where there is a variety of teaching styles within a lecture, as it engages different learning styles and stimulates students. A modern lecture is often a mix of information delivery from both PowerPoint and the lecturers' academic and practice wisdom. It may include videoclips, pictures or music; or guest speakers may be brought in to support and enhance the lecturer's presentation. This is supplemented by asking for students' contributions from a whole-class question or from feedback via peer discussion. Clearly, it is the lecturer's responsibility to provide engaging and stimulating lectures. However, it is important to recognise that you are not a passive learner in lectures.

Both Dina and Isa are engaged with lectures in different ways, but both have areas for development to maximise their critical thinking in lectures.

Lecture etiquette

It is often debated whether quantity or quality is more important. Translating this to lecture etiquette, is just 'being there' enough in an age of attendance monitoring, or is the nature of engagement more important? Klausner et al. (2021) found that arriving late, leaving early, talking in lectures and engaging in non-lecture-related laptop or phone activity were commonplace in lectures. Of note, half of the research participants felt that students arriving late or leaving early impacted on either their or other people's academic performance, whilst it was nearer three-quarters of research participants who felt that students talking in lectures disrupted their learning. Whilst this research focused on perceptions, it provides understanding that lecture etiquette, or lack thereof, impacts on students' ability to critically think in lectures which takes focus and concentration.

It can be helpful to consider the following lecture etiquette suggestions to enhance your critical thinking:

- Attendance. Where possible attend all lectures. Where you cannot attend lectures, it is common courtesy to inform your module team or administrator and critically engage with both the preparatory materials and recorded lecture.
- Punctuality. Arriving on time shows respect to the lecturer and cohort, as well as interest in the subject. It establishes your commitment to your own learning.
- Engagement. Being an active learner develops the commitment to your own learning and enables critical thinking.
- Avoid distractions. Talking, non-academic-related laptop or phone use, music on headphones, noisy food wrappers, etc. cause a disturbance that distracts from students' ability to focus on their critical thinking.
- Be respectful of other learners. When contributing to lectures or listening to the contributions of others, actively and openly listen to the contributions. This will enhance your own critical thinking as you develop ideas.

Adult learners should be orientated to learning (Knowles, 1973; Knowles et al., 2020) and therefore should engage in lecture etiquette to facilitate that learning.

The lecture will be structured with learning objectives and learning materials for students to choose to engage with to enhance their learning.

Lecture learning objectives

Lectures will start with an outline of the learning objectives for the session. These will be linked to the module, level and course learning outcomes and the required learning will be mapped so that you acquire knowledge in a graduated way (Bloom, 1956). You need to learn the basics in year one before you can progress to the more complex issues in year three, and the lecture learning objectives enable you to do this in a supported manner, often called scaffolding. It is therefore important that you pay heed to what you are supposed to be learning in any given lecture.

Critical thinking in preparation for lectures (see Chapter four) will have given you a good idea of the focus of the lecture. Engaging with the learning objectives provides further focus. The case study below will be used as a thread through the chapter so that the benefit can be seen.

CASE STUDY 5.1

Using an example from a History degree, let's consider some example lecture learning objectives.

    To review knowledge of the battle of Hastings.

    To develop understanding of the decisions made in the battle of Hastings.

What do you imagine you would learn in this lecture?

These learning objectives can be seen to develop on students' existing knowledge. The battle of Hastings is on the primary school curriculum, and it is assumed that all students on a BA History course have the basic understanding of how important 1066 was in changing English history. This is indicated in the term 'to review', which indicates that a baseline knowledge assessment will be undertaken, possibly through a quiz or video. If you did not have basic knowledge of the battle of Hastings, this can indicate to yourself that you need to undertake a more robust before or after lecture reading regime and can initiate a discussion with your lecturer to support you in this.

However, the second objective 'to develop' locates the need to learn more than on entry to the lecture. This is personal to your understanding, so if for example you recently did a detailed project on the battle of Hastings, you may acknowledge that you are open to learning new perspectives to enhance your critical thinking and analysis of the situation, whilst if you had not covered the topic since primary school you would identify that this was a new area for you to engage in understanding.

At the end of the lecture, the lecturer may return to the learning objectives to ask you to critically think about your knowledge development or set you a reflective task for after the lecture, which can be linked to the discussion in Chapter seven.

Student engagement

The purpose of a lecture is primarily the sharing of information. As discussed above, the lecturer will provide information in a range of teaching methods and a lecture is designed for students to engage with learning opportunities. It is important here to be aware of your preferred learning style. It is often argued that learning is undertaken in four ways: visual, auditory, reading/writing and kinaesthetic (VARK) (Fleming, 1987).

> **V**isual learners engage with teaching materials that are presented in diagrams and flow charts so that relationships are clearly shown. It can be helpful for visual learners where the lecturer actively writes on a white board or screen.
>
> **A**uditory leaners engage with teaching materials through active listening to lectures, and value explanation by the lecturer. However, this also includes aural learning where learners develop understanding by talking through a topic.
>
> **R**eading/writing learners engage with teaching materials by reading PowerPoints that are presented in lectures. In addition they will find note making assists their learning.
>
> **K**inaesthetic learners engage with learning materials by doing and value experientially learning, so like to try things for themselves to develop understanding.

If you are aware that your learning style is that of a practical learner, you may need to develop coping strategies to ensure that you remain engaged where the teaching method is information-sharing based, as you need to remain actively engaged. The next section will reflect on engagement with lectures materials through active listening, note making and active participation.

Active listening

Active listening is more than listening, it is hearing and reflecting on what is said. Active listening in lectures can appear passive, as it requires the student to be attentively listening which is often inactive in outward appearance. Worse, when combined with note making it can appear uninterested. Nevertheless, students need to concentrate on information delivery in order to actively listen in lectures. The key to active listening is not an eidetic memory so that you can recall every word that was said. Instead, it is about understanding the concepts that are talked about and the key points made so that you can trigger relevant critical thinking.

CASE STUDY 5.2

It can be helpful to practise your active listening skills outside of the lecture theatre. This can be done by sitting quietly within conversations or by listening to a Ted Talk and identifying the key points made. Alternatively, watch this video found at www.youtube.com/watch?v=zigjVCFzZ38 on the battle of Hastings: What were the key historical points that are raised?

- What was the strategic downfall of the English?
- Critically thinking about what you have heard, do you feel that this is a historically accurate account?
- Does this leave you with a question to ask yourself or a lecturer if they were present?

By practising active listening and remaining quiet, you will develop the skill so that you can apply it to lectures. A significant part of active listening skill development is understanding what to listen for, and as you start your skill development it can be helpful to select some prompt questions. This is not a strategic point of only listen when you need to, but instead is about maximising what you do hear.

The role of students in lectures is *not* to be told facts and accept them. Active listening requires the student to concentrate on what is being said, and sometimes what is not being said. It is here that critical thinking during lectures becomes apparent. Instead, the students' role in a lecture is to actively listen and hear the subject information, but it is also to process and filter the information to determine its reliability and relevance to their own learning. No information should be taken at face value and should be considered in light of students' existing knowledge and understanding of the topic.

Nevertheless, students need to be open-minded to listening to information that contradicts their original view or opinion, as it is only by hearing contrary views that the student develops understanding. Critical thinking here should be undertaken that takes your original views and incorporates the new perspective into your understanding, so enhancing your knowledge. An example of this might be that you always thought Harold was a longstanding and respected English king fighting off the greedy Frenchman, whilst the video shows us that William was but one of many candidates who could have taken the throne some months earlier when Harold took it. This may change your thinking about either Harold or William's legacies.

Active listening in lectures therefore requires critical thinking. When a lecturer is covering a topic, it can be helpful to return to the models of critical thinking introduced in Chapter three. You could, for example, apply the RED model (Pearson Education and TalentLens, 2021) and recognise and evaluate assumptions to draw conclusions from the presented materials. Asking open questions – how, why, when, what, where – will facilitate active listening that enables your critical thinking.

Note making

First, it can be helpful to reflect on why note making in lectures is important in relation to critical thinking, particularly when active listening is considered so important. Whilst the obvious reason is to create a record of the information within the lecture to refer back to as your course progresses and aid future learning and assignment construction, here we consider the learning and development achieved through note making. Note making enables the absorption and processing of information (Godfrey, 2023) as it is effectively a selective process where students filter what is important and what should be prioritised for future use. It therefore requires critical thinking about relevance of information. Secondly, it requires critical thinking to analyse and summarise provided information so that a clear and concise summary can be noted. Thirdly, it enables students to record their own critical thinking which can be further developed after the lecture.

Note making from reading materials is discussed in Chapter four, and much of the advice is relevant so will not be repeated verbatim. However, note making in lectures requires a different skill. Instead of reading a page a number of times over until you understand what is being said, lectures are often fast paced and do not allow time to catch up. Nevertheless, with the advent of recorded lectures you can go back to a point to refresh your memory or re-listen to a tricky part after the lecture.

Note making should be clear and concise so that when reviewing them in the future the pertinent points can be easily accessed. If you are producing three to

Top tip 5.1

It can be helpful to either learn shorthand or develop a personal shorthand, for example using abbreviations for often-used words such as bH for battle of Hastings.

But make sure that you remember what it stands for in the future, so it can be helpful to have an abbreviation key.

four pages of notes with no headings, it is unlikely that you will find what you are after in the future. It is absolutely acceptable to use your notes as signposts for future you: re-watch lecture minutes 10–17 or read Chapter nine it's perfect; will enable you to return to relevant points when you are ready to do so. However, it is also good to write the detail so that you do not need to refer to them. These are *your* notes, so they need to work for you. Finally, consider where you will store your notes. This can be stored electronically or on paper and should be accessible for future use until they are no longer needed.

Top tip 5.2

Read/write learners identify that merely making notes in lectures and then typing them up afterwards enables them to remember facts and discussion points.

However, this is not the case for all learners and converting notes into diagrams or verbal recording rather than typing them after lectures up can be just as effective for visual and aural learners.

Most students like to take linear notes in the order that they are spoken, effectively more like minutes of a lecture. This is very helpful with the use of sub-topic headings and concise notes. Similarly, this can be done effectively using pre-printed or electronically accessed Notes Page, where notes are made against each PowerPoint slide. However, it can be important to reflect if you are going to make notes on what is said, or on your thoughts about the subject. If you are taking an active critical thinking approach, a themed note making may be a more appropriate approach for you. A Cornell template can be developed prior to the lecture that enables you to make notes on the relevant points and actively listen without note making in other points.

Worksheet 5.1 A Cornell template for note making in lectures

Lecture Date: Title		
	Notes from lecture	**Further points to consider**
Learning Objective 1		
Learning Objective 2		
Something new I learnt		
Relevant to assignment		
Summary		
Ideas I want to think further about		
Further reading		

In using the Cornell template, it can be seen that the lecture is not considered a distinct learning activity, but that critical thinking after the lecture, as will be discussed in Chapter seven, is beneficial to deep learning.

In summary, note making should not be considered a merely practical activity. It is a means to support your processing of information and a time to critically reflect on the information delivered in the lecture. Notes should form part of the critical thinking after lectures discussed in Chapter eight. Finally, a word of warning in a world of technology. Umejima et al. (2021) recently identified that note making using pen and paper enhanced memory. It appears that a balance between practicality and efficacy will need to be considered.

Active participation

Students who actively listen do not automatically translate to students who actively participate. The students who actively participate in lecture situations are often extroverts (Jung, 1921) who learn through social interaction and aural exploration. In contrast, introverts (Jung, 1921) will learn through quietly thinking and internal reflection. This means that a quiet student is not an indicator of a lack of active listening or critical thinking. It merely represents that critical thinking is undertaken differently by different people.

Active participation in lectures is primarily seen by asking questions to clarify knowledge, answering questions asked by the lecturer, or providing feedback on peer discussion. Where questions are asked by the lecturer, they are often seeking demonstration that the information in the lecture has been heard and understood. In addition, they are seeking to stimulate critical thinking to respond to the question, be that out loud or as a thought. As such, it is helpful for students to actively participate by thinking the answer, even if they are not the one who volunteers or is chosen to respond.

Where students ask questions in lectures, it is often to explore a thought or idea that has developed as part of their critical thinking in the lecture. They are seeking to understand better and are utilising their aural learning style. Furthermore, whilst lecturers are often experts in their own field, it does not follow that they have a monopoly on correctness and should be open to challenge and discussion. However, a word of caution. If you find that you want to contribute every time, pay attention to the other people in the lecture who may also want to contribute. Part of active participation is also an awareness of the impact of self on others. The emotionally intelligent student should be aware of over-active participation and ensure that questions asked are thoughtful and relevant.

Critical thinking is sometimes undertaken in smaller groups in lectures, with a question set by the lecturer that is discussed with peers and then fed back to the lecture. This takes account of the introvert student who feels unwilling to share their thoughts in a larger lecture group. Chapter six reflects on critical thinking in seminars and the same principles should be applied here. It is important that all students in a lecture actively participate in peer discussion.

Alternatively, an exercise may be suggested to stimulate application of theory to practice to engage the kinaesthetic learner. For example, Cerbin (2018) suggests an activity that locates yourself in the situation and asks you to think about 'what if'.

CASE STUDY 5.3

O'Brien (2009) reflects that studying history at universities is often undertaken from a contemporary lens which can be unhelpful. If one applies the understanding of modern warfare to the decisions made by King Harold II and William, Duke of Normandy, critique can be made but nuances are understandably lost.

Instead, if one critically thinks about why Harold may have made a decision or that if he had other options available to him and why he did not take them, an empathic understanding of the learning can be made. Ask yourself …

What if Harold was not exhausted?

What if Harold had access to guns?

In order to maximise learning, students would need to engage in critical thinking in this exercise. Consider different alternatives and how they would have potentially impacted the outcome enhances critical thinking.

In summary, active participation in lectures facilitates understanding through critical thinking, analysis and exploration that embed the subject into students' learning.

Individual learning needs

Students with a disability or health issue may engage with learning in different ways. Students may need longer to process learning materials, may have shorter concentration periods, lack confidence or may be physically or socially fatigued, each of which may impede engagement with lecture materials.

Similarly, ethnically diverse students may experience engagement with lectures in a different way. It is important that recognition is given that lectures are primarily delivered within a white Western perspective. They often fail to take account of ethnically diverse students' educational experiences that provide different foundations. Where students have not experienced critical thinking development at school or have been socialised into being 'taught' rather than engaging in interactive learning, they can be at a disadvantage in lectures where that expectation exists.

Clearly lecturers have responsibility to engage all learners, and inclusive teaching design such as recording lectures for students to relisten to is important (Beesley and Walkden, 2024). However, students will need to both seek support and develop coping strategies to ensure that they are able to engage robustly. University support networks and tutor support is available for all students, and accessing it is often in your best interest to develop academic study skills and enhance your critical thinking in lectures.

Where English is not your first language or those with a learning disability such as dyslexia, note making can be particularly challenging. There may be a need to focus more robustly on what is being said within the lecture to ensure understanding before the move to note making can occur. In such a circumstance, allocating more time to note making after the lecture is often required. The accessing of a lecture recording, be that through university systems such as Panopto or the use of a carefully placed Dictaphone, are likely to be required to facilitate note making. Unfortunately, this places an extra time burden on those students which when also facing additional barriers to accessing education can be considered as an additional layer of social oppression. The use of a support worker or transcription service can address this time imbalance but can take away the opportunity to critically think whilst note making.

Critical thinking action plan

Please reflect on your critical thinking during lectures skills and where you need to develop a skill develop your critical thinking action plan.

Worksheet 5.2   Critical thinking action plan

Critical thinking skill	Action to be taken	Review after six weeks
Engagement with attending lectures		
Ability to actively listen consistently across a lecture		
Note-making skills		
Ability to actively participate as an introvert or extrovert in lectures		

Conclusion

This chapter has considered how critical thinking can, and should, be undertaken in lectures, the third stage of the experiential learning loop. Whilst the emphasis is on the lecturer to provide interesting and engaging teaching materials in lectures, it is the student's responsibility to engage with critical thinking and subsequent learning. Critical thinking in lectures begins with an understanding of lecture learning outcomes and how they direct students' understanding of the focus of the lecture.

Active listening enables students to hear and critically think about lecture content so that they not just hear but understand the subject matter. Note making is an important part of the learning process as it requires critical thinking and processing of the heard information to transfer it to written form. Finally active participation, be that as an introvert or extrovert learner, facilitates critical thinking as it stimulates further consideration of the subject matter.

However, Cerbin (2018) argues that it is not just being actively involved in the lecture that is important. Critical thinking before and after the lecture needs to happen to ensure deep learning, which serves as a reminder that this chapter should be read in conjunction with Chapters four and seven.

Further reading

Fleming, N. (1987) *VARK: A Guide to Learning Styles*. Available at: http://vark-learn.com
   This website provides insight into different learning styles and how they can be used to enhance learning.
Hopkins, D. and Reid, T. (2018) *The Academic Skills Handbook*. London: Sage. Chapter fourteen provides lots of useful tips for getting the most out of your lecture.

6
Critical thinking during seminars

CHAPTER OBJECTIVES

- Understand how to maximise learning during seminars
- Develop critical thinking skills by collaborating with peers
- Appreciate how others' views and interpretations expand and enhance your own critical thinking skills and therefore improve assessment performance

Introduction

This chapter will consider how to think critically in seminars to develop your knowledge and skills, and reflection in action (Schon, 1983) skills, which will be required within seminars. It will consider some approaches to maximise your learning in these contexts in order to enhance your ability to demonstrate critical thinking skills.

Like critical thinking in lectures, critical thinking in seminars is the experiment part of the experiential learning loop, where you are required to reflect in action. However, seminars also require effective interaction with others. Remember that performance in exams and coursework is only part of what you bring to university level study: learning through experiences is just as important and valuable. In a seminar, you may be asked to construct an argument, compare and contrast evidence and reach a 'balanced' conclusion.

Critical thinking in seminars: the doing and reflecting in action part of the experiential learning loop

Generally, a *seminar* refers to small group sessions which are designed to promote interaction between students supported by teaching staff; it is the *attending*, *participating* and *critical thinking during* section of the experiential learning loop. Seminars (sometimes called tutorials in some universities) provide opportunities to develop your understanding of concepts or theories which might have been explored in larger group sessions like lectures. They involve *active* learning rather than simply listening and provide opportunities for you to check your understanding (McMillan, 2021).

Working with others enables us to discuss and explore key concepts, see things from different perspectives and consider how we might apply that learning to real world situations. Seminars provide important opportunities to make and test your progress towards achieving the learning outcomes which your assessments are designed to measure. This process requires you to develop your critical thinking skills: skills which are best developed and tested when you consider others' views and experiences, not just your own. Hopkins and Reid (2018) suggest that seminars are multi-faceted as they develop communication skills, problem-solving skills, and confidence whilst facilitating deeper learning and greater peer connections, which strengthen your emotional resilience.

In addition, active participation is required where your tutor poses questions rather than simply providing information. You might be asked to consider problems by applying theory, content from lectures and/or your preparatory reading. Finally, as you progress through your course, active participation may increase to include where your tutors will expect some parts of seminars to be led by you and your fellow students.

Research has shown that students who actively engage in seminars are much more likely to succeed on their course and have more confidence in themselves (Hauck et al., 2020). However, some students find seminars more difficult to engage in than others.

Both Anya and Harry are anxious about engaging with seminars: many students are. However, they now have a choice to participate or to avoid seminars. As an adult learner (Knowles, 1973) you will need to take responsibility for your own learning, and engaging in all learning opportunities is paramount here. Taking a brave leap into the unknown and attending and engaging with seminars will enhance your critical thinking, learning, knowledge, skills and ultimately academic grades. Furthermore, critical thinking about why you are not engaging will enable you to start to recognise barriers and start to address them.

Critical thinking during seminars

WHICH STUDENT IS CRITICALLY THINKING?

Anya and Harry are Secondary Education university students. Consider if you can identify their behaviour patterns in yourself or course mates.

Anya attends all the lectures but only some of the seminars.

She travels from home and doesn't tend to socialise with the other students on her course who live in university accommodation.

She is nervous that no one will sit next to her and want to work with her in small group work. Now she is noticing that other students seem to have more confidence answering questions in lectures.

Harry prefers lectures where he can just sit and listen and make notes.

He avoids seminars because he is nervous that others may disagree with his views or he might ask a 'silly' question.

He is finding that other students are making better progress towards the assessments than him.

Group working takes lots of different forms and often groups are formed by your tutor rather than students being permitted to self-select. It is really helpful for you to have begun to think about what relevant skills and experiences you have to offer groups you work with. Maybe

- you are skilled at producing diagrams or visual aids;
- you have more advanced searching for information skills and are confident using online databases;
- you are good at summarising information;
- you are a fast reader;
- you would make a very effective group leader, gathering ideas from others and allocating different parts of the task fairly;
- you excel at keeping your group to time and on task.

There are lots of other strengths you might have but it is very important to be ready to volunteer to 'play to your strengths'. Several researchers have attempted to categorise and model the range of strengths which might be evident in human behaviours related to group and team work. One of these is Belbin's Team Roles model. You can complete the official Belbin® Self-Perception Inventory online in order to see what approaches and functions you seem most likely to contribute to group work. Similarly, you might prefer to discuss with your fellow students what strengths they think you bring to group work in seminars. They might identify strengths which surprise you. Spending time critically thinking on this might enable you and your fellow students to adopt the types of roles which best play to your strengths in seminars. For example, if, according to Belbin (1981), you are a 'Coordinator' or a 'Completer' you could be best placed to ensure that your group maximises their efficiency and completes tasks in time. If you are a 'Specialist' you may have valuable prior experience, whilst a 'Resource Investigator' may be most adept at finding the information you need from other sources.

A further way to embrace your participation in seminars is to consider Fink's (2013) six groups of learning activities, similar to those noted by Bloom et al. (1956), but which additionally include a focus on emotional aspects of learning.

Table 6.1 Participation in seminars (adapted from Fink, 2013)

Significant learning category	**Explanation**
Foundational Knowledge	What key information (facts, terms, formula, concepts, relationships …) is important for you to know in your own subject area?
	What do you need to remember in the future?
Application	What kinds of thinking are important for you to develop in your own subject area?
	Do you need to be a critical thinker? Creative thinker? Practical thinker? Problem-solver?
	What skills matter in your own subject?
	What projects do you need to learn how to manage, for success in your own subject area?
Integration	What connections (similarities and interactions) do you need to know about and recognise when thinking about the ideas on your course?
	How do the concepts on your course relate to you own life?
Human Dimension	What do you need to learn about yourself as a student?
	What do you need to know for interacting with people in the future, for example for your future employability?
Caring	What changes do your tutors suggest that you need to make about your approach to learning, and life beyond higher education?
	What are your interests? Values? Feelings?
Learning How to Learn	What should you know about learning specifically in your own subject space to be a good student on your course? What are the best ways to learn, and to develop critical thinking in relation to your own subject matter?
	How do you become a good self-directed learner?

Here, you can see that participation is not just turning up for the seminar, it requires critical thinking about yourself, strengths and areas for development so that you can maximise your contributions and learning within the seminar. Of course, in order to work effectively you should ensure that you are as clear as you can be first about what the group work entails and what your tutor's expectations are. If you aren't sure after reading through the information provided for the group-work activity, you should check with your tutor.

Group tutorials

Whilst this chapter focuses on seminars, you may also have group tutorials. Universities allocate students a tutor, sometimes called advisor, instructor or coach and may have personal, academic, study or practice prefixed to indicate role. You should access your tutor for individual support, which will enable collaborative critical thinking with them on your personal, academic and professional development. However, they may also provide regular group tutorials, where all students allocated to the tutor meet and the tutor facilitates group discussion on a given topic. All of the advice provided within this chapter, as well as Chapters four and seven, should be applied to critical thinking before, during and after group tutorials.

Barriers to participation in seminars

It is true to say that most learners find seminar and small group work daunting at first and there are a number of reasons for this:

- If you have previously succeeded mainly by learning facts about your subjects, you may not be used to expressing an opinion about something. In seminars, you are required to develop an opinion through discussion and debate by considering the available evidence and hearing a range of perspectives. Learning to gather information and evidence and assess its relevance and value is vital for success in university level study. Doing this with others maximises the development of your own critical thinking skills.
- Sharing your own opinions or values can feel risky because others may not agree with you or might even say negative things about your views (Race and Pickford, 2007).
- Some of us have *imposter syndrome*: we wonder whether we are 'clever' enough for a university education. Imposter syndrome can be where you don't feel that you deserve to be at university or are not clever enough to be participating in a seminar. Similarly, knowledgeable students often feel imposter syndrome where they feel anxious about the debate element of a seminar if they struggle to verbalise thoughts. Remember that your university would not have offered you a place if they didn't feel you had the potential to succeed on your course.

- Seminars involve discussion and weighing up evidence about complex issues. It is not unusual for this to feel confusing, and you may conclude that you don't quite understand, so it may feel like hard work for you. You may need to continue to critically think after the seminar (see Chapter seven) to process this information, but don't be put off: usually when things are challenging there is better learning potential.
- There may be no *right* answer. If you are someone who likes definitives or facts, this might deter your attendance. If this is the case, you will need to think about how you reduce your anxieties and embrace uncertainty. Talk to your tutor about your feelings.
- Some students' voices might dominate the group. It can be quite off-putting if one voice dominates a seminar discussion, and it should be remembered that dominance does not equate to a correct perspective. Working on challenge can be an important learning task within seminars: approaching that person sensitively and tactfully can be transformative for all involved as it will stimulate critical thinking on group-work skills.
- If you are someone who likes to share their opinions through external critical thinking (see Chapter five), seminars are a great learning opportunity, but remember to ensure that you are letting everyone have equal airtime.
- If you are someone who prefers internal critical thinking, seminars may feel daunting, particularly if some students' voices dominate.
- If you are struggling to overcome feelings of isolation or anxiety about small group work, sometimes writing down ideas, e.g. on sticky notes, is easier than having to say them out loud.

It can be useful to reassure yourself that others will be feeling similarly challenged. Even if they seem to have a very good understanding of the topic, they might find working with others difficult or vice versa. Remember that you have lots of life experience to draw upon not just your prior subject-related learning. You will have developed skills in other situations that you can apply to seminars. These could include transitions to new schools or other places of learning or a part-time job where you have managed to work with others who are not in your immediate circle of friends. However, you should find that your university offers lots of free additional support and online resources for developing the requisite academic skills for participation in seminars.

Nevertheless, teaching staff will not expect you to 'have all the answers', otherwise there would be no point in the session. Seminars are for trying things out, exploring ideas further and considering what they might mean for yours and others' practice. Interpreting evidence and ideas with your fellow students should mean that you are all much better placed to succeed in your assessments and demonstrate critical thinking. Remember too that working effectively with others is something you will usually need to be adept at in the workplace after you graduate. Being able to work effectively with others requires 'emotional intelligence': the ability to recognise and manage your own emotions and empathise with others so you can manage or reduce conflict. It is important to recognise, develop and test these skills as part of seminar activity.

Top tip 6.1

Seminars require you to use your critical thinking and critical evaluation skills. Working as part of a group and being able to contribute confidently and hear other people's views, awareness of your strengths and areas for development will help to develop your critical thinking skills.

Appreciating more diverse views and perspectives than your own leads to enhanced critical evaluation and critical thinking. This means you need to make a big effort to understand a wide range of perspectives even if you don't agree with them.

Ensure you hear other perspectives.

Ensure all voices are heard in group discussion and contrasting views are respected.

It is important to be able to invite others to contribute, without putting them on the spot.

Use open questions that are non-judgemental, like 'That's interesting. Can you say why you think that?' or 'That's a new way of thinking about this for me. Could you explain it a bit more?'

If you see that someone in your seminar is not engaging support them to develop their confidence.

Offer them the opportunity to speak.

Give them time to think critically. Jumping into silences can stop people from contributing.

Listen when they do contribute, valuing what is said is important for developing confidence for future contributions.

Talk to them after the seminar and ask if there is anything that would assist them to contribute in a future seminar.

But be aware that not everyone wants to speak, and respect students who politely decline to contribute.

Critical thinking in seminars

Seminars provide an ideal environment for practising and expanding your ideas before they are tested in your formal assessments. As we have already explained in earlier chapters, demonstrating critical thinking skills requires you to first show you have a good grasp of existing subject knowledge and evidence from authoritative sources. It also means you will need to express your understanding in ways which show you can find your own voice. We call this Academic Assertiveness (Moon, 2009) and it is a fundamental requirement for academic as well as professional success.

Being mindful of the instructions from your tutor and the intended learning outcomes for your session here is a possible sequence of activities:

1. Ensure your group is clear about the task you have been set.
2. Begin by sharing the relevant evidence and or ideas which your group has collected and noted. These could be theories or evidence or arguments.
3. Map or organise these in some way, perhaps visually on a board or flipchart paper or sticky notes, or suitable electronic device. Identify similarities and differences.
4. You will need to take account of the *context* in which that evidence was collected. This might lead you to observe that there is a *range* of findings, interpretations and views.
5. Do you need to consider the *credibility* of your evidence? Consider what might have influenced these differences, e.g. who the authors are, who they are writing for (their intended audience), how and when and where they collected their information (see research methods), whether it has been peer-reviewed.
6. Using your mapping and taking account of context consider whether some arguments or theories are more relevant or better evidenced and/or analysed more effectively than others.
7. Return to the task and share your understandings in the light of your group discussions. Assess and develop your arguments/solutions.
8. Ensure that you consider all contributions from your group in order to provide a balanced response to the task which you have been set.

Critical thinking requires us to demonstrate that we are fair minded. So we need to present and consider a range of views, not just those with which we agree. Working in groups in seminars is a really effective way of enhancing your ability to do this and to transfer other ways of thinking to when you are working on your own assessments for example. Using processes like those described above you will be much better able to organise information, identify similarities and differences and reasons for these. In so doing you will be demonstrating some key aspects of critical thinking, deepening your understanding and appreciation of the complexity of your subjects and therefore enhancing your performance in assessments.

Active listening in seminars therefore requires critical thinking. When involved in a seminar discussion, it can be helpful to return to the models of critical thinking introduced in Chapter three. You could, for example, apply De Bono's (1985) six thinking hats and try to explore the discussion topic from a range of perspectives. You could adapt the hats to suit the discussion or activity.

Critical thinking skills in action

It is important for the group to understand what is required of them. This can be done through taking the seminar activity and unpicking it before you begin.

Consider this example of a seminar activity from an Education Studies degree. Using the examples from the research we have considered in the lecture, identify and discuss how refugee children might be marginalised by traditional pedagogical practices in schools.

Working together in your group using the examples provided:

1. Define who refugee children are.
2. Gather some explanations of how they are (often) marginalised in schooling.
3. Choose one of the projects we have discussed in class and analyse the design in terms of how it addresses some of the disadvantages they may experience.
4. Critically evaluate the outcomes of the project in relation to Paulo Freire's ideas about empowering learners.

By picking out the verb in each task, you can begin to understand what is required of you:

1. The first task would be to *define* these terms.

    You might want to define what you mean by children and by refugee.

    This involves appreciating that these young people are not all the same so you would need to share your interpretations of what you are reading. It might lead to a discussion about what their needs may be and how they may vary.

2. This requires *discussion* in your group not only of what marginalisation means but also identify the mechanisms which may result in disadvantage (*how*).
    This may require some researching, and you may nominate a group member to refer back to your previous learning to facilitate presentation (or reminders) of pertinent ideas to stimulate discussion.

    You may not all agree at the end of the discussion; the intent is to stimulate critical thinking not to come to a consensus.

3. This requires *analysis* as together you will need to relate the key components of the design of the intervention to how it is intended to help young people overcome disadvantage. This is unlikely to be an 'exact' science. Some aspects may be obvious and others less so.

Other verbs in this task include 'choose', 'addresses' and 'experience'. Don't be put off by multiple verbs, and definitely do not disregard them. But from a critical thinking perspective, the seminar group-work task is to 'analyse'.

4. This requires *critical evaluation*, which would include an assessment of the outcomes of the intervention including identifying any practical and other limitations. It would be helpful to ensure that you have access to Freire's concepts so that you had the correct framework to critically analyse the project against: How does it conform to the ideas? How does it contradict the ideas? How does it vary away from the framework?

   This might also require considering a range of perspectives of the relative success of the intervention including policy makers, practitioners and the young people themselves. What might have been learned from this intervention?

It can be seen that by understanding each task, and what is required to be done, the seminar group are able to work through the task efficiently. Yet had they not understood the task they could have misunderstood the activity, or worse not undertaken the activity, missing out on structured learning that might impact on their ability to embed learning from a previous lecture or develop further their understanding in the next lecture.

This quote helped some students engaging with the seminar task above to appreciate why critical thinking skills are essential: 'Teaching is as much about compromise and the imperfect reconciliation of competing imperatives as the implementation of ideals' (Alexander, 2001, p. 84).

What does this mean? Simply put, the author is arguing that being an effective teacher is difficult because even if you have a clear idea of what effective learning looks like, there are lots of different demands you must manage which prevent you from being as effective as you might wish to be. Although guiding principles might provide a basis for designing solutions, we don't live in a world with unlimited resources and, in the case of education, different stakeholders apply different success criteria. More broadly, there are rarely simple solutions to being effective as a professional. Showing you can recognise, articulate, discuss and even embrace complexities like this in your seminars should be seen as valuable opportunities to develop your critical thinking skills and therefore your ability to demonstrate these not just in your assessments but in life outside of university. The key aim of a university education is the development of intellectual and moral autonomy (Yorke, 2006); in other words, the confidence to be able to contribute to discussion and problem-solving based on sound evidence but whilst avoiding appearing to underestimate the complexity of the problem. There is no better way to test out these critical thinking skills than in seminar settings.

Individual learning needs

Seminars are undertaken in smaller groups and often require the active participation of all students. This may be challenging for some students, perhaps because they have a reasonable adjustment, they become anxious when interacting with others and especially if they are expected to talk in front of others, or because English is not their first language. Seminars can be a more challenging learning activity for the quieter student or the student who is an introvert learner (Jung, 1921), as discussed in Chapter five. Whilst an initial reaction can be avoidance, this restricts your learning and the collective learning of the group, as your perspective is not presented and explored. It can be helpful to explain to peers that you will attend but will contribute as you become more confident with the group.

In addition, some students find seminars particularly difficult to learn from because there are less likely to be slides or automatic recordings of the discussion. Finding ways to capture both your learning and the advice which your tutors offer becomes especially important therefore because notes may not be provided.

Top tip 6.2

You can

- make notes as you go along;
- take photos of the whiteboard or flipcharts;
- ask if you can make a recording on your phone;
- compare notes and thoughts with peers;
- clarify understanding with seminar leader.

In addition, Hopkins and Reid (2018) argue that intercultural awareness of similarities and differences in communication styles in seminars is critical to their success. Indeed, because students attend with a variety of experiences, knowledge and skills, where a range of identities meet for a seminar, it is beneficial as they can share their expertise and learn from each other Boud et al., (2001). However, that is easier said than done and if your personal social, cultural and educational experiences are of oppression and isolation it may take more than just building confidence in the group before speaking. Wong et al. (2022) suggest that ethnically diverse students adapt through emotional detachment and desensitisation; however, whilst this coping strategy may be effective, it may not be an emotionally intelligent way to engage with a seminar as all views should be aired, heard and critically thought about by the rest of the seminar group. Talking to the seminar leader about safe ways for you to participate can be helpful in creating a safe space.

Critical thinking action plan

Please reflect on your critical thinking skills within seminars and where you need to develop a skill to add to your critical thinking action plan.

Worksheet 6.1   Critical thinking action plan

Critical thinking skill	Action to be taken	Review after six weeks
Preparation for seminars		
Contributing within seminars		
Facilitating others to contribute to seminars		
Hearing different perspectives in seminars and reflecting on their worth		

Conclusion

Sharing your understandings and ability to apply underpinning theories in seminars is key to being able to demonstrate critical thinking in your assessments and realise your potential whilst at university and as a graduate. This involves you being able to show you appreciate that most of what you are learning is context-specific and requires multiple 'solutions'. Participating in group processes in seminars is key to developing your ability to consider more than one perspective and to show the value in accepting the thinking behind others' views. That doesn't mean we all need to agree but it does mean we appreciate and can show that effective teamwork is based on valuing and combining a range of perspectives, skills and experiences. Critical thinking in seminars also enhances your ability to deal with unforeseen challenges, respond to change in your external environment and embrace complexity in all its forms. These elements are key features of critical thinking.

Further reading

Hopkins, D. and Reid, T. (2018) *The Academic Skills Handbook*. London: Sage. Chapter twelve is on communicating in seminars and Chapter thirteen is on working in groups, both of which are useful when undertaking critical thinking in seminars.

McMillan, K. (2021) *The Study Skills Book*. London: Pearson. Chapters 17–19 are about active learning in groups, including seminars, tutorials and practicals.

7
Critical thinking after lectures and seminars

CHAPTER OBJECTIVES

- Understand how to maximise learning after lectures
- Understand how to maximise learning after seminars
- Develop understanding of how learning can be applied to future tasks

Introduction

In this chapter we will first consider the ways in which you can maximise your learning after both lectures and seminars, reflecting on action (Schon, 1983). We will consider some approaches to maximise your critical thinking skills following on from classroom discussions so that you can consolidate your learning and complete the experiential learning loop. It is important to continue to critically think after learning in lectures and seminars to ensure that you work on further developing your knowledge and skills, to feed this forwards by taking it with you into your future classroom sections.

Critical thinking after lectures and seminars: completing the experiential learning loop

Your approach to critical thinking after lectures and seminars can be aligned with strategies that suit your own learning style to enhance your ability to actively learn.

Chapters two, five and twelve outline different learning styles, so as you develop your critical thinking after lectures and seminars, you should consider using strategies that suit your style and preferences. Earlier chapters also discuss the importance of you working to actively learn in lectures and seminars, and so you can continue your active learning journey after all forms of classroom contact.

> **WHICH STUDENT IS CRITICALLY THINKING?**
>
> Sarah and Nick are Sociology students who have attended a lecture.
>
> Sarah printed out the lecture slides provided to her and took them with her to the lecture. She added some points to them during the lecture, and afterwards she files away her notes in date order in her folder.
>
> Nick printed his notes and added to them during the class.
>
> After the lecture, Nick listens to the lecture recording and then revisits his notes to make sure that he has not missed any key points.
>
> He considers and compares the various theories that he has been introduced to in this week's lecture content.
>
> He also follows up with actions that his tutor suggested during the lecture; for example, visiting websites with information about the topic and watching online tutorials.

Both students are engaged with their lectures in different ways, but Nick is working more effectively to consolidate his learning after the classroom session has ended because he continues to engage in activities to develop his knowledge and understanding of his subject matter.

Thompson and Thompson (2008) outline a model of reflection called CIA (control, influence and acceptance) which is intended to support reflective learning. Consider using this after your lectures and seminars as a way to reflect, creating notes about each of these areas:

1. Firstly think about *control*: here you need to identify the issues or elements of the situation (after lecture learning) that you control/change.

    You might consider that you cannot control the range and breadth of theories that are presented in lectures and seminars; this may feel overwhelming at times.

    However, you can control how you engage with the materials after lectures and seminars so that it is most productive for you.

2. Secondly, think about *influence*: here you need to focus on identifying the elements (of after lecture learning) that you can't control, but that you can influence.

   You may not be able to influence what time the next lecture starts, reducing your time to critically think about the lecture content before starting another topic.

   You might consider what time you have available to you and chose an ergonomic approach of note making that enables you to return to bullet points of interesting things to think about and indicators of further reading when you need it.

3. Finally, you need to *accept*: this means noting the things that you are unable to control or influence.

   You might not accept that a concept is baffling you and this may make you angry or frustrated.

   But you can accept help from those who do understand it.

In using this model to reflect on lectures and seminars, you can work on developing your learning in the areas that you can both control and influence.

Critical thinking after lectures

There are many ways that you can build upon the strategies outlined in Chapter five, about critical thinking during lectures, to enhance your learning after your attendance, as illustrated in Table 7.1.

Table 7.1 Critical thinking after lectures

Before lectures you should …	During lectures you can …	After the lecture consider …
Familiarise yourself with the learning objectives for your lecture.	Use active listening.	Reflecting further on what was said during the lecture.
		Do you understand the key concepts being discussed? Where do you need to develop your understanding?
Complete any preparation outlined by your tutor, such as reading key texts, making some notes.	Develop your note-making skills.	Revisit the notes that you made, what are the key points that you can summarise from them?
		How do these key points link to the learning objectives that your tutor highlighted for the lecture that you attended?
		Is there a need to learn more in more areas based on gaps in your notes?

(Continued)

Table 7.1 (Continued)

Before lectures you should …	During lectures you can …	After the lecture consider …
Consider any questions that you have about the learning objectives and reading materials before you attend the lecture.	Actively participate.	Were there questions that you or your peers asked that have helped you to understand the lecture content?
		Do you need to discuss some of the material further, for example with your peers?
		Did your tutor suggest any follow-up activities for you to pursue such as reading, or further questions for you to consider?

Chen (2021) discusses an after-class note-making strategies scale which is outlined in Table 7.2, to detail the numerous ways in which you can continue to work with notes.

Table 7.2 After class note-making strategies

After class note making strategy	Example of this
Elaboration	Reading supplementary materials.
	Writing down examples.
	Writing down explanations of concepts and theories.
	Listing key words.
Organisation	Putting notes into outlines and/or plans.
	Combining all notes from reading tasks and lectures.
	Annotating notes to further develop points.
	Looking at relationships between the lecture content and your own notes.
Help-seeking	Speaking to other students in your class to clarify your own understanding.
	Comparing your notes with your class mates' notes to see if there are any differences.

As you develop your own approach to actively learning after attending lectures, you should consider these suggestions as a starting point but then adapt them to suit your own learning styles and preferences, to develop your critical thinking in a way that feels most suited to you. Fleming (1987) outlined four ways of learning: visual, auditory, reading/writing and kinaesthetic (see Chapter five for more on these).

Critical thinking after lectures and seminars

CASE STUDY 7.1

Four first-year students on a Sociology degree attended a lecture.

After the lecture, they each critically think about the lecture, but take different actions to achieve this. They choose their action according to the way in which they preferred to learn.

- Kayla prefers a visual approach to learning, so her action was to adapt her notes into mind maps and diagrams.
- Luke likes to learn through hearing (auditory methods), so his action was to re-read his notes aloud, and to listen to online tutorials about his lecture topic. He found helpful resources free online.
- Zainab is a reading/writing learner, so she decided to read her own notes again and engage with other written sources on the topic of the lecture (supplementary reading materials), whilst writing further notes.
- Caleb learns by experience, kinaesthetically. This can be more challenging in subjects such as sociology, so he decided to develop his own strategies by incorporating movement into his learning. He started by walking and listening to a podcast on the weekly topic after the lecture.

Engaging in learning strategies after lectures is an important part of your critical thinking, because you will continue to question the knowledge that has been presented to you. Indeed, sociology as a subject supports students to develop their critical thinking, because the subject matter applies multiple lenses to society (Plummer, 2021).

To develop your critical thinking after a lecture, you can consider areas of the lecture you can argue against, using academic evidence that presents a different viewpoint or you can assess your own understanding after a lecture by thinking through what you heard and noted. Assessing your own understanding will support you in consolidating your learning and identifying areas that you need to work on to enhance your understanding even further – this is deep learning (Craik and Lockhart, 1972).

Top tip 7.1

> Most of us learn through a combination of learning styles, therefore it is important to use a toolbox of strategies to develop your critical thinking after you have attended lectures.
>
> Remember to try a range of strategies to ensure that you are encouraging yourself to think more deeply, question your assumptions and explore new ideas.

Critical thinking after seminars

It is also important to know that you can further maximise your learning again after you have attended seminars. Earlier chapters demonstrated the importance of critical thinking skills before and during seminars, and Chapter six offered a sequence of activities for you to use in seminars. These can also be applied later on, following on from your attendance at and engagement with seminars. Table 7.3 outlines follow-on strategies for supporting your critical thinking after seminars.

Table 7.3 Critical thinking after seminars

Before the seminar you can …	During the seminar you can …	After the seminar consider …
Prepare according to the instructions that your tutor has provided you with, completing all required tasks.	Ensure your group is clear about the task or the 'problem' you have been set.	How the seminar discussion has enabled you to expand upon your understanding of the 'problem' set, and the topic being discussed. Are there are still areas of challenge that you need to work on to develop your response to addressing the problem?
Reflect upon the evidence that you have been engaging with.	Share the relevant evidence and or ideas which your group has collected.	Can you now summarise the evidence that has been presented to you? Do you fully understand it, and if not might you need to do some further critical thinking, critical reading and critical reflection?
Make notes to summarise the key points arising from the completion of your tasks.	'Map' or organise these notes in some way … Identify similarities and differences.	Revisit any notes or mapping that you developed before attending the seminar and consider if you need to add further points. It is also useful to summarise the key points from any notes, post-seminar attendance.
Consider the quality of evidence you have been reading.	Take account of the context in which that evidence was collected. This might lead you to observe that there is a range of findings, interpretations and views.	Did you learn anything else about the context, and what does this tell you about the interpretation? For example, Foucault, a sociological theorist, wrote theories about power, knowledge and social control. He was born in 1926 and was homosexual. This context informed his analysis of power and social control, though many of his ideas are still argued to be applicable to society today (Pollard, 2019).

Critical thinking after lectures and seminars

Before the seminar you can …	During the seminar you can …	After the seminar consider …
Apply analysis approaches to the evidence that you are working with (e.g. CRAAP and REVIEW, as discussed in Chapter four).	Consider the 'credibility' of your evidence?	Consider the evidence presented to you in the seminar, and the value of the research underpinning it – are there issues with the evidence? For example, Laud Humphreys authored a sociological book, called *Tearoom Trade*, in 1970, which focused on men meeting in public toilets to engage in sexual activities. His work had many ethical issues (was he really just an observer?), and resulted in harsh consequences for him, including his degree being revoked. Despite the ethical and methodological problems with his work, his evidence was important as it presents participant voice (Nardi, 1995).
Make notes on the results of your analysis of evidence, considering authority, accuracy and purpose.	Consider whether some arguments or theories are more relevant or better evidenced and/or analysed more effectively than others?	Are there gaps in the evidence, or the arguments made? If the theory was written some time ago (many classic sociological theories are older than most students), consider if the key points of it still apply now or if some elements are no longer applicable. For example, Marx wrote about socialism and the need for revolution. He predicted a revolution, which has not occurred; however, his criticisms of capitalism remain relevant to understanding contemporary social inequalities (Singer, 2018).
Reflect on what you think about the topic and the tasks.	Return to the task and share your understandings of the question or problem in the light of your group discussions. Assess and develop your arguments/solutions.	So reflecting back, you can start to consider – have your ideas changed? Have they developed in some way? What else do you *now* know following on from the seminar?
Put yourself in the shoes of an imaginary student who does not agree with your viewpoint.	Ensure that you consider all contributions from your group in order to provide a balanced response to the task which you have been set.	Did all of your group members agree? Did anyone offer a challenge or a different opinion? How did your peers use evidence to support their points?

These seminar follow-up activities are again just a starting point for you to use and adapt, supporting your critical thinking development. You can also reflect on how the seminar itself went, and consider if there was anything that you would like to do differently, so that you can get even more out of it next time. All of the strategies discussed are approaches that you can use to make judgements, challenge your thinking and develop new ideas, key components of critical thinking.

CASE STUDY 7.2

First-year students on a Sociology degree attended a seminar to discuss different ideas of how some of the classic theories about inequalities can be used to explain contemporary issues in society.

Golden struggles with sociological theories. He has tried to engage with preparatory reading, attended and listened in lectures, and in the seminar is quiet but attentive.

After the seminar, Golden writes down the key theories and concepts using his own words. He sketches a pattern note to make sure he is capturing all of the perspectives that were discussed and, importantly, how they were applied within the discussion.

He is able to reflect on how he feels about the different theories as he has lots of ideas to consider, and he can now start to consider his own perspective on the topic of inequality. He feels that he has a starting point to develop from.

Here we develop the benefit of collaborative learning in seminars, where multiple ideas are suggested which prompt critical thinking through evaluation to develop your own perspective on a topic. The reflection on these ideas after a seminar should be seen as the continuation of the critical thinking process and as much a part of the learning as the actual seminar. As you process ideas your deeper learning occurs.

Critical thinking after lectures and seminars enhances future learning

To enhance learning after lectures and seminars therefore requires critical thinking. When reflecting after a learning activity, it can be helpful to return to the models of critical thinking introduced in Chapter three. You could, for example, apply the FRISCO model (Ennis, 1996), where you consider the materials covered to consider the Focus and Reason for their inclusion by teaching staff, which will support you to understand the Inference that is being made and apply it to the Situation, which will give you Clarity and enable you to have an Overview for application to future learning.

Evaluation strategies are part of critical thinking as they assist us in placing ourselves at the centre of our learning and help us to reflect. Many of the post-seminar strategies outlined will support you in reflection, enabling you to share your knowledge with others, and reflect upon the ways in which you can put your new knowledge into action. For example, you can use your new knowledge to inform your understanding of the topic and draw on it as you start to prepare for your next seminar. You can also consider the ways in which your learning is useful for assignments. Critically thinking after seminars can be enjoyable!

However, it is important to remember that not all learning after lectures and seminars happens independently, and peer support can be seen to be an excellent way to develop your critical thinking skills.

CASE STUDY 7.3

After the sociology seminar, the seminar group go for a coffee.

Noah is finding the transition to being a self-directed learner challenging. He finds it difficult to concentrate, he is not enjoying reading the course materials and he feels overwhelmed. He feels that this has become a barrier to critical thinking after lectures and seminars.

After the seminar, his peers all discuss what they are finding hard about studying at university. Whilst they experience challenges in a variety of ways, Noah feels less worried, following the conversation, as he knows that he is not the only student taking time to adjust to new ways of learning. In addition, everyone shares tips and ideas on what they have found useful and discussion continues that develops these ideas constructively.

Noah starts to revisit and reorder notes after both lectures and seminars and allows himself time to reflect on his learning. He becomes clear about what he understands and where he needs to invest more time to develop his learning.

The group recommended podcasts on key sociological topics and he now listens to these whilst travelling home after each learning session.

What is important here is that Noah has completed the experiential learning loop. He has tried to read before the seminar, contributed and developed ideas within the seminar, and reflected on how hard he finds it, but then has identified new ways to critically think and engage with seminar material in the future. Overall, he has enhanced his ability to critically think after lectures and seminars and he is able to learn more effectively.

Individual learning needs

Remember that it is important to be proactive in your approach to learning. If you have a health issue or disability, you may find both lectures and seminars tiring, and sometimes struggle to concentrate during these. To make sure that you continue to learn, as soon as you have left lectures and seminars spend some time writing or recording a short summary of the content from them. Always reflect on and revise any of your own notes or recordings, working to find a strategy that supports you in doing this effectively, for example using a template to help you to organise your notes (see Godwin, 2012). It is helpful to consider what your lecturer said at both the beginning and end of each classroom session (lectures and seminars alike), because these are often the times when key bits of information are provided. Remember to allow yourself to take short breaks, time to 'recharge' when you are working to consolidate your own learning post-classroom (University of Reading, 2024).

> **Top tip 7.2**
>
> Whilst your own institution will make reasonable adjustments for you to support your learning, you should also consider how to make your own reasonable adjustments to support the continuation of your learning after lectures and seminars. What strategies work best for you? Test different options and then apply those that you feel benefit you the most.

As earlier chapters have discussed, ethnically diverse students' experiences of learning may involve much adjustment (Bunce et al., 2021). As an active participant in your own learning, you can develop your own strategies after lectures and seminars to enhance your critical thinking. If supplementary material is biased, in terms of authorship and focus of research being in the Global North, you can search for follow-up learning materials written by ethnically diverse academics and authors. If these are not available, you can develop strategies to critically think about the material that you have been presented with in both lectures and seminars. Sociology, for example, is much criticised for being based on the ideas of Dead White Men (Bancroft and Ferve, 2016). Reading critical analyses of content is also a useful post-classroom strategy. Lim (2022) notes that it is important to have support in several areas, to ensure that your wellbeing, confidence and ability to engage in learning are all present, as this will enhance your student journey. Consider the ways in which you can use strategies after both lectures and seminars to ensure that you are meeting your needs in all of these areas.

Top tip 7.3

> Lim (2022) suggests that 'ethnic capital' (first described by Modood, 2004) is a powerful resource to support student learning at university. This is linked to supportive networks and shared heritage.
>
> It can be helpful to consider joining with other ethnically diverse students on your course, or within your own institution, and using these networks to continue your learning after classroom interactions.

Critical thinking action plan

Please reflect on your critical thinking in relation to how you will implement actions related to developing your critical thinking after seminars and lectures.

Worksheet 7.1 Critical thinking action plan

Critical thinking skill	Action to be taken	Review after six weeks
Ability to reflect after lectures and seminars.		
Ability to revisit notes and re-use them (condensing, summarising and mapping them to learning outcomes).		
Ability to continue to actively participate in learning, using strategies suited to you own learning style.		
Ability to understand and assess evidence and its credibility.		

(Continued)

Worksheet 7.1 (Continued)

Critical thinking skill	Action to be taken	Review after six weeks
Ability to understand the context in which knowledge and evidence was created.		
Ability to assess arguments and solutions.		
Ability to develop arguments and solutions.		
Ability to consider all perspectives.		
Ability to manage the emotional aspects of learning.		

Conclusion

In this chapter we considered the ways in which you can maximise your learning after both lectures and seminars, by outlining a range of strategies for you to implement to support your ongoing learning, after you have left the classroom. The chapter also considered some approaches that can be used to maximise your critical thinking skills following on from classroom discussions so that you can consolidate your learning and complete the collaborative experiential learning loop, by becoming self-directed students.

Further reading

Chatfield, T. (2022) *Critical Thinking*. London: Sage. This book comprehensively covers lots of areas, so you can select those most relevant to your own needs. Chapter twelve on 'putting it all together, critical thinking in study, work and life' has really helpful content to support your ongoing learning post lectures and seminars.

Cotterill, S. (2023) *Critical Thinking Skills: Effective analysis, argument and reflection*. London: Bloomsbury. This is a comprehensive book, but perhaps pay particular attention to Chapter eleven on mapping and evaluating argument, as well as Chapter twelve on critical reflection, as these areas are most useful after lectures and seminars.

Greetham, B. (2016) *Smart Thinking: How to think conceptually, design solutions and make decisions*. London: Palgrave. This book has three sections, firstly one on conceptual thinking, secondly a section on creative thinking and finally a section on making decisions, all of which are useful for developing your critical thinking after lectures and seminars.

PART III

CRITICAL THINKING IN ASSESSED WORK

So far in this book we have considered what critical thinking is, how to do it, and applied it to learning in lectures and seminars. This part turns its attention to the points where you are required to demonstrate your learning within your course. Assessments are often daunting and can create anxiety across all student groups. The third and final part of the book turns to critical thinking in assessed work.

Assessments are best when they are varied across a course, so that they include assignments, essays, exams, presentations, practical assessments and placements. This means that irrespective of your learning style, there will be an assessment strategy that plays more to your strengths. It is fair to say that an exam favours those who have excellent memory and the ability to regurgitate facts, whilst a presentation favours those with strong communication skills. A course where it was all practical assessments would be unfair on the student with dyspraxia who struggled with fine motor skills, but they may thrive with a written assignment that they can take time to engage with and reflect and review.

Irrespective of the type of assessments, critical thinking is beneficial in preparation for, during and after assessments. The principles of the experiential learning loop can be applied here too, with critical thinking and preparation before and for assessments enhancing your knowledge and skill base that will inform your assessment completion; critical thinking during an assessment enhancing your engagement with the assessment and produce better results; and critical thinking after assessments using feedback and feedforward as a way to enhance future assessments.

This part will support your critical thinking in relation to writing for assessments (Chapter eight), particularly assignments and essays (Chapter nine) and exams (Chapter eleven). It will consider critical thinking in practical assessments, particularly presentations (Chapter ten) and placements and practical assessments (Chapter twelve). It concludes with guidance on how to apply critical thinking to feedback.

8
Critical thinking and assessments

CHAPTER OBJECTIVES

- Understand the importance of module learning outcomes and marking criteria
- Reflect on critical thinking to develop your academic skills
- Reflect on how best to use artificial intelligence tools

Introduction

This chapter will help the reader to engage effectively with written assessed work. It will reflect on the importance of developing an *active* understanding of a module's learning outcomes, marking criteria and assessment questions in order to fully appreciate what the learner is actually being asked to do. Such an understanding is key to working more efficiently and unlocking higher levels of academic achievement. It will provide guidance, reflective prompts and practical examples – a toolkit to guide a learner's engagement with their work, scaffolding effective academic writing. It will consider the use of artificial intelligence (AI) in critical writing. This chapter will provide a foundation for later chapters' discussion on effective engagement with specific forms of critical writing.

Learning outcomes

Module learning outcomes, or learning objectives, describe the intended result of your programme of study – what you should know, understand and be able to apply at the end of your module or other programme of study. They will usually be stated in your module handbook or covered in early classes or lectures. If you are unable to identify the intended learning outcomes for your studies, you should ask your lecturer or module leader as soon as possible.

Why are learning outcomes important?

One useful way of thinking about learning outcomes is to see them as a road map, showing the intended direction of travel. Think about going on a journey. If you know where you are going from the start, you will be able to be active in your travelling, consciously concentrating on reaching that destination more effectively, paying more attention to key details and waypoints along the way. Let us apply this analogy to academic study:

- Being aware of the intended learning outcomes for your studies will enable you to focus your attention on them – like in a journey, it helps to be clear about where you are heading.
- Academic assessments are used to assess whether you have achieved learning outcomes – they are how you will demonstrate you have reached your learning destination.

So what does this mean, and how do we apply this active awareness in practice? Quite simply, being aware of the specific intended learning outcomes for your studies informs your understanding of what an academic assessment will be asking you to evidence. This will allow you to hone in on key points in lectures and seminars, and also while reading, listening and reflecting more generally.

WHICH STUDENT IS CRITICALLY THINKING?

Nihal and Michael are students on a Tourism degree.

Nihal is a hardworking student who attends every lecture, takes copious notes and engages fully with reading before and after teaching.

He is thoroughly enjoying his course and learning a lot, but occasionally gets anxious that he is unable to discriminate between what is important information for his studies, or just something that is interesting general knowledge.

Michael has limited time to engage with his studies. He has a part-time job and carer responsibilities. Despite his best intentions, these external pressures mean that he does not make it to every lecture and rarely completes all of the expected reading for his course.

Knowing the challenges he will face, the first thing Michael does on starting a module is to check the learning outcomes and assessment instructions. This means he can focus his limited time on the absolute essentials.

Everyone is different and the salient point is that, in their own individual ways, both students are critically thinking about how to work effectively. Nihal has realised that his engagement lacks focus and will hopefully soon engage with his module learning outcomes and assessment instructions to help him concentrate on key details. Michael has already done so, and has acknowledged that when he has capacity he needs to engage with the broader learning available from his course.

Taxonomy of learning objectives

Benjamin Bloom, the American educational psychologist, led the production of some of the classic models used to categorise different forms of learning objectives. The taxonomy of educational objectives (Bloom, 1956) introduced in Chapter two identified that learning objectives should be progressive, becoming more complex as the student's knowledge and academic skills develop. The key elements of Bloom's taxonomy, adapted by Anderson et al. (2001), are, in sequence:

- *Remember*: Recall facts and other basic concepts.
- *Understand*: Explain ideas or concepts.
- *Apply*: Use information in new situations.
- *Analyse*: Draw connections among ideas.
- *Evaluate*: Justify a position.
- *Create*: Produce new or original work.

CASE STUDY 8.1

Let us now look at a course-specific example. The learning outcomes from a Tourism module concerned with the ethics and practicalities of responsible tourism:

At the end of the module, students will be expected to:

1. Understand and use Responsible Tourism as a marketing tool.
2. Identify appropriate customers for Responsible Tourism.
3. Develop creative marketing solutions to attract and expand a customer base for real-world Responsible Tourism products.

The first task is to establish what these learning outcomes actually mean the learner needs to do. In plain English, students will be expected to demonstrate:

(Continued)

(Continued)

1. That they **understand** what Responsible Tourism is and how it might be used in marketing.
2. That they can **identify** potential customers.
3. That they can consequently **develop** appropriate marketing materials.

Paraphrasing learning outcomes so that you understand them is a useful way to highlight what you need to do (Chatfield, 2022).

Applying Bloom's (1956) and Anderson et al.'s (2001) taxonomy of learning objectives, it is safe to assume that this would be a first-year module as it asks the student to understand, identify and develop. This is clearly a very practically focused set of learning outcomes, which might be assessed by a case study or business report, showcasing the clear real-world applications of learning. Knowing the learning outcomes from the start would enable a Tourism student to focus their studies on being able to achieve the three clear intended outcomes.

So what next?

Top tip 8.1

If you have not already, it is helpful to take **action**.

- Look up and note the learning outcomes for each of your modules or other programmes of study.
- Consider if you understand them, and if not talk to your module or course leader.

Reflect on how you might evidence your achievement of your learning outcomes in your assessments.

With an established understanding of the module learning outcomes, the next step in critical thinking and critical writing is to consider how to demonstrate your understanding and knowledge against the learning outcomes in academic written work. Your assessment marking scheme provides further clues as to what you need to do to get the highest marks.

Understanding assessment instructions

Once you know the learning outcomes you are working towards, you can critically engage with your assessment instructions, further ensuring that you understand *exactly* what is being asked of you. Language is a complex tool, and similar sounding instructional words can in fact mean subtly different things.

The best way to begin this is to identify the instructional words in your assessment brief, the key words which will tell you what you need to do.

Ten common examples are given below, together with what they might be telling you to do:

1. **Analyse:** Examine a topic by considering each aspect of it in detail, assessing their implications and importance for your conclusions.
2. **Assess:** Weigh up the worth, significance or implications of something.
3. **Compare/Contrast:** Examine the ways in which two or more things are similar or different.
4. **Comment:** Give your views, backed up by the evidence, analysis and research which formed them.
5. **Criticise:** Assess something, discussing the evidence you have engaged with in formulating your judgement.
6. **Evaluate:** Give an opinion on something, providing the evidence which informed that opinion.
7. **Explain:** Give reasons for something.
8. **Identify:** Pick out and state something.
9. **Review:** Critically examine and assess something.
10. **Summarise:** Give a brief account of the main points of a topic.

Please remember that exact specifics will depend on the particular details of your particular assessment. Going beyond this, you can then look for more specific clues as to what you actually need to do in your assessment brief. For example:

- *'With reference to appropriate data, identify likely trends in the South-East Asian luxury market in the next decade ...'*
    - You will need to include statistics or other forms of quantitative information.
- *'Given Khan's study (2023), assess the potential impact of "climate anxiety" on tourist decision-making ...'*
    - You will need to relate your answer to a particular study or publication.

- 'Assess the influence of television documentaries or travel blogs on the growth of Dark Tourism in the period 2010–2020 ...'
  - Your answer must be related to a clear timeframe.
- 'Using at least three real-world scenarios ...'
  - You must provide a specific number of actual examples in your answer.

CASE STUDY 8.2

Let's consider a real example, the first assessment from the Tourism module whose learning outcomes we considered above:

'Research and write a Responsible Tourism marketing blog for a social enterprise and non-profit website created to tell sustainable tourism stories.'

As we predicted, this is clearly a practically focused assessment, and there are some clear clues in the question as to what is required. The instruction word 'Research' highlights that research is required, so even in blog format you will need to provide citations. Being told the nature and purpose of the platform gives you a clue as to the required tone and style of writing as well. So even a student who only read the question would hopefully understand that they had to write a research-based blog, on a specific topic, to fit with the theme of a particular website.

However, a student who had also read and remembered the module learning outcomes would know that they also needed to demonstrate their understanding of:

1. Responsible Tourism as a marketing tool.
2. How to identify appropriate Responsible Tourism customers.
3. How to devise marketing solutions to expand a Responsible Tourism customer base.

Recalling these three outcomes would further inform the student's planning of what to include in their blog. Note how the three learning outcomes give a significant steer as to what to include compared to the assessment instructions alone.

Ultimately, understanding assessment instructions is a simple process of determining precisely what you are being asked to evidence. Time spent determining this early on will save you significant time later, also guiding your studies. After all, once you have identified the key words in your assessment brief, you can consider what they mean you need to do in practice. This will then inform the general plan you make for writing your assessment, from your initial reading to the content you include.

Applying your understanding of learning outcomes

A common mistake that students make in their writing and assessments is to list everything they know about a topic. This is understandable, as it might reflect what they have been asked to do at school or college, demonstrating that they have learned and can repeat information. However, at university, a higher level of understanding needs to be developed, where you apply the information you know by critically engaging with a topic. Critical thinking about your assessment question – looking for specific instruction words and other clues as to exactly what you need to do – will help you deliver an assessment answer which demonstrates that higher level of understanding, ultimately by making an informed judgement rather than simply sitting on the fence (Cottrell, 2023).

So how do you actually demonstrate your achievement of intended learning outcomes in your assessments? Given the topic of this book, you will not be surprised to have it reiterated that criticality is the key! Whatever the assessment, a few core principles apply:

- **Read around the topic:** You will naturally have your own preconceptions and opinions about the topic of the assessment. However, it is important that before you formulate your answer, you read around the topic (as we explored in Chapter four), engaging with a range of sources and perspectives. This will ensure that the position you adopt is the correct one, and that you are aware of potential counter-arguments.
- **Back up your arguments with evidence:** Review your work to make sure that you are not making unevidenced statements, or simply describing a situation. A statement needs to be backed up by evidence about why that is the case. Or a description of a situation needs to be followed up by comment on the implications of that situation for your overall argument.
- **Discuss key points:** As you develop your position, discuss it with your fellow students, tutors and perhaps even your friends and family. While your answer ultimately has to be your own work, the very process of explaining what you are working on will further help you to formulate your position. The responses of the people you talk to might also influence your thinking!
- **Show your working out:** A good way of ensuring that you are working critically, and backing up your arguments with evidence, is what some students call 'showing your working out', like in a primary school maths class. When you proofread and edit your work before submission, you can look at each statement and ask yourself: Is this statement supported? Does the reader have the information they need to understand how I reached this conclusion?
- **Join the dots:** It can be a little too easy to run through the list of points you want to cover in your assessment answer one after another, almost like a shopping list. Instead, to

provide a truly critical, high-level answer, demonstrating your attainment of the intended learning objectives, you need to do what some students call 'joining the dots'. This means showing the links between different pieces of information or different aspects of your argument. In later chapters we will look at how to highlight such joining of the dots in your written arguments.

- **Acknowledge counter-arguments:** Almost inevitably, there will be a counter-argument to your position, whether an alternative option or simply another point of view. Good critical writing might well overtly acknowledge this alternative perspective, briefly outlining it before explaining why it is not in fact correct or applicable. The very act of doing so demonstrates criticality, strengthening your own position.
- **Beware of over-scepticism:** We live in age of public scepticism, from distrust or loss of faith in traditional hierarchies and information sources to conspiracy theories, deep-fakes and AI-generated content of sometimes dubious accuracy. In critically questioning traditional conclusions and conventions, it is important not to over-correct. We need to avoid listening to alternative voices without applying an equal critical eye (such as the CRAAP or REVIEW frameworks covered in Chapter four) to them, remaining alert for potential biases, misinformation or unevidenced statements. In being critical, we need to strike a balance between what we expect and what we will in fact accept (Wallace and Wray, 2021).

As we will explore in later chapters, there is more to critical assessment writing than this – but if you first ensure you understand your learning outcomes and assessment instructions, and then remember to apply these core principles in your work, you will be supporting yourself in more effective critical writing.

> Top tip 8.2
>
> Reflect on how you might incorporate these core principles of understanding your learning outcomes into your assessment work; for example:
>
> - You could include them in your assessment plan.
> - You can use them in your Cornell template when note making.
>
> You could use them as a checklist when proofreading and editing your work as the extent to which you have answered the question is as important a point to check for as spelling and grammar.

Using sources: critical thinking to develop your academic writing skills

It is worth reflecting on how you use sources to construct an effective academic argument which both demonstrates your understanding of the topic and that you have achieved the intended learning outcomes of the exercise. As we have already noted, you need to back up your arguments with evidence, sharing the information which leads to your conclusions with the reader and talking them through your interpretation of it. However, the actual choice of sources and evidence which you use can also more subtly support your argument.

For example, if a Tourism student like Nihal or Michael included lots of travel blogs and influencer social media posts in their work, it would demonstrate engagement with contemporary experiences of travel. However, if this was all that they cited, it would imply to the reader that they had perhaps not fully engaged with the academic or professional literature contextualising the lived experiences of individual travellers. If they instead provided a diverse range of citations in their work, from travel blogs to academic textbooks, from professional trade body reports to academic journal articles, this would support a far stronger academic argument, a position clearly based on a broad understanding of the full range of literature relevant to the topic.

> **Top tip 8.3**
>
> Looking beyond your choice of sources, how you comment on them and incorporate them into your work can also help you unlock higher marks.
>
> If you are including a social media post as an example of real-world lived experience of travel, while aware it is one individual's experience and perhaps not reflective of the broader literature, then state this. Equally, if sharing an academic journal theory while aware it may not map to all cultures and locations, then acknowledge this as well.
>
> 'Show your working out' as we said earlier, help the reader understand your interpretation of the source – this is just another way of demonstrating your critical analysis in your writing.

Critical thinking in assessed work

When planning and reviewing your work, you may find these prompts helpful to ensure that you have used an appropriate range of references appropriately:

- What sources have you used to support your arguments? Have you used an appropriate range of source types, including appropriate academic journal articles and/or textbooks as well as professional information and online search results?
- Have you incorporated these sources into your work appropriately, acknowledging their strengths and weaknesses while explaining how they relate to your overall argument?
- Have you also considered how you will critically proofread your work before submission?

Let us consider this last point a little further. There are obvious key points to check for and correct when proofreading an assessment submission; for example:

- spelling;
- grammar;
- use of colloquialisms or informal language;
- use of unexplained acronyms and abbreviations.

However, have you also considered proofreading for:

- the strength and cohesivity of your academic argument;
- the flow of your work from paragraph to paragraph, with one point leading to another to build a strong argument;
- if you fully demonstrate accomplishment of the module learning outcomes;
- if you fully address the assessment marking criteria.

Top tip 8.4

> It can help to approach proofreading as a separate task to writing. Some students find it helps to finish writing an assessment, then revisit the work a day or two later in a different context to edit before submitting.
>
> For example, if you typed an assignment on a laptop in your room, or a computer in the university library, you might proofread it as a hard copy in a cafe or on a park bench, changing the font as well as the format from on screen to on paper. This should help you spot points you might otherwise miss.

If this particular tip does not work for you personally, you may wish to reflect upon how else you might revisit your work in a different context, helping you to spot points to change before submission that you might otherwise miss.

However you approach the task, just remember to proofread for strength of argument as well as for spelling and grammar.

Artificial intelligence (AI) and other forms of technological assistance

There are an increasing number of artificial intelligence tools available to help with writing and other aspects of academic study. Consequently, it is important to understand what tools are available, how they might help you, and how they might not help you, and when their use is permissible in your studies. For any form of technology designed to help with your studies, helpfully you can ask yourself three simple critical questions to guide your use of it:

1. *Will this technology actually help me? Or would it be quicker or produce higher-quality work if I just do the job myself?*

It is always tempting to think that there is a 'silver bullet' or some other kind of magic solution to a complex or time-consuming task. There are online tools available to help with academic tasks such as paraphrasing, referencing, note making and even generating example assessment answers. However, many such systems require a significant investment of time to set up, or to learn how to use effectively. So it is important to consider if a tool you are considering will in fact save time, or if exploring it could in fact just be another form of procrastination.

2. *Do I actually understand how to do the task I am asking a computer to do? And how the computer will accomplish it?*

It is important to make sure that you are not cheating yourself. Ultimately, you are at university to study, learn and grow your understanding. If you know how to accomplish a particular task and have found an ethical way to accomplish it more effectively using technology, then that would be an excellent example of growing and applying your understanding. If, on the other hand, you are using technology for a task because you don't know how to do it yourself, then that is not in fact helping you long-term. As we'll explore below, you also need to understand how a computer is accomplishing a task to ensure that it is doing so correctly.

3. *Is the technology's use actually ethical and permissible under my university's academic integrity guidance?*

It is important that you understand what is or is not permitted on your course. For example, using a tool such as ChatGPT to generate an assessment text you submit is clearly cheating, like copying someone in an exam or paying someone to write an assessment for you. Not everything is that simple, though. Using tools such as the spelling and grammar checkers in Microsoft Word or Grammarly is long-established academic practice. However, if such tools are now suggesting alternative forms of phraseology and text, would adopting their suggestions constitute cheating, as the words are no longer your own? Arguably yes, it would – demonstrating the importance of understanding what is or is not permitted on your particular course.

So how can artificial intelligence tools help you in your work? Well, that will ultimately vary from individual to individual! However, there are a few common acceptable uses:

1. as a creative prompt, to generate ideas around a topic before you start writing;
2. to generate examples of specific styles of writing;
3. someone with a specialist learning need might use an ai tool to help with that – for example, a dyslexic student using an article summarising tool in addition to reading an article abstract.

In such cases, you still need to know how the tool works. In some cases, it is less helpful than it appears to be, for example, many tools which generate text produce very reputable-sounding academic paragraphs. This can include citations which are often in fact non-existent – the system has included 'Gregson, 2023' not because any such work exists, but because the models which inform its outputs imply that a citation is needed at that point in the same way a full stop might be needed at another point. The system is mimicking good practice, not making a conscious decision which citation to include.

All of which returns us to our three key questions of if technology will actually help, if you understand what you are trying to do and how the computer will do it, and if such a solution is actually permissible. Think critically before you click to generate text!

You can apply the same three core questions we applied to artificial intelligence to other forms of technological support as well. For example, there are many tools available to assist with academic referencing including the 'Cite' button on Google Scholar and academic databases. Once again, it is worth matching the tools to the job as you cannot guarantee that their citation is correct or matches your university requirements but it can be a good foundation to develop your citations from.

> **Top tip 8.5**
>
> If you are writing a first-year undergraduate 2,000 word assessment, with 10-20 references, you would be better off writing the references manually to support you to develop and understand the principles of academic referencing. For this length assessment, spending several hours setting up and learning how to use a complex reference management system would in fact once again be a form of procrastination; the technological equivalent of claiming you can't possibly start writing until you have done the food and drink shopping for a party and tidied your desk!

As such, critical thinking is required when using artificial intelligence: use it to enhance your academic practice, not replace it. Such an understanding will also help futureproof your ability to work effectively, both academically and in the world of work. Ultimately, the nature of the assignments discussed in this book is likely to change as technology evolves. For example, written assessments may have to be conducted under exam-like conditions, or shifted to verbal assessment or specific tasks involving application of knowledge, testing understanding rather than requiring submission of written work which could have been computer-generated by AI. The tasks which employers value in graduates may also change. As such shifts occur, maintaining a solid critical understanding of what you are being asked to achieve and how artificial intelligence tools work is your best way of being prepared for them.

Individual learning needs

This is the time to critically think about yourself, your individual learning needs and your academic skills.

Take a moment to reflect critically upon yourself:

- Are there any personal circumstances of yours which might speed or slow your capacity to work on your assessments?
    - How might you adapt?
    - What assistance might you need, or changes might you need to make?
- Do you have any special knowledge, or a different perspective on any aspect of the assessment?
- Are there any adjustments you can make to your working practice to support yourself in working more effectively?

The result of these reflections might, in turn, cause you to revise how you approach assessments. By being emotionally intelligent and aware of your strengths and areas for development, critical thinking will enable you to enhance your engagement with your assessments and improve your grades.

Critical thinking action plan

Please reflect on your critical writing skills and where you need to develop a skill, develop your critical thinking action plan.

Worksheet 8.1   Critical thinking action plan

Critical thinking skill	Action to be taken	Review after six weeks
Developing an active awareness of module learning outcomes		
Understanding *precisely* what an assessment is asking you to do		
Making a plan to achieve that goal		
Checking you have followed your plan and written critically, focused on the assessment requirements		
Your understanding of the use of AI		

Conclusion

This chapter has explored how critical engagement with module learning outcomes, assessment instructions and marking criteria can support critical writing, one of the classic ways of demonstrating your learning and consequently achieving academic success. In practice, this means being an *active* thinker, reader and writer. You need to *engage* with your module learning outcomes, *understand* what you are being asked to achieve, and then *demonstrate* this in your assessment writing.

In university-level study, this will generally involve applying your understanding of a topic, based upon critical analysis and reflection, not just repeating everything you know about a topic. This chapter has highlighted some simple means of doing so.

Being able to apply your knowledge effectively in this way will demonstrate your high-level understanding of a topic, a prerequisite of gaining higher marks.

In the following chapters, we will look at how to apply your critical thinking skills to specific types of academic assessment.

Further reading

Chatfield, T. (2022) *Critical Thinking: Your essential guide*. London: Sage. Chapter ten outlines the key aspects of critical thinking and working, also providing further top tips.

Cottrell, S. (2019) *The Study Skills Handbook*. London: Macmillan International. Chapter thirteen explores the topic of writing at university level in more detail.

Williams, K. (2022) *Getting Critical*. Basingstoke: Red Globe Press. Part III offers a useful overview of getting critical in your writing.

9
Critical thinking in essays and assignments

> **CHAPTER OBJECTIVES**

- Understand how to structure an essay and apply the same principles to other assignment types.
- Consider the importance of a plan and critical thinking in preparation for essay and assignment writing.
- Understand how to embed critical discussion in the structuring and writing of an essay or assignment.

Introduction

This chapter will help the reader to think critically when writing academic essays. It will explore practical ways of embedding critical thinking into the whole process of academic writing, from formulating an initial plan for an essay assignment to writing critical paragraphs and even individual sentences. The aim is to ensure that university-level criticality occurs in a student's essay writing as standard working practice.

Practical examples and reflective prompts will guide the reader in working more critically while writing essays in general, as well as encouraging students to reflect on how they might develop their own writing style in future. The chapter starts with the core principles of essay structure, before moving on to cover planning and time management and then revisiting critical reading as a basis for effective critical essay writing in detail.

Essay versus assignment

Essays were traditionally one of the most common forms of university assignment and remain a common assignment type on many courses. Quite simply, an essay is a piece of writing in which you build an argument based upon information in order to answer a specific question or topic. Typically it will have an introduction, conclusion and a main body of text. This main body of text needs to be structured in a logical way, to support the development of your argument and lead the reader to the same conclusions as you, but it will not usually have subheadings.

Of course, different forms of written assignment also exist, such as scenario or problem-based assessments, reflections, reports, literature reviews or various forms of deep dive into specific pieces of information or lived experiences. You might even encounter hybrid assignment types, where, for example, you are expected to incorporate a literature review or reflection into your essay in order to inform your conclusions.

In this chapter we will consider critical thinking for essays in particular, although happily many of the broad underlying principles will apply to other forms of written assignment as well. However, if working on another form of written assignment you should also check the standard expectations for that particular form of writing as well, looking at past examples and reviewing your assessment instructions and marking scheme.

Now let's look at two different approaches to the task of essay writing.

WHICH STUDENT IS CRITICALLY THINKING?

Sara and Karl are on an English Literature degree.

Sara's previous educational experience was very practical and she is new to the discipline of essay writing. Consequently, she's understandably a little worried about her essay, so she's approaching it in a very methodical, practical way.

Karl loves his course and has been focused on studying it for years, his A-level choices and leisure reading reflecting his engagement with key aspects of his subject. Consequently, he has an unusually broad general knowledge of key aspects of the essay question.

Sara looked at the online guidance her university library provides about good essay writing and also read a short book on the topic. She's checked her module learning outcomes and assignment mark scheme. Then she has made a detailed plan of what to say in each section of her essay, and at what length, also noting when she will have written each section by, and when she will proofread and edit.

Sara now feels more in control of the process.

In practice, this has led to Karl working in a relatively unfocused way. The evening after his lecturer first discussed the essay he typed multiple thoughts into a first draft. Since then he's drawn a mind map of other points to cover, adding extra thoughts as they occur to him, and he knows that at some point he'd better revisit the module learning outcomes.

Karl's doing OK, but he is a little worried that his remaining time is limited and that he'll probably finish a long way over the word limit and need to edit down significantly. It'll be fine, though, he thrives under pressure!

As your critical mind will doubtless tell you, both Sara and Karl are exaggerated archetypes and although hopefully both will write good essays, you can appreciate the salient points of their examples. Sara's strength is her structured planning, Karl's is his enthusiasm and background knowledge. A good personal essay writing process should provide an effective means of positively channelling such enthusiasm and creativity, while also providing useful structure, as we will consider throughout this chapter.

Essay structure

Let's begin by reminding ourselves of the first principles, the core components which make up an essay.

An essay conventionally has three main sections, an introduction, the main body of text and a conclusion. Even if you are an experienced essay writer, it is worth reflecting on the traditional requirements for each section, so you can consider how best to fulfil them in your work.

Introduction

Your introduction should inform the reader how you will answer the question. It sets out your argument and the points and topics you will explore to justify that position. 'The introduction to your essay should encourage your reader to read on.

It should also manage your reader's expectations about what is to follow' (Day, 2023, p. 41). The introduction might also outline any data, texts, methodologies or theories you will particularly engage with. It tells the reader what to expect and the marker what to look out for.

Top tip 9.1

The introduction should be based on a close reading of the module learning outcomes and the essay's assignment mark scheme. There is an old academic cliché that the introduction should be the final part of the essay to write, tying everything you've done together.

That is perhaps a bit extreme, but you can see the point. Wingate (2012) noted that not appreciating the need to develop your own position is one of the most common failings in undergraduate essay writing. Some students fall into the trap of writing a vague introduction as a form of procrastination, advancing towards the word count before truly engaging. Instead of this, the text of your introduction should tightly reflect your planned answer to the essay.

Main body of text

This is where you demonstrate your broad knowledge and critical understanding of the topic and that you have met the module learning outcomes.

Top tip 9.2

Each paragraph should generally make a different point that develops the overall argument, be presented in a logical order and be of an appropriate length, avoiding the classic pitfall of spending too much time on one point and not enough time on another.

Crucially, rather than just summarising information you have learned, you will also add critical comment and analysis relating that information to the essay question. We will explore ways of doing this in individual paragraphs later in this chapter. We will also look at ways of repeating this process as many times as required, dependent on depth of discussion required on each topic, how many topics are advised to be covered and your word count.

Conclusion

Your conclusion sums up your answer, linking back to your introduction by once again highlighting any particularly salient points. You summarise and explain why the points you have analysed in the main body of your answer back up your position, despite any potential counter-arguments. You may also briefly highlight potential ideas for future research, or comment on the broader implications of your findings.

Top tip 9.3

> Do not introduce significant new information or ideas in your conclusion. It is a summary of the discussion already provided.
>
> Beware the banal or fence-sitting. You have just argued for a particular position at some length. A final line like 'What the future holds, no-one can say' may seem like a fine rhetorical flourish, but will in fact undermine your overall seriousness (Roberts, 2017, p. 130).

As we noted earlier, this chapter is about essay assignments. Consequently, if using it to guide your work on another type of written assignment, you should consider how its structure might differ from an essay. Your assignment mark scheme should provide a guide here, as well as your module handbook, assignment instructions, and any past examples or specific guidance for the particular form of writing that you can access, even if for a different question. However, let us briefly look at a few practical examples:

- **Reflection:** A written reflection would probably still contain an introduction and conclusion. However, it might also have specific sub-sections or even headings, relating to the information or experiences under consideration and the reflections arising from them.
- **Report:** A report is generally a formally structured document with headed sections. Longer reports might well contain a table of contents, an abstract or executive summary, an introduction, the main body of the report (split into relevant sections relating to the topic), a summary or conclusions, any recommendations, a reference list or bibliography and an appendix or appendices for any additional information.

- **Literature reviews:** Literature reviews are where you consider the available information relevant to a given topic and summarise it. Generally, they are formatted in a comparable manner to an essay, with an introduction, main body and conclusion. However, it is important to remember for your planning that the slightly different focus – on summarising information rather than answering a question – will influence both what you say and how you structure it.

Given the diversity of assessment options in academic study, naturally there are other forms of written assignment available. However, the same key principles generally still apply: Check the assignment instructions and mark scheme, ensuring that you know what you are being asked to do and how to format and present your answer for a particular form of assignment – and then make a plan for how to do this!

Formulating a plan

Next, to inform your essay plan-making, we will consider the key factors relevant to a good essay plan. It is helpful to return to how we summarised the critical writing process at the close of Chapter eight: 'You need to *engage* with your module learning outcomes, *understand* what you are being asked to achieve, and then *demonstrate* this in your assignment writing.' In practice, once you have deconstructed and understood the question, you are then ready to make a plan that ensures that you demonstrate the required level of critical thinking in your answer. A plan is crucial as it will keep you on track, organising your arguments and keeping your writing focused on the intended outcomes. This will help you avoid common traps, such as merely summarising everything you know about a topic rather than fully answering the question or providing the critical analysis necessary to unlock the highest marks. Quite simply, a plan is your way of scaffolding your academic success in an essay-type assignment.

Here are two popular essay plan templates to get you started. It is important that you have an approach to planning that works for you, so you should treat these examples as templates for you to adapt as you see fit.

Arguably the most common plan is the PEAL method, as seen in the template below and as we will discuss further later in this chapter. It can be a helpful way to construct a clear plan for answering an essay question point by point. In particular, it provides the structure that is often considered necessary within an essay.

> **ESSAY PLAN TEMPLATE 1**

Introduction

Point 1 (repeat as many times as necessary)

- Point:
- Evidence:
- Analysis:
- Link:

Conclusion

> **ESSAY PLAN TEMPLATE 2**

Introduction

- What this essay will cover
- Brief definition of key terms or concepts

Section word count:

Complete section by:

Essay section (repeat as many times as necessary)

- Key point:
- Evidence:
- Analysis/critical comment:

Section word count:

Complete section by:

Conclusion

- What you have found:
- How the evidence supports this:
- Any further implications for your overall argument/the topic in general

Section word count

Complete section by:

This second essay plan format has been adapted to include more detail and you might adapt each one further to suit your individual style of thinking and working. For example, you might want to use a mind-map-style visual approach instead. However, it is important to understand the basic plan components first.

For another form of written assignment like a literature review or reflection, you will probably need to use a different plan template, to reflect the different structure of that particular form of writing. However, the same underlying principle applies. You are using a template to structure your initial plan and in turn your written work, ensuring that you cover the key points, in an order which supports your overall position, including critical comment or analysis and naturally leading the reader towards your conclusions or closing summary.

CASE STUDY 9.1

Karl is a student on an English Literature degree. One of his first-year module assessment is:

Explore the concept of 'human bondage' in work of the period 1900–1950. You are encouraged to show the range of your reading, but you should also address a set text in detail (3,000 words).

Karl decides to use an essay plan template to plan a response to this question. He considers:

What might he include in the introduction?

What key points might he include in the main body of text?

How many key points might he make within this essay?

What might he include in the conclusion?

Even without checking the learning outcomes of the module, there are already a lot of prompts in the question to inform a draft essay plan. While instructed to address a set text in detail, the writer is actively encouraged to answer more freely, demonstrating the extent of their learning and knowledge, which opens up multiple potential options. Given the potentially broad scope of this essay, it would also be particularly important to set out an approach to answering it in the introduction. Karl could perhaps turn to 'the concept of "human bondage"' itself first. The phrase alludes to W. Somerset Maugham's 1915 novel *Of Human Bondage*, a powerful account of a young man's quest for happiness while troubled by unrequited love and both money and employment troubles. There are already plenty of universal themes there to explore in the essay, to say nothing of the 'bondage' of class, gender and race in the time period in question, each of which could be taken as a critical discussion point and explored using the PEAL method.

Finally, Karl could critically think about the question to 'show the range of your reading' which may prompt him to consider authors as diverse as, for example, George Orwell and Virginia Woolf, while noting that they need to be from the set period of 1900–1950.

CASE STUDY 9.2

A rough draft of an essay plan.

Introduction:

- Note origin of the phrase, but highlight broader connotations in literature of period, citing several other examples of human bondage.
- State which set text will be considered in particular and why (drawing in any relevant literary theories).
- State which other forms of bondage will be examined and why, including any other key texts or authors which will be considered in particular detail.
- Trail conclusion that the diversity of the essay's coverage highlights that 'bondage' is as diverse as the human experience itself, as represented in literature.

Point 1

Point: Phrase refers to a Somerset Maugham novel.

Evidence: Details about novel.

Analysis: The forms of bondage experienced by the main protagonist.

Link: However, even in one novel, multiple forms of social and personal bondage are outlined …

Point 2

Point: The female protagonists also experience human bondage.

Evidence: Relevant plot details.

Analysis: Shows that human experience is multi-faceted and open to various interpretations (discussion of characters' motivations, etc.). Tie in to any relevant literary theory.

Link: As can also be shown in other works of the period …

Point 3

Point: An obvious example of literal human bondage is George Orwell's *1984*.

Evidence: Salient plot details.

Analysis: However, even within Orwell's stark political fable, interpersonal and gender-based bondage forms comparable to Maugham's work are discernible. Tie in to any relevant literary theory.

Link: Back to overall argument, or cue up another diverse example.

Points 4, 5, 6 …

Further points might then be found by revisiting the module learning outcomes.

Module learning outcomes:

1. Develop a critical understanding of a range of literary texts from the period 1900–1950.
2. Understand the cultural traditions and contexts in which the literature of the period was written and read.

Engage in close reading and analysis of core texts.

In our rough draft of an essay plan, we have already covered the first two module learning outcomes, although both could probably benefit from more detail. Perhaps further texts could be cited, and more relevant cultural and social context. However, the third learning outcome is a real clue – if possible, we should provide some more detailed textual analysis of key works. Rechecking the module reading list and/or teaching materials might then highlight key literary concepts or theories to include. It is worth remembering that teaching staff do spend time preparing the most appropriate materials for the module so to ignore them would seem foolhardy.

Theorists such as May and May (2011, p. 114) recommend six key steps in formulating a critical academic argument:

1. Identify the key issues.
2. Anticipate all the sides to an argument.
3. Research all sides, using authoritative sources.
4. Weigh the evidence for all sides, and build support for your position.
5. Identify and respond to counter-arguments.
6. Communicate your conclusions.

These six points would be a good starting point for making an essay plan. You can see how they might guide your planning, making sure you do not miss any key perspectives or tasks. They might also stimulate initial reflection on what points to include in your essay, and what order to include them in. That is a good thing, and you should make a note of anything that occurs to you at this point in your draft essay plan.

With a finite number of words available, and finite time in which to write the essay, even if you are not an English student you can see the need for an essay plan to ensure that you do not overlook a key factor or spend too long on any one point.

How to read and critically think in preparation for writing an essay

At this stage you may wish to revisit the advice in Chapter four on critical reading. The first two of May and May's six points above are part of the initial planning and brainstorming process. The third and fourth points comprise the critical reading part of the essay writing process. In the fifth point you might then return to your plan, adapting it on the basis of your critical reading, before finally writing your essay, the sixth point, 'communicate your conclusions'.

As we said in Chapter four, it can be helpful to have questions in mind when reading a chapter or article critically. In this particular instance, the question could be: 'How does this relate to my essay question?' or 'What are the implications of this text for my argument?' You can also use models such as the CRAAP tool we considered in Chapter four to further inform your critical reading. For example, if you note that everything you are citing is a novel of the period in question, you may also wish to cite some academic commentary, demonstrating the breadth of your reading and understanding of the topic.

The key point is to apply your critical brain to direct your readings. You should ask yourself:

- What do I need to cover in the essay?
- What key authors or topics do I need to refresh my memory of?
- What might I be missing?

In a discipline as subjective as English Literature, you will never cover every aspect of the topic. That is one of the joys of academic study and research, there is nearly always something new to say or a fresh perspective to unveil! However, if you plan and read critically, you can ensure that you cover a representative sample of the discourse. Crucially, as Godfrey (2018) notes, critical reading is an ongoing process. This will give you a sound basis for providing a reasoned and logical – if never wholly definitive – position on your essay topic.

Top tip 9.4

> As you write your essay, fresh ideas are likely to occur to you as you critically think about the subject matter.
>
> They, in turn, will trigger thoughts of lecture notes, books or articles you may wish to revisit or topics you may need to seek out fresh information on, further extending your critical thinking.

Crucially, as Godfrey (2018) notes, critical reading is an ongoing process. As you write your essay, fresh ideas are likely to occur to you. They, in turn, will trigger thoughts of texts you may wish to revisit, or topics you may need to seek out fresh information on. This, in turn, will inform amendments to your plan, with critical reading, planning and writing working as a fluid and ongoing process right up until you finally hit 'Submit'. Indeed, the critical process even extends beyond submission, with any belated thoughts that occur to you and your eventual assignment feedback informing your future work. Equally, as in other cases in this chapter, you can apply this approach to other forms of written assessment, just changing the focus of your critical reading and ongoing reflection to fit the needs of that particular question or form of assignment.

How to write a critical discussion in an essay

> Critical thinking is a practical, hands-on process, not just abstract theorising. (Kirton, 2012, p. 135)

For critical thinking to be demonstrated in an essay, ensure your work is analytical rather than descriptive. Happily, there are a number of straightforward techniques and prompts you can use to help embed criticality in your essay writing:

- **CRAAP:** As we considered in Chapter four, the CRAAP method can guide initial critical engagement with information. Remember that it stands for *Currency, Relevance, Accuracy, Authority* and *Purpose*, five factors which can aid your critical evaluation of information. That might then inform how you comment on that information; for example:
    - 'Although dated in their social attitudes, Jenkins' overall conclusions remain relevant ...'
    - 'The social media comments helpfully contextualise academic commentary by reflecting a contemporary audience's personal responses to the play ...'

You can see the critical thinking in action. The first bullet reflects the Currency and Relevance aspects of CRAAP, the second bullet is addressing a potential concern about Authority by emphasising the Relevance of the content cited. Essentially, in each case, the student is showing the reader what they feel is important about the information, while also highlighting that they have taken into account its potential weaknesses.

Finally, reflection on CRAAP style comments might influence further reading and adjustment to essay plans – for example if you realised you were only citing one particular type or age of source.

- **PEAL:** The PEAL method is an easy way of structuring paragraphs to ensure that you include critical comment. It stands for:
    - *Point:* The one key point you are making in this paragraph.
    - *Evidence:* Include information from reliable sources to support your point.
    - *Analysis:* Explain the relevance of your point and evidence, perhaps linking them to broader discussions of the topic.
    - *Link:* Link back to your overall argument and/or on to the next paragraph.

Let's look at a brief hypothetical example, based upon our W. Somerset Maugham *Of Human Bondage* case study.

Point: The term 'human bondage' in the essay question is an allusion to W. Somerset Maughan's classic novel of 1915.

Evidence: The novel is essentially a classic 'coming of age' tale, an account of a young man's pursuit of creative and personal happiness while beset by romantic and financial concerns.

Analysis: However, as Phipps (1991) has noted, the exact form of the 'bondage' that the protagonist endures is open to question. It could be the unhappy love affair with Mildred, the financial struggles or even the relationship and career the protagonist eventual acquiesces to. Or as Munro (2005) comments, 'bondage' could also allude to the forms of class and gender subjugation endured by significant female characters in the novel. Strikingly, these views are not mutually exclusive, with 'human bondage' a multi-faceted and diverse concept.

Link: This phenomenon can also be found in other literature of the period.

> **Top tip 9.5**
>
> Remember, the 'analysis' section is where you will earn the majority of the marks, so even in this concise example it should generally be longer than the descriptive 'evidence' section.

Now let us consider a few further prompts to ensure you are truly critical in the analysis section.

- **The Yes/No angle:** Does the evidence support or refute your argument? How might you critically comment on this?
    - 'Sheldon's work (2014) further demonstrates that ...'
    - 'This is a valid counter-argument, however, it is not in itself enough to contradict our overall findings ...'
- **The language angle:** As the preceding examples show, you can use language to scaffold the inclusion of discursive critical comment in your work rather than just making simple statements of fact.
- 'Chen's conclusions (2021) may be based on a relatively small body of literature from a distinctive genre, but they can nonetheless be applied more generally ...'

> Top tip 9.6
>
> In your reading, look out for key critical phrases you can adopt. The Manchester Academic Phrasebank is a good source of academic vocabulary, with a whole section on critical language (www.phrasebank.manchester.ac.uk/being-critical/).

- **The Sherlock angle:** Identify an author's position and then interrogate it. Does the evidence support their position? What are the implications of their information for your essay answer? You might even need to suspect the question itself! Some essay questions deliberately make naïve or misleading generalisations in the hope that you will question them (Roberts, 2017).
- **The proofreading angle:** As we said in Chapter eight, when proofreading your work, you can also check for strength of argument. You could even check paragraph by paragraph for if you are spending too much time analysing rather than describing, and if your overall argument is effectively supported by the organisation of your essay.

It can be reassuring to remember that none of this is new. Staying with our literature case study example, Rudyard Kipling was a journalist before he was a successful author of the period, his professional background perhaps influencing prompts he may have used for his own critical thinking:

I keep six honest serving-men

(They taught me all I knew)

Their names are What and Why and When

And How and Where and Who.

While many of his other views might seem dated in modern society, his use of questions as essential critical thinking tools remains relevant.

Of course, for the long term it is a little too simplistic to approach essay writing in the relatively rote-like manner these prompts suggest. However, in the short term, the prompts will help you incorporate key aspects of critical thinking in your writing process, perhaps employing the contemporary saying *fake it till you make it* as we again said in Chapter four. Indeed, research (for example, Bennion et al., 2020) shows that the very process of writing an essay aids the process of developing a deeper understanding of a topic.

Later on, as you evolve as an academic writer, you will develop more of your own voice, deploying these and other techniques in a way which best reflects your own individual style. Once again, you can apply these prompts to other forms of written assignment as well. While an evidence-based writing model like PEAL may not be wholly appropriate for a narrative reflection (although it would still support transition from narrative description of an event to analysis of its significance), tips such as the proofreading angle and the language angle are more generally applicable. The very process of considering which prompts, templates, plans and models best support your particular critical thinking in different forms of academic assignment will also help you to develop as a writer.

Individual learning needs

In the same way that a good essay plan will incorporate subject-specific or assignment-specific requirements, it should also incorporate any relevant factors from your personal circumstances and identity. This is important as a way of supporting yourself to have the best possible chance of doing well in the essay. Ultimately you want to make sure that you play to your undoubted strengths, while supporting any relative weaknesses and also continuing to develop and stretch yourself.

Let's consider a couple of practical examples.

CASE STUDY 9.4

Claire has a Reasonable Adjustment Plan (RAP) for her studies due to a specific learning difficulty: she has dyslexia. Her RAP states that she can ask for an additional ten working days to complete the essay, but she knows that she also has to start engaging with a plan earlier than some students as she needs longer to read, take notes, write a plan, write the essay, proofread and amend it, before being able to submit it. Claire needs to be organised and

(Continued)

(Continued)

plan. She finds *Of Human Bondage* (Somerset Maugham, 1915) difficult to read in anything more than 15-minute chunks, so needs to take longer to read it to ensure that she is able to write a robust essay answer.

To aid her critical thinking she plans to read for 15 minutes every hour on the days she allocates to write her assessment. In between she knows that she needs exercise or relax and plans for this. She is delighted at how effective this strategy is in writing her assignment, also now recognising more fully why she is provided with additional time to write it. Such critical thinking will, in turn, help her with planning her future work and indeed wider life.

CASE STUDY 9.5

Shamima is an international student and English is not her first language. Studying in a different language and culture to her previous experiences means that her critical thinking is helpfully informed by a diverse range of perspectives. However, speaking a language effectively is a distinct skill from being able to work in it.

Consequently, Shamima may wish to clarify with her tutors what is specifically meant by critical thinking in the local context of her UK university course, and reflect on how she can further support herself in essay writing in English. Depending on her previous knowledge of English literature, she may also want to ask her tutors for further recommended concise readings or commentaries which would help her contextualise *Of Human Bondage* in the wider canon in a comparable manner to someone whose pre-university career had been in the UK.

Both Shamima and Claire will hopefully write good essays, informed by their particular life perspectives. However, you will note how they have actively reflected on their particular circumstances and proactively considered what actions they might need to take to best support themselves in effective study.

Take a moment to reflect critically upon yourself:

- Are there any personal circumstances of yours which might speed or slow your capacity to work on your essays or other forms of written assignment?
    - How might you adapt?
    - What assistance might you need, or changes might you need to make?
- Do you have any special knowledge, or a different perspective on any aspect of the essay or other form of assessment?

- Are there any adjustments you can make to your working practice to support yourself in working more effectively?

The result of these reflections might, in turn, cause you to revise your essay writing plan.

Critical thinking action plan

Please reflect on your critical thinking skills in relation to writing essays and where you need to develop a skill, you can further develop your critical thinking action plan.

Worksheet 9.1 Critical thinking action plan

Critical Thinking Skill	Action to be taken	Review after six weeks
Making a plan		
Ensuring you write critically		
Critical proofreading		

Conclusion

This chapter has considered how effective planning can support critical essay writing. It has explored means of embedding criticality in your essay-writing process, from formulating an effective plan and structuring your work to providing practical tips and prompts to ensure that critical analysis and comment is not an 'add-on' but a standard part of your writing process. It has also encouraged reflection on how to apply these strategies to other forms of written assignment, along with reflection upon your individual characteristics and the implications they might have for your critical working plan and writing process.

Ultimately, essay writing is a distinct form of academic work, but you can prepare for it like any other key task or skill. After all, in this chapter we have really just applied the lessons of Chapter eight in a specific context. Having first understood what we were being asked to achieve, we have then planned towards that goal. Equally, as we noted earlier, contextualising the general principles of good critical working to specific assignment types can be done with any form of academic work. As we look at two more assignment types in the following two chapters, you will be able to recognise many of the same broad principles of critical working being applied.

Further reading

Greetham, B. (2023) *How to Write Better Essays*. London: Bloomsbury Academic.
Maugham, W.S. (1915) *Of Human Bondage.* London: William Heinemann.
Roberts, J.Q. (2017) *Essentials of Essay Writing: What markers look for*. London: Palgrave.
University of Manchester (2023) Academic phrasebank. Available from: www.phrasebank.manchester.ac.uk/

You should also consult your library for the good range of subject-specific essay-writing guides which are also available.

10
Critical thinking in presentations

CHAPTER OBJECTIVES

- Understand why university learning and assessments take the form of a presentation
- Consider what makes a good presentation and how this includes critical thinking skills
- Identify and analyse criteria specific to critical thinking in presentations

Introduction

This chapter will consider what a presentation is and how to approach it critically to enhance your engagement and performance. It will consider both individual and group presentation and offer strategies to develop presentation skills. It will consider the importance of understanding marking criteria to maximise outcomes.

Advantages of presentations

Most students will be required to deliver a presentation at some point during their university course. A presentation usually means some sort of oral account (using spoken rather than written word) which makes use of some sort of visual aids (mood board, PowerPoint, poster, etc.). A presentation can be delivered by an individual or in a small group, be online or face to face, and live or pre-recorded upload. However, they are usually delivered to an audience of tutors, other students and/or experts by experience. A presentation can be assessed, and that will be the focus of this chapter; however, it can also be part of a seminar to share information and stimulate discussion (Chivers and Shoolbred, 2007).

It is not unusual for students to wonder why presentations are included as part of the educational repertoire. It is helpful to remember that a presentation enhances not just knowledge of the subject, but also communication skills, organisational skills, confidence and often group-work skills. The advantages of presentations are:

- Preparing and assessing presentations can be more engaging for students and staff than creating and marking lengthy written assignments.
- Presentations can work better for presenting and analysing visual content.
- They can involve group work and collaboration and therefore provide opportunities to enhance your group-work skills.
- On the basis that several heads are usually better than one, the quantity but also the quality of what students can produce can be greatly enhanced.
- Presentations allow for immediate feedback and where assessed a mark.
- Questions from an audience can be used to provide additional opportunities for students to clarify content or demonstrate further understandings.

In short, it is not surprising that presentations are a common mode of learning and assessment activity in higher education. The better you understand how to create an effective presentation including one that demonstrates the required critical thinking, the more likely you will be able to realise your potential and have a good experience. In this chapter we consider some practical tips for critical thinking and success in presentations.

Where a group presentation is required, if you share out the work effectively, combine the skills and knowledge of your group, and work as a team you will achieve even greater outcomes. Nevertheless, some students find presentations very stressful and a small number experience considerable anxiety. Many presentations are organised around small groups and group work has its challenges. It is not always popular with students especially if the same mark is awarded to each member of the presentation group. This may be because not all students might have contributed equally, and some students might feel that their mark has been affected by a lack of understanding or lack of preparation by others in their group which may feel unfair.

However, empathic critical reflection should be given to *why* some students are not engaging. They may be just lazy, in which case the frustration is justified.

However, be careful not to jump to this conclusion. If they are avoidant because they are anxious about working with someone or the work itself, then you will need to work together to support and nurture them to enable them to develop in confidence and academic skills, which will in turn develop your own empathy and group-work skills as group presentations are not just about developing presentations skills.

> **WHICH STUDENT IS CRITICALLY THINKING?**

Olivia and Andrzej are students on a primary education degree, they have been asked to pair up to create and present a summary of a research paper in a seminar.

Olivia has read the paper and used the CRAAP model to evaluate it and has lots of ideas on the presentation.

Andrzej has read the paper and used the CRAAP model to evaluate it and has lots of ideas on the presentation.

She presents them enthusiastically to Andrezej and insists that her way is correct. She feels that he is not participating and feels cross that he is not as enthusiastic as her in the planning or actual presentation.

However, he feels that Olivia is not listening to his ideas and is talking over him. He withdraws and feels disempowered and disinterested.

Both Olivia and Andrzej undertook preparatory critical thinking for the task, but once working together the critical thinking evaporated. For both students it would be beneficial to reflect on how they participate in group work, with Olivia needing to be more open to other people's ideas and use her listening skills and Andrzej needing to be more assertive, confident and maintain his enthusiasm in difficult situations. If they had taken an empathic approach to each other, their critical thinking would have developed not just their presentation, but also their academic and personal skills.

Presentation design features

When designing your presentation there are some basic features which are relatively easy to include and others which are more difficult. The latter includes demonstrating critical thinking but unless you attend to the basic features of effective presentations the critical thinking skills will be less evident. Sirazova (2019) found that confidence in preparing for a presentation impacted on the success of the presentation, so it is time well spent. First, you should ensure you are clear about your tutors' expectations for presentations:

- How are judgements going to be made about the quality of your presentation?
- Do you need to show some creativity, innovative approaches, a more friendly, engaging and informal presentation?
- Can you (or are you expected to) 'ad lib' (talk to your notes and slides rather than read them out word for word)?
- Alternatively, is a much more formal or more tightly scripted conference-style presentation required?
- Are you expected to make good use of visual aids, graphs, tables, pictures, etc.?
- Is there an expectation that certain key concepts or theories need to be presented? Do correct technical terms or legal/procedural foundations need to be explored?

By understanding the task parameters or assessment criteria you are ensuring that your presentation meets the brief, which is the first step to success in presentations.

Presentation method

Firstly, you need to decide what method the presentation will take. This may be part of the assessment brief, or you may have flexibility. It can be a PowerPoint presentation or a flipchart paper. It can be all words, or it can be a more creative approach where, for example, pictures or audio represent what you will talk about. If you need to include statistics or a graph, think about their management. A presentation requires you to demonstrate the ability to communicate your knowledge gained through the module in a clear, coherent and concise way. This is your opportunity to be innovative and creative in doing so. It can be helpful to consider:

> Is the content appropriate to your intended audience?
>
> Do your visual aids complement and enhance your ability to demonstrate the quality of your thinking rather than detract from it or simply repeat it?

If it is a team presentation, you will need to consider and demonstrate the ability to interact professionally with group members and work as a team. It is helpful to agree a running order and have a nominated person to co-ordinate the presentation materials from each person to ensure that it is cohesive.

Structure

A logical and clear structure with appropriate introduction and conclusions or summary will enable you to better highlight where your critical thinking skills are in evidence. Xuwei and Feipeng (2021) researched successful TED Talks, aligned them to presentations and recommended the importance of a strong clear introduction that introduced self and topic to engage the audience and can be applied to assessors. This should lead to development of the topic, present a particular position and then end by summarising what you have said.

It is beneficial to determine a clear focus of your presentation. Align this task to an assignment plan (as discussed in Chapter nine): taking the time to think about what you want to achieve is invaluable. Hopkins and Reid (2018) argue that a presentation should include introduction, main discussion and conclusion, which forms a clear structure to develop.

CASE STUDY 10.1

University students on a primary education course have been asked to create a presentation (maximum 15 minutes) as per this brief:

Choose two different theories, models or perspectives of learning associated with outdoor adventure education and identify potential learning (personal and social) outcomes and how they might be measured.

Andrzej is undertaking the presentation. First, he considers presentation method and structure. He knows that he needs to use a PowerPoint presentation and reflects that in 15 minutes six main slides is enough to create a presentation plan.

Slide 1: Introduction of self and topic (30 seconds)

Slide 2: Development of topic and introduction of two theories (2 minutes)

Slide 3: Theory 1 (3 minutes)

Slide 4: Theory 2 (3 minutes)

Slide 5: Potential learning associated with outdoor learning (3 minutes)

Slide 6: Measuring learning (2 minutes)

Slide 7: Conclusion (1 minute)

Slide 8: References (30 seconds)

Returning to PEAL (Point, Evidence, Analysis, Link) outlined in the previous chapter, if slides 2–6 follow this principle, a clear structure and plan is formulated.

If it is a group presentation, consider how you will structure each person's contributions from the agreed plan.

Will you share out the presentation content and order to ensure that everyone has equal responsibility?

Will each person have equal time or will a subject require more time so this becomes agreed but unequal?

Will you consider taking turns in a planned manner or multiple small contributions each, or will it be a 'free for all' during the presentation?

This will require discussion to ensure that everyone feels that they have the time that they want. Critical thinking can be given to the question of what you will do as a group if one person exceeds their time and the presentation time cannot overrun. It may be that you wish to allocate a timekeeper who knocks discreetly or who holds up an agreed symbol when it is time for each person to wrap up their section and hand over to the next person, as Sirazova (2019) found time management to be the most common area for development in presentations.

Presentation content

Deciding on your topic is crucial here. It may be you can see how some of the topics are more complex or more controversial, or perhaps they have interesting implications or challenges with professional applicability. Remember that your enthusiasm may well influence your engagement with the topic. It may also influence how engaging your presentation is when you come to deliver it.

> **Top tip 10.1**
>
> Make a quick list of possible topics within your presentation brief. Consider how well you understand each of these in considering which one to choose.
>
> Are you more familiar with some than others?
>
> Do you have some useful prior experience or knowledge to draw upon?
>
> Are some more interesting to you?
>
> Are any more relevant to the presentation brief?

This can start to identify which topics will be in your presentation. Remember that you cannot cover everything and depth of discussion on a couple of topics is more important than naming lots of topics. If it is a group presentation you will need to reach a joint decision: a topic which best fits your *combined* strengths, interests and experience as well as your skills. Time spent critically thinking about choice of topic and focus will make your presentation both easier for you to prepare and present, and more engaging. Some topics will lend themselves better to you engaging in critical reflection, critical evaluation, analysis or synthesis. However, the choice here is taken by critically thinking about what you want to achieve, what you need to achieve and what you can achieve in the presentation. You should consider these and similar questions in the context of the assessment guidelines, assessment criteria, learning outcomes and the mark scheme, if there is one. In addition, it is worth critically thinking:

- Have you addressed all aspects of the brief/question?
- Are you using a range of appropriate and authoritative sources?
- Are you showing the explicit relevance and importance of the information and evidence you are including?

Use of relevant theory is a key feature of critical thinking. Therefore, in your presentation you should show how theory can help you explore or even unpack what might otherwise be taken for granted. In our case study example, it specifically requires you to link theory to evaluating your experiences. This might mean you can critique current practice or current thinking but more often it enables you to show deeper understanding and hence critical analysis. Deeper thinking can enable you to critically reflect upon and justify your own thinking or arguments, rather than jump to conclusions. It can also enable you to provide explanations for why things are as they are or may appear to be and/or offer possibilities for change. In this way critical thinking could be demonstrated by identifying points of tension or points of possibility. Depending on your subject, demonstrating critical thinking might also require you to show that you appreciate that your chosen topic may be:

- viewed from multiple perspectives;
- influenced by various contexts;
- explained through supporting evidence and relevant theory.

Often, as in the case study, there will not be a right answer or only one solution to the presentation task and it is unlikely that your tutors have a model presentation in mind. In fact, tutors are often looking for a range of creative presentations across the cohort that engage them and stimulate their thinking. You can see in this example, that in applying his knowledge and chosen theories and suggesting other possibilities, Andrzej may also need to suggest that some of what he concludes is not clear cut or is context specific.

CASE STUDY 10.2

Andrzej made a quick list of possible theories, models and perspectives in relation to a) learning and b) outdoor activities. He then considered which he was more familiar with, which he had useful prior experience or knowledge to draw upon, which he was interested in and which were more relevant to the presentation brief.

He returned to his initial presentation plan after critically thinking about presentation content to update the plan with more depth of what will go on each slide. He notes in italics further information or ideas that he needs to explore.

Slide 1: Introduction of self and topic (30 seconds)

Make clear here what the presentation will cover

Outline what audience can expect.

Find picture of child in outdoor activity

Slide 2: Development of topic and introduce two theories (2 minutes)

Introduce Comfort, Stretch, Panic model

Explain why they are relevant/important to the topic

Why have I chosen them?

Possibly name a theory I discarded?

Slide 3: Theory 1 (Comfort, Stretch, Panic model) (CSP) (3 minutes)

Leberman and Martin (2002) developed a model to show three zones of learning: 1) comfort, 2) stretch and 3) panic.

Learning happens best when we are in the middle zone called the stretch zone.

Explain each zone, with extra focus on stretch zone

Slide 4: Theory 2 (Zone of Proximal Development) (3 minutes)

Vygotsky's *(need to find year)* zone of proximal development (ZPD) theory is similar but different from Leberman and Martin's theory.

His is a much earlier work based in psychology and children's learning.

He suggested that the ZPD represents the gap between what a learner can already do and/or understand and what they can do with appropriate support.

Should I swap these two around as V is older and explains CSP?

Slide 5: Potential learning associated with outdoor learning (3 minutes)

Potential learning includes:

Increased reading, writing and maths skills (Quibell et al., 2017) and science (Fan et al., 2024) *(that surprised me, so reflect on why)*

Social and emotional learning (Molyneux et al., 2023)

Self concept, self confidence, self control (Fiennes et al., 2015 *(but this is old, can I find anything newer?)*

Increased student engagement and ownership of their learning (Mann et al., 2022)

Development of collaborative skills (Mann et al., 2022)

Slide 6: Measuring learning (PEAL) (2 minutes)

This is the hardest slide! I need to think and read about this more

Possibly test before and after? Use reflection postcards?

But I need to think about how I can show learning

Slide 7: Conclusion (1 minute)

To optimise learning we must set appropriate levels of challenges and match that with appropriate support.

Primary school students benefit holistically: educationally, socially and emotionally from outdoor activities.

Outdoor environments provide an ideal environment for this type of activity. But these same principles can be applied to learning in general.

Slide 8: References (30 seconds)

Check referencing strategy is correct

Confidence in presentation

How you present is just as important as what you present. It is helpful to make sure you show not just knowledge but also understanding. This can be demonstrated by using (and describing where appropriate) any key terms appropriately and by avoiding oversimplifying content or a reliance on superficial description. Examples of a critical and cautious stance might include:

> 'can be questioned in terms of', 'fails to consider the possibility that ...', 'this may or may not demonstrate ...' 'there is a lack of consensus'.

You could use words or phrases which signal that you are thinking critically:

> *Furthermore, in addition, alternatively, similarly, conversely, by contrast, not only ... but also, thus, it would seem therefore that ...*

However, it is wise to avoid absolutes as words like

proves, always, never, is, every ...

which are likely to annoy your tutors (unless you have strong evidence to back up your claim). Instead be more 'tentative' and use words like

suggests, may indicate that, it would appear that, has argued that, claims that

as they show critical thinking rather than closed thinking.

Top tip 10.2

There are some helpful phrasebanks, which gather together similar phrases which you can use to show you are thinking critically. An example of this is one from the University of Manchester, which includes a whole section on phrases you can use to signal critical thinking. You can access it here: www.phrasebank.manchester.ac.uk/being-critical/

Top tip 10.3

Ensure you know how to use the IT, or whatever other visual aids you are using.

Arrive early enough to get set up and settle in.

Think about how you will represent yourself in the presentation as your attire, posture, pace of your delivery and tone of voice will communicate confidence (or lack thereof) that will enhance your grade and/or feedback.

Taking a few slow breaths before you begin can really help to calm you. If you lose your place in your presentation, take a moment and carry on: your assessor is unlikely to notice and they always take account of nerves anyway.

It is helpful not to 'read' your presentation if you have the confidence not to do so. Having notes to refer to is always good, but reading out loud is less engaging than talking about your points.

Presenting in front of your tutors and, if required, in front of other students, can feel quite daunting. Sirazova (2019) found that confidence enhanced oral presentation outcomes both as an individual and within group presentations. The best way to develop your confidence, as individuals and as a group, is to practise and polish your presentation lots of times and invite people you know well to give you kind but honest feedback, so you can improve it. Like other university work, you should always avoid relying on what is a first draft, completed the night before. To achieve to your potential you need to be prepared to draft and redraft your work multiple times, just like your tutors do with work they submit for publication. This means setting deadlines for a first and subsequent drafts well before you are due to present. You could consider recording your practice presentations so you can see and hear how it comes across.

If it is a group presentation, remember to support each other. Constructive feedback will be helpful to build each other's confidence and presentation efficacy, so be open and honest but tactful and sensitive.

Preparing for assessed presentations

Let's look at assessment criteria for the case study presentation above.

CASE STUDY 10.3

The presentation has the following marking criteria:

Table 10.1 Assessment criteria and their weighting

Assessment criteria	Weighting
Demonstrate critical analysis and understanding of two theories, models and/or perspectives of learning associated with outdoor adventure education	40%
Identify potential learning (personal and social) outcomes from outdoor adventure education and how they might be measured	20%
Demonstrate how you will ensure that an outdoor activity is inclusive	20%
Presentation, communication and referencing	20%

In preparing for the presentation, primary education students would consider that theory was weighted heavily, but also recognise the importance of the quality of the presentation.

Usually each of the assessment criteria will have a 'weighting'. This indicates that some are assigned more importance than others. In assessed presentations your skill in presenting will often form part of the marking criteria, and if it is a group presentation working in a group could also be part of the marking criteria. As such you might consider:

1. Demonstrate critical analysis and understanding of two theories, models and/or perspectives of learning associated with outdoor adventure education.

   Here you need to show your knowledge of the key theories or models associated with learning in outdoor adventure education (Prince and MacGregor, 2022). This has the greatest weighting and returning to the presentation plan shows us that Andrzej has allocated three specific slides to this and will apply theory to his evaluation.

   You only have a short amount of time in which to present so you will need to aim for depth rather than breadth. It is a skill to be able to say what you need and to omit what you don't, so check with your module team if they can clarify what is expected of you if you are unsure. You will need to do more than describe the theories; make sure you explore the relevant strengths and challenges/limitations. Rather than simply reporting what you have read, you should aim to evaluate it. You need to be able to demonstrate that you can make judgements about the value, purpose, relevance, authenticity, logic and weight of the ideas, works, solutions, methods, and materials which you choose to include. To do this you should show how they compare/their relevance to one another and explain their relevance to your chosen topic.

2. Identify potential learning (personal and social) outcomes from outdoor adventure education and how they might be measured.

   This is outcome related, and you would explore the benefits to primary education children. You might link it to the wider curriculum requirements (Prince and MacGregor, 2020), which might include social development and behaviours, fine motor skills, group work, etc. You might consider that developing a child's confidence and allowing them to identify and develop their own interests in new areas could be measured by feedback, SMART goals or observation of social interactions before, during and after a residential outdoor activity event.

3. Demonstrate how you will ensure that an outdoor activity is inclusive.

   In your presentation you will usually need to show you can use key terms relevant to the topic. These terms often have a variety of meanings. For example, the word 'inclusive' is used in different ways. It could mean everything is provided, or everyone is welcome, or more specifically it could mean designed to be accessed in lots of different ways to accommodate different abilities. This then enables you to explore from your defined standpoint how you would ensure the activity was inclusive.

   You will see from the case study in this chapter that Andrzej did not identify inclusivity in his presentation plan. If he did not notice this before presenting, it would impact on his grade and potentially mean that he would not pass the assessment. Being aware of the assessment requirements is that important.

4. Presentation, communication, and referencing

This is all about the presentation itself: the planning and delivery of it.

In this assessed presentation example, you will need to show your ability to communicate your knowledge in a clear, coherent and concise way. In most university-level presentations, you will need to make reference to key authors or researchers (just as you do elsewhere). Ensure you show how the referenced works link to the points you are making or the examples you are choosing. Critical thinking whilst undertaking preparatory reading (see Chapter four) will enable you to consider how a reference helps explain what you are arguing/describing. Finally, ensure that you adhere to your university referencing standards.

If you aren't sure about what the assessment criteria mean, or how they will be interpreted, you should always seek guidance from your tutors. Remember, they will respond much more effectively if you have critically thought about your presentation first yourself and create specific questions. Avoid asking something like 'I don't understand this assessment' or 'Can you give me some help?'. Instead make a suggestion for feedback like 'I am considering the models for change, am I on the right track?'. This gives your lecturer a baseline assessment of your understanding and presentation focus to build on and develop.

After your presentation

At the end of your presentation there may well be questions or some sort of discussion. This is sometimes called a *plenary*. It is useful to consider the sorts of questions your tutors might ask, based on the task parameters or assessment criteria. However, it is critical that you hear and respond to their questions rather than a different question. Questions after presentations are often to either give you the opportunity to address something that is an assessment requirement or are based on genuine interest from the assessor, so don't be afraid to respond with enthusiasm rather than anxiety.

Top tip 10.4

You can write down the question to ensure that you have understood it.

You can ask them to repeat or clarify the question if you are not sure about what they are asking.

You can take a sip of water to give yourself time to construct an answer to the question.

If the question suggests there are limitations or complexities do not be afraid to acknowledge these: you only had a certain amount of time and had to make decisions about what to focus upon so do not be afraid to own the focus you took. They are not trying to trip you up but to decipher your thinking to enable clearer understanding of your presentation. However, use their questions to develop your critical thinking. They are asking questions to stimulate your thinking and understanding further, so see them as beneficial to your learning and performance.

If you are working on a group presentation, a group debrief is critical. Remember to be positive with all group members; blaming and shaming is not helpful and can cause longer-term damage to students' confidence and future engagement.

Individual learning needs

Presentations are a form of verbal communication and students who find expressing themselves in writing more difficult than others may prefer this means of communicating their knowledge, understanding and their critical thinking skills. Conversely, students who lack confidence or oral communication skills may feel that this assessment strategy penalises them. If you find yourself unable to face the prospect of presenting in front of others, you should seek support and advice from your tutors and/ or support services. A reasonable adjustment, for example if you experience anxiety, may be the pre-recording and playing of your presentation or recording audio rather than video.

An additional point for consideration is where a group presentation requires additional meetings than your timetabled sessions to plan, review and agree a presentation. It can be difficult for students who have childcare, a job, live away from the university or health needs that create fatigue to engage with extra-curricular activities over and above timetabled lectures. In today's society where remote communication is easily accessible, it may be that such sessions could be held online to support individual learning needs.

Critical thinking action plan

Please reflect on your critical thinking skills within presentations and where you need to develop a skill to develop your critical thinking action plan.

Worksheet 10.1 Critical thinking action plan

Critical thinking skill	Action to be taken	Review after six weeks
Critical thinking in decision-making of presentation mode and structure		
Critical thinking about content of presentation		
Confidence in presenting		

Conclusion

This chapter has considered what you need to do to showcase your critical thinking skills in presentations. Demonstrating critical thinking skills is vital in order to avoid falling into the trap of simply gathering lots of information and arranging it in a logical order so you can present it back to your tutors. Presentations offer you the opportunity to show what you have *learned* rather than simply what was taught to you. In other words, you need to be able to show understanding and learning gained: what can you do now and what do you understand which you may not have been able to before. Remember that understanding does not mean you know all the answers. It means you appreciate the complexities and subtleties of your chosen topic. In this sense presentations provide a really effective way to 'test' your critical thinking skills. They are also more likely to involve the types of learning that are retained long after the assessment.

Further reading

Anderson, C. (2016) TED Talks: The Official TED Guide to Public Speaking. Available at: www.youtube.com/watch?v=HN0hkfD6c_c. Effectively TED Talks are the specialists in short presentations, and this one is a great ten-minute guide to public speaking.

Chivers, B. and Shoolbred, M. (2007) *A Student's Guide to Presentations*. London: Sage.

Cooper, H. and Elton-Chalcraft, S. (2022) (eds) *Professional Studies in Primary Education*. London: Sage. This is a helpful book for any student studying primary education. Chapter sixteen (Prince and MacGregor) on outdoor learning is relevant to the case study.

Hopkins, D. and Reid, T. (2018) *The Academic Skills Handbook*. London: Sage. Chapter eleven on giving effective presentations is helpful to engage with here and Chapter thirteen is on working in groups which is helpful for group presentations.

11
Critical thinking in exams

> **CHAPTER OBJECTIVES**
>
> - Understand how to approach exams with a critical and positive eye
> - Explore a range of tips and coping strategies for exams

Introduction

This chapter will assist the reader in applying their critical thinking skills in the pressurised scenario of an academic examination. As most students will have sat exams before, at school or at college, this chapter will support learners in reflecting and building upon those experiences in order to work more effectively. This will hopefully reduce some of the stress of exams and support the reader in gaining higher marks.

As in previous chapters, a range of practical tips and critical prompts directly linked to the assessment type are provided. The reader will be guided through the process of preparing for an exam before considering various tips and strategies for critical thinking in the exam itself. Some further prompts are provided for students with a Reasonable Adjustment Plan (RAP) or whose first language is not English.

Overall, the intent is to minimise the element of chance around exams, enabling the reader to critically engage with them in a controlled manner, like any other form of assignment.

Think about yourself and exams

It is helpful to start by thinking back to your previous experiences of exams. Honestly reflect upon what has – and has not! – worked for you in the past, so that you can learn from those experiences and support yourself more effectively this time around. This does not just include how and when you revise. You should also apply your emotional intelligence to considering how you might support your wellbeing around exams. This will support your exam success, but more importantly your overall wellbeing at a potentially challenging time.

It might even be helpful for you to begin by conducting a brief exam audit of your previous exam experiences. This will support your reflections on how best to approach your next exam.

1. What worked for you previously?
2. Can you repeat any previously successful strategies?
3. What did not work for you previously?
4. How can you avoid or minimise past problems?
5. What else will you do differently this time?
6. What are you confident about approaching the exam?
7. What gives you that confidence in particular areas? Is anything transferrable?
8. What are you worried about?
9. What can you do about this (if anything)?
10. What actions will you now take to prepare for the exam?

Now let's consider the practical example of a pair of medical students.

WHICH STUDENT IS CRITICALLY THINKING?

Ben and Zoe are medical students, who have an exam as part of a module in their first year of study. Both are worried about the exam.

Ben has been hiding from the exam. He's worked hard at his part-time job, exercised a lot, partied a lot, and even in the final few days before the exam he has spent a lot of time on 'important' tasks like tidying his desk and arranging summer work before starting to revise.

Zoe has engaged with the exam head-on, directly addressing the points of most concern to her.

The night before the exam Ben's working hard, long and late, frantically re-reading everything that might be relevant in no particular order, scrawling notes to refer to on his bus journey into the exam as crucial last-minute support.

She had a long chat with her tutor about previous feedback she's received about her written work and created a clear plan to develop her academic skills in general.

She's also carefully studied the module learning outcomes and checked how they relate to past exam paper examples.

As a result of that background work, she now has a tight revision plan to systematically follow, giving her reassurance.

Both students will hopefully be successful in their exams, reflect on their approach and do even better in future. However, the hopefully obvious point is that Ben will have had a more stressful experience than Zoe, having left more of his success to chance. While the part-time job and partying are individual lifestyle choices, the points he was worried about were in fact clues as to what he needed to address, both for the exam and to support his overall wellbeing.

Top tip 11.1

Look after yourself

Acknowledge that most people find exams at least a little stressful, so take steps to look after yourself, as you would at another challenging time in your life. Good mental health and emotional wellbeing are paramount to effective revision and exam success.

Be proactive

Particularly if you have sat many exams before, many of the tips in this chapter might just sound like common sense. That is completely true, they are!

However, the challenge for you now is to consider how to apply the tips in real life. What will you actually change in your revision practices and exam techniques?

Earlier on in this book we discussed learning styles, noting the range of literature and perspectives on the topic. Being truly critical, we might even note how some question if they actually exist at all. Of perhaps more immediate relevance is the work of Feeley and Biggerstaff (2015) with medical students, who noted that while learning style does not correlate with exam performance, learning approach does. How Ben and Zoe work will have an impact on their overall results, but related factors such as motivation and wellbeing remain important.

Before the exam

As we quoted in Chapter four *to fail to prepare is to prepare to fail*. Like many old sayings, it sounds like a cliché because it is true. In fact, it is particularly true of exams, where the crucial detail to remember if worrying is that you have much more agency and understanding of the process than might sometimes seem to be the case. As Ashokka et al. (2021, p. 80) noted in a study of postgraduate medical students, 'non-academic attributes impact success in postgraduate examinations'.

The same might be said of undergraduate exams and other subjects. You can support yourself through exams by applying your university-level critical thinking skills to your whole approach to them. You can use the critical thinking skills you have developed throughout your studies long before you start an exam, building upon your previous experiences and reflecting upon what you might need to do in any particular exam to increase your chances of success. After all, you are now likely to have more control over your time and learning than you did in your previous studies. In practice, there are the three following main areas to consider.

Exam content (and revision)

> Exams are designed to test the bringing together of your surface learning, your memory of key facts and data, and your deep learning, your understanding of key facts and data. (Burns and Sinfield, 2022, p. 258)

If you've read the previous chapters, you can perhaps guess the advice that is now going to follow! It is important to remember that like an essay, assignment or a presentation, an exam is designed to test your attainment of a module's learning outcomes. An exam is not trying to trip you up or trick you, it is actively designed to enable you to showcase your learning. A critical and active appreciation of this key fact can guide your revision, enabling you to focus on important topics. While perhaps of little consolation now, it has even been suggested that exams requiring higher-level thinking skills like criticality can help learners unlock deeper levels of understanding (Jensen et al., 2014.

Take a moment to revisit your module learning outcomes yet again. These are the points that you will be expected to demonstrate that you have achieved in the exam. It can help at this point to consider your learning like a return bus or railway ticket, rather than a single ticket (McIlroy, 2005). You are not preparing for your exam in isolation, you can revisit your notes, lecture materials and assignments from earlier on in your course, refreshing your memory of key points. Once you have done so, you are in a good place to make a revision plan. You can use these prompts as a checklist in making your revision plan, making sure that you don't miss any key details:

- Have you revisited your module learning outcomes and understood what you are being asked to evidence?
- Have you revisited your notes, lectures, readings and assignments to refresh your memory of key points?
- Have you checked the format of the exam and consulted any past examples so you know what you are working towards?
- Have you made a realistic timetable of when you will study?
- Have you reflected on your past experiences and considered how you personally revise most effectively? For example:
    - Would a mind map help, linking key points?
    - Would cue cards of key facts and figures help?
    - Would re-reading some key texts as well as your notes help?
- Have you considered how best to support yourself through the revision process?
    - Will you reward yourself for effective study?
    - How will you avoid procrastination?
    - What will you do to regain control if you start to panic or worry?
    - Will you check in with friends and family to ensure you are supported more generally?
- What other factors are applicable to your particular subject and your personal circumstances?

Ultimately a revision plan might be very simple, but to focus and structure your work it should cover:

What you need to do: The topics you need to understand.

How you are going to do it: Your working methodology, whether mind maps, notes or memorising key points.

When you are going to do it by: Your timetable, so you can actively adjust your schedule depending on your progress.

Top tip 11.2

Remember that effective revision is a distinct academic skill in itself, and you can train yourself in it just like you can referencing or essay and assignment writing. There are some good general books on exams listed at the end of this chapter which cover revision in more detail. However, you should also look online and in your university library for additional texts on revision and exams, in case there are any further useful prompts which help you fine tune your revision techniques.

Exam format

As well as actively considering the exam content to guide your revision, it is equally important to critically reflect upon the exam format you will encounter. This will enable you to steer your wider preparation to give yourself the best possible chance of success. Let's consider some practical examples of factors which might influence effective preparation in a particular direction.

- Location

    It's an obvious point, but again, apply that critical brain. What could seriously trip you up at the start of an exam? Perhaps being stressed after failing to find the room in time? If you know that without food you do not concentrate and there is not a café close to the exam room, plan ahead. Similarly, if you have childcare and the exam room is a distance from dropping your children at daycare, arrange support for the day if you can as it is a factor you don't want to impact on your prompt arrival.

    If an exam is in a physical location or online platform you haven't used before, make sure you investigate how to access it in advance.

- Open or closed book exam

    Another simple point, but whether or not you will be able to refer to a key text during the exam is crucial to your preparation. In either scenario, you will likely need to demonstrate critical understanding of your topic.

    If it is a closed book exam, you may need to spend more time memorising key facts and quotations to base your academic arguments upon.

    If it is an open book exam, familiarise yourself with the layout of the book so that you know roughly where to turn to, but remember to ensure that the copy you take into the exam does not have notes or highlighted sections in it unless you are told that is permitted.

- Format of the exam

    Exam format can take the form of written or online, long or short, and it is important that you know what is expected of you.

If it is a written exam, in the age of smartphones and laptops, it is helpful to consider how used you are to writing by hand for a long time. If you haven't written quickly for a prolonged period of time recently, you may wish to practise doing so.

Equally, even for an online exam, you may wish to practise working in a concentrated manner without procrastination or distractions on a laptop for an equivalent time period to the length of exam.

If it is a long exam, even if you are not allocated official breaks, you may want to plan to give yourself regular brief breaks. Practise a technique of shutting your eyes and singing a song or picturing your favourite holiday memory with your first thumb and a finger touching and return to this strategy in the exam to give yourself a break and a boost of positivity. However, it is important not to linger for too long: ensure that you make the break brief not get lost in happy memories at the expense of the exam questions. In contrast, if it is a short exam, it can be helpful to practise concentrated focus.

- Multiple choice, short questions or essay?

    The type of question will also influence your preparation, so take steps to clarify from your module handbook or exam briefing, as this might influence your revision topics.

    An essay examination conventionally tests general understanding of key points and principles, with a choice of questions and specific examples left to the learner's choice. Here you might take an educated guess (based on critical thinking about the teaching, learning objectives and hints given in the exam briefing) to narrow down to say six topics for an exam with three essay questions on the day. This is a risky business and does leave you open to anxiety that the topics won't come up, so don't ignore other topics completely and learn how your chosen topics can be linked to less revised topics so that you can always apply the tactic of 'similarly [revised topic] can be applied here ...'. Whilst this is not perfect it will mean that you have a better chance of not panicking and hopefully will enable you to pass even if you don't get your best grade.

    On the other hand, a multiple-choice or short-question exam won't be testing analytical understanding as deeply, but it will still be checking your capacity to recall and apply certain key facts and principles. Always answer every question, even if it is an educated guess: an answer is better than no answer as you may just beat the odds and get it right.

    Chapter twelve will focus on practical assessments and it is worth reading this chapter in conjunction with it.

These are only a few examples and exam formats do vary. As we've already noted, it is helpful to consult a past paper as an example where possible to see the format and develop your understanding of what will be required of you. The salient point is to pre-emptively and critically consider the challenges you will be facing and then tailor your preparation accordingly. As we saw with Ben, if you are worried about a particular aspect of an exam, then that is actually useful information. It is probably a clue to some additional revision or preparation you need to do!

Revision preparation

Having considered the content and format of the exam you are likely to encounter, it is also helpful to reflect critically on how you might structure revision to support both your academic success and your personal wellbeing as you approach a potentially stressful task.

- Throughout the semester or term

    Revision is not just a retrospective process. Your proactive listening skills can help you prepare for an exam throughout your course. When key learning points or particularly notable facts are mentioned, make a note of them; such points or facts are what you'll probably need to evidence your understanding of in the exam. The ability to refer back to such points quickly and efficiently will speed up your exam preparation.

CASE STUDY 11.1

Ava began her medical exam preparation by not even thinking about the exam, or so she likes to joke.

First, she broke with the habit of a lifetime and loosely scheduled her life for the weeks until the exam, ensuring she has time to work, study and relax. She's even considered some mindfulness activities to help her unwind. This was Ava's way of laying the foundations for her success, and it wasn't a form of procrastination like Ben's, as she moved on from it quickly.

Second, Ava revisited her module learning outcomes, rechecked her lecture, seminar and reading notes, and revisited key materials online. She wasn't reviewing them in detail, she was scanning for headline-level key points to emerge from her module.

This was Ava's way of preparing before she even begins to consciously think about the exam. She's ensured she is well-prepared to study and has reminded herself of the key learnings from her module. Now she knows what her medical exam will expect her to evidence.

- A month before:

    If possible, do you need to adjust your work, leisure or family routine to allow adequate revision time at key periods in the run-up to your exam? In the same way that you need time to write a presentation, assignment or essay, you need time to prepare for an exam.

    It is helpful to consider the time and space to be in the right frame of mind for it, which might include going to the library, the best time of day for you to revise or turning your smartphone off for a period.

    You might also want to consider tangible motivation for successful revision, such as rewarding yourself for completing certain tasks.

CASE STUDY 11.2

Ava has already identified the key points that have emerged from the module teaching and learning outcomes. She identifies six of these and breaks each one into four further sub-categories.

She has critically reflected that she learns best by revising for a couple of hours every day and that first thing in a morning is a productive time for her. She plans accordingly and gets up an hour earlier each day to revise when the house is quiet and before her day 'starts'.

She also knows that she learns best when she writes things down, so each day creates postcards for a different sub-category. She has more days than sub-categories, but this allows her to have a day off if she wants, or if she's ill.

- A day before

    Obvious as it may sound, you are more likely to perform better if you are well-slept, hydrated and not hungry in the exam. You know how your body and mind works and you can plan accordingly, actively adjusting your routine to support yourself.

    A night out the day before an exam is probably a bad idea! However, some people actually prefer to do some brisk exercise and then stay up quite late the night before an exam, knowing that they'll then sleep better than if they try to get an early night and then lie awake worrying.

CASE STUDY 11.3

Three days before the exam Ava clears her days to enable her to review her revision cards. She knows there was no point in doing it sooner as she would forget the content, although is aware that her friend has found it more useful to review all the cards quickly on a daily basis for the last week.

She continues her routine: she gets up early and begins to review the postcards of her sub-categories that she has created over the last month. She decides to allow an hour per category, and knows that some will take longer than others, so plans to do an active console game in her quieter hours and goes for a walk in her lunch break.

She rewards herself with a gentle night out with friends.

- An hour before

    First and foremost, you need to ensure that you get to the exam in a timely manner. If you know that you are often late to most lectures and appointments, you need to adjust your routine and arrive early. It is better to sit and have a coffee on campus than run in late and miss exam time, or even worse not be able to sit the exam at all if it has a cut-off point for late arrivals.

Consider if you need to make any short-term changes to your communications with family and friends to ensure that you are not disturbed at a crucial moment. An hour before the exam, you might want to turn off your phone, or at least some key apps, so that you don't see any personal messages that might distract you.

CASE STUDY 11.4

Ava is at university an hour before the exam: she knows her bus route can be unreliable. However, she does not want to see her friends who have decided to meet for coffee to share anxieties.

Instead, she goes to the library and sits with headphones in listening to her favourite music. She decides at one point to review her revision cards of one sub-category that she just wants a reminder of, but overall feels calm and confident.

In the exam

Preparation complete, now let's look at a case study of an actual exam. As with your revision, how you approach the exam will of course depend upon your subject. A clinical suite based practical exam will be very different from a multiple-choice test on pharmacology. In this case we'll look at one of the most common formats, a written exam in the essay or multiple long questions format.

Top tip 11.3

Help! The invigilator has just told you to begin, and everyone in the room has turned over their paper to look at the first question - what do you do now? As with other assignments, you can in fact scaffold your success with a firm structure:

1. Prepare
2. Breathe
3. Plan
4. Write

Prepare

Before acting, you should ensure you fully understand what you are being asked to do. You should start by *carefully* looking through the paper, checking the questions, how many you have to answer, and how much time you have to answer them. If there are multiple questions you might work out how long to spend on each question and what order to answer them in, while in an essay scenario, you might read through the choice of question several times, deciding which one gives you the best chance of showcasing both your learning and the critical thinking skills which will allow you to unlock the highest marks.

In essence: *Make sure you understand what you are being asked to do.*

Breathe

At any stage in the exam, you may feel pressured or overwhelmed. To an extent, this is normal. As Cottrell (2012) notes, stress is a result of coming under threat from an exterior force – such as an exam! It is OK to take a moment to pause, gather your thoughts and prepare yourself to continue as best you can in a given moment, acknowledging that this is all any of us can ever do. We should also acknowledge that not every coping strategy will work for everyone every time and that is also OK; we will then just need to adjust accordingly later on.

In purely practical terms, if you get stuck, remember that you can always move on to an easier question or essay section. This should enable you to return to the trickier question, having given yourself time to consciously or unconsciously consider your response to it.

Plan

It may help you to underline key words in the question and make a short answer plan, similar to how you write a normal assignment plan. As with standard assignments, this will keep you focused and ensure you don't spend too long on one area at the expense of another. As Tracy (2006, p. 144) notes, 'at higher levels you can never know everything about your subject', but you can use your critical planning skills to apply even 'a little knowledge' more effectively in support of your arguments. The condensed exam-planning process could be characterised as:

a. **Brain dump:** Jot down the key points, thoughts and connections that occur to you about the question.
b. **Organise:** Use mind maps, numbers or arrows to organise the key points by priority, setting out the order in which you will connect them and work through them to build an overall critical argument, as in a regular written assignment.

c. **Revisit:** As you write, other points may well occur to you. It can be helpful to briefly jot reminders of them into your plan before your mind moves on to another topic.

Write

Remember that you are not just showcasing your recall of facts and subject information, but your capacity to critically apply them. The same prompts and techniques you have used in standard assignments still apply in exam conditions, so make sure you use them!

a. *Critical structure: CRAAP/PEAL/Yes–No and Sherlock:* Remember the critical evaluation, overall argument and paragraph structuring methods you learned in Chapter nine and throughout your course. They still apply here, so make sure you actively use them and avoid the low-level answer trap of merely listing everything you know on a topic. Critical comment is still required!
b. *Critical language:* Remember everything you have learned about building an argument and using critical language. Now is the time to deploy those linking, hedging and boosting words which connect sources and points and ease your path to making appropriate evaluative comments and supported judgements.
c. *Critical self-support:* As we've already acknowledged, for most people exams are stressful situations. However, you can take control if an exam situation ever becomes too challenging. For example, if you feel yourself panicking, it might well be a worthwhile investment of five minutes of exam time to control your breathing. You could deliberately concentrate upon your breathing – in and then out, in and then out, in and then out – as a means of calming yourself, slowing your heart rate before beginning to work on the exam again. Equally you can also consciously challenge unhelpfully negative thoughts by reminding yourself of your past achievements, that you are not alone in finding exams challenging, and so on.
d. *Critical proofreading:* Your exam plan should include time to proofread at the end, as ever not just for spelling and grammar but more importantly for strength of argument. You may wish to add an asterisk or two, further emphasising a certain point or linking your reasoning back to the overall question.

Top tip 11.4

> Answer the questions you feel most confident about first! This will score you as many marks as you can early on, before you then consider trickier questions in more detail.
>
> Make sure you answer every question. You'll gain more marks writing a little or answering a few questions in one section than chasing the final few marks in another.
>
> Make sure you leave yourself time to proofread and add any final thoughts which occur to you on reflection and re-reading. This is as much part of exam technique as an initial 'brain dump' of key thoughts.

Individual learning needs

As we have considered in previous chapters, it would be misleading to presume that everyone approaches any form of assessment on an equal footing. As in other scenarios, everyone has their own preferred assessment types and everyone has their own strengths and weaknesses. The important factor is how we acknowledge those factors and prepare accordingly. Let's look again at some examples of students from the medical course we mentioned earlier, considering how they might now prepare for their forthcoming written exam.

CASE STUDY 11.5

Maya has a Reasonable Adjustment Plan (RAP) which covers dyslexia. In the case of exams it states that she can have additional time. She can also be provided with any key readings in advance, under supervised conditions, so that she has adequate time to engage with them.

She knows that she will need to carefully organise and plan her revision and exam practice to keep herself on track, even more than most students. She has good strategies in place to enable her to engage within the additional time her reasonable adjustment affords her.

CASE STUDY 11.6

Em has a RAP, which covers her anxiety. Her understandable concern is becoming overwhelmed by the rapid reading and writing required in her exam and having an anxiety attack, impacting on her capacity to answer effectively. Consequently, she has taken control of the process in two ways:

1. She has considered calming factors such as breathing techniques which are within her personal control and that she might apply in an exam.
2. She has proactively discussed her situation with her university's student support services, ensuring she has received all possible support and equitable adjustments. As a result of her engagement, her RAP now gives her the option of sitting the exam in a calmer, less public environment and she can also take supervised breaks as required.

CASE STUDY 11.7

Tendai's first language is not English and she has a relatively low reading speed in English. This means that it takes her longer than others to decode key ideas and concepts. She may also be unfamiliar with the exam format of being asked to comment on a key reading in relation to wider module learning.

She cannot reasonably ask for additional time or advance sight of key readings like Ava and Ellie, as ultimately it was her choice to enrol at an English-speaking university with assessments in English.

However, she can effectively support herself in other ways. She can focus her revision on generally applicable quotations and 'big picture' key points of the module. Such work would be useful for any student, but in Tendai's case she can practise how she might flexibly connect her key points and quotations to specific past exam questions. This will prepare her for the sort of nimble mental work she'll have to complete under pressure in the exam. She can also talk to her course team to ensure that she has fully understood how the exam will operate and what she will need to do to succeed in it.

This is ultimately yet another area where you can support yourself by being active and critically assessing your personal situation. Whilst we are all different, with different strengths and weaknesses, you should never be unfairly disadvantaged in an exam because of your personal circumstances. If you think that you require a reasonable adjustment to your exam conditions you should raise this with your university as soon as possible, as it is generally easier to make adjustments in advance than make allowances retrospectively. While everyone's desired adjustments are not always possible or equitable, it is always worth having the conversation – you do not want to disadvantage yourself by missing out on support to which you are fairly entitled.

Critical thinking action plan

The key takeaway point from this whole chapter is that you have a lot more control over your experience of exams than you might initially think. You can exercise that control by critically reflecting on the steps you can take to support yourself in working more effectively. You might adjust your preparation, exam technique or family circumstances for example. What you do is up to you, but the key point is that you have at least some agency over your situation and can take steps to support both your academic success and personal wellbeing. An exam remains designed to showcase your knowledge – all you need to do is consider how best to do so. An adaptation of one of the critical thinking action plans we've already used in other chapters may again help you with this. Please reflect on your revision and exam skills and where you need to develop a skill, further develop your critical thinking action plan.

Worksheet 11.1 Critical thinking action plan

Critical thinking skill	Action to be taken	Date to review progress
Understand what is required of you		
Focus your studies		
Support yourself		

Conclusion

This chapter has considered how you can actively apply the critical thinking skills you have developed throughout your studies to performing more successfully in exams. It has supported critical reflection on your revision process and exam preparation, as well as your actual exam technique, guiding you in positive engagement with what is widely acknowledged to be a stressful experience. In particular, you have been encouraged to reflect on your personal approach to exams and consider what small changes you can make to support your academic success and personal wellbeing. Your next challenge is to ensure that these good intentions actually occur in practice.

The key point is that while examinations are a unique academic challenge, the skills you are developing throughout your course are preparing you for them. Chapter four supports your understanding of effective preparation and reading strategies. For essay-style exams, the planning processes, prompts and writing techniques of Chapters eight and nine apply. Similarly, for oral presentation exams, the guidance of Chapter ten applies. As with any other essay or assignment, all you really need to do is recognise the challenge you are facing, reflect upon what the marker is expecting of you, and then consider what practical steps you need to take to reach that goal. You can best support yourself by first understanding what a good exam answer looks like and then focusing your activity on delivering it.

Further reading

Anderson, L. and Spark, G. (2020) *Pass Your Exam*. London: Sage.
Becker, L.M. (2018) *14 Days to Exam Success*. London: Palgrave.
Cottrell, S. (2012) *The Exam Skills Handbook: Achieving peak performance*. Basingstoke: Palgrave Macmillan.

12

Critical thinking in practice learning and practical assessment: skills practice, role plays, experiments, placements, volunteering hours, apprenticeships

> CHAPTER OBJECTIVES

- Understand the importance of critical thinking in practical learning opportunities
- Develop critical thinking when undertaking experiential learning, collaborative experiential learning and practical learning assessments

Introduction

Many practical university courses have an element of practice learning opportunities, where skills practice can include role plays, field trips, experiments and creative productions. Similarly, many professional courses have a work-based learning element including practice placements, volunteering hours and apprenticeship on-the-job hours. Skill development can be enhanced by not just practising the task, but also by critically thinking about how the task was undertaken. The chapter will begin by introducing practical learning opportunities, consider critical thinking through experiential learning and collaborative experiential learning, and conclude by exploring critical thinking in practical assessment.

> Ever tried. Ever failed. No matter.
>
> Try again. Fail again. Fail Better. (Beckett, 1983, p. 4)

This quote from Irish novelist and playwright Samuel Beckett is a more realistic twist on the 'practice makes perfect' saying, where we recognise that we will make mistakes as we learn through practice. However, it is critical thinking on these mistakes that develops our knowledge and skills every time we 'try' an activity for a further time. It is the importance of experiential learning (Kolb, 1984) that practice learning is built upon.

Practical learning activities

It can be helpful to start by thinking about what is a practical learning activity: do you undertake them in your course? We have spoken in Chapters five and six about critical thinking in lectures and seminars and highlighted that often lecturers will supplement 'teaching' with a question, case study or task for students to complete. These require students to critically think about their perspective to develop their understanding and interact with their peers to develop this further. In many ways this external critical thinking is a form of practical learning. However, this chapter focuses on practical learning activities that are both skills practice and work-based learning.

Skills practice: role plays, experiments, practice sessions

Students undertake a wide variety of practical learning tasks in many university degree subjects. This includes role plays, field trips, experiments, and creative practice and productions.

> **SOME EXAMPLES OF SKILLS PRACTICE**
>
> On a Nursing degree, students engage with simulated learning in a mock-ward and take blood pressure or give injections on a dummy.
>
> On a Music degree, students practise their violin for three hours per day to apply their learning from lessons and embed their skills.
>
> On a Sports Injury degree, students role-play to each other a case study to elicit where and when a patient hurts and if there are stimuli that cause the pain.
>
> On a Geography degree, students go to Iceland for a week to study geysers.
>
> On a Biomedicine degree, students spend time in the lab to undertake experiments to practice skills and understand consequences.
>
> On a Film Studies degree, students work together across six weeks to act, film, produce and edit a short video.

The common thread here is that students are asked to undertake a practical learning activity that involves their active participation to learn a skill.

Work-based learning: placements, volunteering hours and apprenticeship on-the-job learning

Professional and vocational courses often require students to undertake a practice placement or volunteering hours to enable their skill development and apply learning from in-university teaching. This can take many forms: some courses require a full year in practice whilst others have multiple short placements; some are pre-allocated by university whilst others are organised by students themselves; some are local whilst some are international.

In any work-based learning activity, it is important that the student *does*. This means that it is an active learning experience, which can be through actively observing a mentor or by actively undertaking the task with support and guidance. However, equally important is that the student critically thinks about what they can learn from the practical learning activity.

Critical thinking in assessed work

WHICH STUDENT IS CRITICALLY THINKING?

Basil and Clarissa are law students who have been asked to arrange volunteering hours in a legal setting across the first year of their course.

Basil engages with the advice and support of the module leader and identifies a role as a volunteer in a local legal advice centre.	Clarissa organises her volunteering hours late in the academic year and barely squeezes them in.
He very much enjoys the opportunity and is able to apply for a part-time job that he continues for the rest of the period of his course.	Her lack of enthusiasm is read by the organisation, and she is left to file documents most times that she attends.
He can see that the application of his legal knowledge to the role is beneficial to both his understanding of how it is applied and to the clients who gain his support.	She feels that the volunteering hours were not beneficial to her.

Basil was proactive as he made early efforts to find a volunteering opportunity which turned into a job, beneficial for both his development of skills and his financial stability. This shows how valuable a volunteering opportunity can be when engaged with robustly and enthusiastically. In comparison, Clarissa puts nothing in and gets nothing out, making this a lost learning opportunity. This is the first lesson about work-based learning: it is your learning opportunity, and you will need to engage with it robustly to ensure that it is beneficial to you.

Top tip 12.1

To maximise your learning within work-based learning, it is helpful to:

Engage with the specific requirements of your practice placement or volunteering experience to understand what is expected of you.

Know what you want to achieve within the experience.

Be enthusiastic and engaged.

In addition, there is a growing trend towards higher education (university-based) apprenticeships in the UK, where learning is divided into off-the-job training in university and on-the-job training in an employer-led work base. During the on-the-job hours, apprentices are required to apply their off-the-job learning to develop their knowledge, skills and behaviours (KSBs) requirements.

> **Top tip 12.2**
>
> It is important as an apprentice to really see and value the learning in both the off-the-job and the on-the-job periods of the apprenticeship.
>
> After each lecture or seminar, take time to critically think about how the learning from the session can be applied to your role, to enable you to make the links between theory and practice.

The commonality across all practical learning opportunities is that students are expected to develop knowledge and skills through experiential learning (Kolb, 1984) and critical thinking. Whilst it is important to recognise that work-based learning can be challenging where university expectations in relation to learning activities and learning outcomes are different than the host employer's priorities (Minton and Hadfield, 2021), critical thinking enables you to fit your university learning requirements to the agency's needs.

Experiential learning

In Chapters one and five we discussed Kolb's (1976) and Fleming's (1987) learning styles. Whilst they remain relevant, in practice learning activities students also learn in practice as an activist, reflector, theorist or pragmatist (Honey and Mumford, 1982).

Activists: learn through doing an activity and immerse themselves in day-to-day activities.

Reflectors: learn by critically thinking about how they would do an activity or did do the activity.

Theorists: learn by applying knowledge and understanding to the activity.

Pragmatists: learn by applying new ideas to activities and prefer variety of tasks.

It can be helpful to understand how you learn best, but it is important that you do not become so entrenched in one learning style that you forget to ensure rounded learning through application of all four strategies.

Experiential learning can be seen as critical thinking applied to practice learning opportunities and the four learning styles above link to each of the four stages below. Kolb (1984) suggested that learning is undertaken not just by doing an activity (concrete experience), but also by reflecting on the activity after it has been undertaken and considering what went well and identifying areas for development (reflective observation). This is supplemented by developing an understanding of why the activity had gone as it had, through the application of academic knowledge and practice wisdom to the activity (abstract conceptualisation) in order to plan how you would take a future similar activity and apply learning from the original activity (active experimentation).

It can be argued that the definition of insanity is doing the same thing in the same way and expecting a different outcome. In contrast, Kolb (1984) argues that it is only by doing the same thing and critically thinking about how you could do it differently that you can expect a different outcome.

Experiential learning in skills practice

In practice learning activities in university, students are expected to undertake an activity and afterwards reflect on how the learning activity went. To illustrate the experiential learning model a case study will be presented, using Case Study 12.1 of Jack who is a student on a Film Studies degree, and has just been set a group task across six weeks to act, film, direct, produce and edit a short video.

Using Kolb's experiential learning model, Jack is able to critically think about the first rehearsal and how he participated in the role of director:

Concrete experimentation: he acted as director for the rehearsal. Jack provides a brief description of what he did at each stage of the rehearsal.

Reflective observation: Jack reflects that his directing skills were unclear and that he would like to think about how he could develop this before the third session.

Abstract conceptualisation: He decides to watch directing videos and return to taught materials on directing. This includes reading Kelly (2023) who reflects on the importance of creative decisions in such an activity. Jack recognises from this the importance of both understanding what is expected of him as the director and each of the film-making stages.

Active experimentation: He plans how he will be more confident and assertive in the following week's rehearsal and attends having made creative decisions that he can implement.

Here experiential learning is taking place. The student critically thinks independently about his original performance as a director and is able to identify and address his areas for development to be a more informed and skilled director as a result.

Experiential learning in worked-based learning activities

In work-based learning, students are also expected to undertake an activity and afterwards reflect on how the learning activity went. To illustrate the experiential learning model a case study will be presented, using Case Study 12.2 of Kimaya who is a social work student on practice placement in a team that supports older adults, when she undertakes a home visit to Mr and Mrs Cook.

Using Kolb's experiential learning model, Kimaya is able to critically think about a home visit and identifies:

Concrete experimentation: she undertakes a home visit to Mr and Mrs Cook to discuss a referral by their daughter for residential care. The daughter feels that this is necessary as they are both at risk of a fall due to increasing infirmity.

Reflective observation: she felt she was able to engage with Mr and Mrs Cook well using her communication skills but found it difficult when they asked specific questions about the process of moving into residential care which made her feel that she had let them down.

Abstract conceptualisation: she spent time talking to experienced social workers in the team to gather knowledge about residential care, read procedures and read Lee and Oliver's (2023) chapter on working with older people.

Active experimentation: Kimaya felt prepared the next time she took a similar referral for the potential questions in the next home visit.

It can be argued that Kimaya applied her existing knowledge and skills when she undertook the home visit. However, an area that she had not anticipated or experienced previously was raised. She reflected on both her strengths and her areas for development and through critical thinking she was able to develop her knowledge which she would apply to future home visits.

> **Top Tip 11.3**
>
> It is worth noting that there are a significant number of reflective models that have developed from Kolb's (1984) model of experiential learning, as outlined in Chapter three. Identifying the one that engages you is time well spent. These include:
>
> Gibbs (1988) Reflective Cycle: Description, Feelings, Evaluation, Analysis, Conclusion, Action Plan
>
> Jasper (2013) ERA model: Experience, Reflection, Action
>
> Driscoll's (2007) What? Model: What? So What? Now What?
>
> Greenaway's (2014) 4Fs model: Facts, Feelings, Findings, Future
>
> Apply each of these reflective models to a practice learning activity that you have just undertaken by using the headings. Reflect on which one 'works' for you and apply it to enable your critical thinking when undertaking experiential learning in the future.

Irrespective of the style of practical learning activity, the expectation is that the practical element is not an isolated incident. Instead, the expectation is that you will take time to critically think about your practice using a reflective model to enhance your knowledge and skills, so that next time you practise you are able to 'fail better' (Beckett, 1983).

Collaborative experiential learning

The model of collaborative experiential learning (CEL) (Beesley, 2024) develops Kolb's (1984) experiential learning and layers in reflective discussion with peers or the mentor before and after the learning activity. Figure 12.1 shows it relating to a mentor, but peer discussion can be supplemented for mentor.

The CEL model enables students to enhance their critical thinking (experiential learning) by both thinking out loud and by bouncing ideas off a peer or a more experienced mentor.

Critical thinking in practice learning and practical assessment

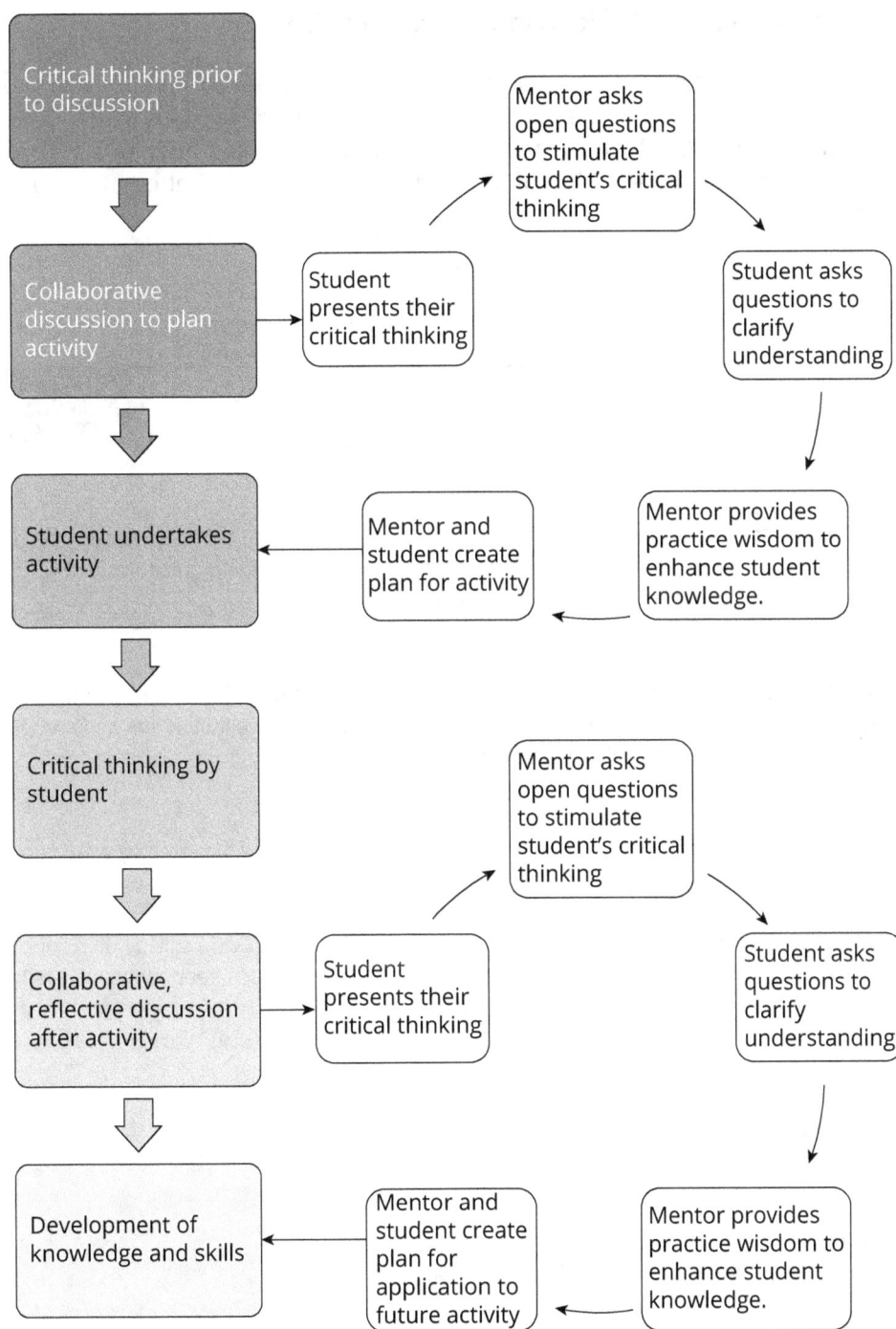

Figure 12.1 Critical thinking in collaborative experiential learning (CEL) (adapted from Beesley, 2024)

Collaborative experiential learning in skills practice

After practice learning activities in university, you may have formal or informal group debriefs and peer discussions that facilitate development of ideas, knowledge and skills. To illustrate the CEL model a case study will be presented, Using Case Study 12.1 of Jack who was introduced above to enable comparison of impact.

CASE STUDY 12.3

Critical thinking prior to discussion

Before the first session begins, Jack reflects on what he would like to achieve, focusing on his interest in film directing. He considers the activity instructions and learning outcomes and aligns them to his reading of Kelly (2023) and creative decision-making.

Collaborative discussion to plan activity

The students meet for the first session and Jack is able to contribute ideas articulately as he knows what he wants and what the brief is. Other students contribute their ideas and creative decisions are taken to develop the project plan.

Students undertake activity

The students meet for the second session, which is a first rehearsal of the clip they will video.

Critical thinking by student

Jack identifies that his directing skills were unclear and that he would like to critically think about how he could develop this before the third session. He chooses to use Greenaway's (2014) 4Fs model and uses the following questions.

Facts

- What was expected and what actually happened?
- Which factors influenced my involvement?

Feelings

- How did I feel when I was contributing well?
- How did I feel when I recognised that I was unclear?

Findings

- What would I like to have done differently?
- How did other people's involvement influence my feelings?

Findings

- Did my learning change what I will do in the next rehearsal?

Collaborative reflective discussion after activity

After each session, the group go for a coffee and talk about how it went, what they could differently and what they have learnt. They are able to both reflect on their own performance and provide constructive feedback on each others' involvement.

Jack apologises for a lack of clarity on his directing. Zoe acknowledges that it would be useful to be better, but also praises his organisational skills which she had valued. Zoe asks him questions as to why he had not been clear when he had been organised and Jack asks Zoe if there is anything that she would have valued him doing.

Jack begins to understand why he was unclear when directing because he is supported to develop his initial thoughts to think critically.

Development of knowledge and skills

Jack feels more confident because Zoe provided positive feedback, but also heard her questions and reflected further on why clarity is important and how he can be clearer whilst he watched videos on how to direct and accessed taught materials on directing. He feels more knowledgeable and confident for the next week's practice session.

Here experiential learning is taking place collaboratively. The students independently critically think about their own ideas and performance; however, this is enhanced by developing their ideas together as 'the goal is for each shoot to be more efficient and productive than the last one before' (Kelly, 2023, p. 215).

Collaborative experiential learning in work-based learning activities

In work-based learning you are likely to be allocated a practice educator, work-based teacher, supervisor, peer support, buddy or mentor. These have various names across different subjects and courses, but for the purpose of this chapter they will be referred to as mentor. A mentor is designed to offer you support and guidance in your learning opportunities, and some will also assess your development. It can be helpful to consider how a mentor can enhance your critical thinking in practice learning. In addition, Minton and Hadfield (2021) advocate that collaborative learning meets both the student's learning needs and supports the development of the agency and mentor as they develop too from the student's work.

To illustrate the CEL model a case study will be presented, using Case Study 12.2 of Kimaya who was introduced above to enable comparison of impact.

CASE STUDY 12.4

Critical thinking prior to discussion

Kimaya is planning to do a home visit to Mr and Mrs Cook following a referral by their daughter for residential care which stated that they were at risk of a fall due to increasing infirmity.

She reflects on previous home visits that she has observed and is confident in her communication skills. However, she is unsure about the procedure for admission to a residential home and requests a discussion with her mentor to support her preparation for the home visit.

Collaborative discussion to plan activity

Kimaya and her mentor have a reflective discussion. She is able to suggest what she might do in the home visit but also asks questions to clarify her thinking. The mentor is able to talk her through the procedure and how she does such a visit herself, but also asks Kimaya 'how might you respond if …' questions to prepare her for what might happen.

Kimaya takes notes and together they create a plan for the home visit, which she feels confident in.

Students undertake activity

Kimaya undertakes her home visit to Mr and Mrs Cook. She feels confident because she has a plan and she feels knowledgeable because she prepared collaboratively with her mentor. Her confidence enables her to undertake an effective visit.

Critical thinking by student

Kimaya chooses to use Driscoll's (2007) What? Model to critically think about the home visit.

> What? Kimaya describes the home visit concisely.
>
> So What? Kimaya reflects that she felt she was able to engage Mr and Mrs Cook well using her communication skills and that when they asked specific questions about the process of moving into residential care she felt anxious but able to answer their questions. She reflects that she wants to continue to build her confidence in undertaking home visits, and that this can be done by developing her knowledge further.
>
> Now What? Kimaya wants to talk this through with her mentor to see if she can offer any further advice. In preparation for the discussion, she reads Lee and Oliver's (2023) chapter on working with older people.

Collaborative reflective discussion after activity

Kimaya meets with the mentor to reflectively discuss the visit to Mr and Mrs Cook. Kimaya describes the visit and is able to explain to the mentor how she is feeling, but also discusses the ideas she has had to improve her practice and confidence after reflecting and reading.

The mentor is happy that Kimaya has been proactive in her critical thinking and asks her open questions to develop this further. The mentor is able to make further suggestions to develop Kimaya's ideas.

Together they create a plan as to how she will approach future visits confidently using Kimaya's initial ideas from her independent critical thinking and enhanced by collaborative discussion that developed these ideas further.

Development of knowledge and skills

Kimaya has developed her knowledge and skills to a greater degree than the first Case Study 12.2 example above, but has also developed her confidence which will assist her in future visits.

The principle of the collaborative experiential learning model (Beesley, 2024) is that 'two heads are better than one'. Where both participants approach the practical learning activity open to reflective critical thinking and hearing each others' perspectives to develop their own, then learning is enhanced.

Practical learning assessments

Often the practical learning activities are development towards a practical learning assessment. This is the opportunity for the lecturer to test what you have learnt from the teaching and practical learning activities and assess your knowledge and skills.

Practical skills-based assessments in university

Practical learning assessments in university are often designed to assess your knowledge *and* skills development. This means that you will be assessed on your skill base from a practical perspective as well as your understanding of the knowledge that underpins your actions.

As such, first there will be a practical element which will often reflect real world examples of practice related to your degree subject. This can take many forms:

Case study: this is designed to assess what you *would* do in a given situation.

Completion of a task: for example, software development tasks can demonstrate and enable assessment of programming skills.

Delivery of a performance: this can be a set or created piece, and is intended to assess your creative skills.

Direct observation of practice: here students are observed undertaking a set task with a clear assessment criterion.

Experiment: where you are asked to set a hypothesis, test it and evaluate your results, often undertaken in a lab.

Group work: it can be problem-solving in a group to identify a solution, where assessment may be on the task outcome or on group-work skills.

Objective structured clinical examination (OSCE): this is a simulation situation where actors, people with lived experience, teaching staff or even fellow students play a role for you to respond to and be assessed in your actions.

Oral language exam: this can be a conversation or the ability to answer questions in a different language to assess development of language skills.

Peer assessment: where an activity is set and all members of the activity rate each other, much like may be seen in competitive TV reality programmes.

Presentation: as outlined in Chapter nine, a group or individual presentation can be assessed.

Production of a product: here you are set a product to design and deliver.

The practical assessment will link to your practical learning, which should have been scaffolded to enable you to develop the skills that are required in the assessment. As with exams, discussed in Chapter eleven, it is important that you understand what is expected of you, practise to develop confidence, knowledge and skills, and critically think within the practical assessment to maximise your effectiveness.

The benefit of developing your critical thinking in practical learning activities is that you will be able to apply your enhanced critical thinking skills in a practical assessment activity. By critical thinking throughout your practical learning tasks, students develop deeper understanding of the topic and transfer knowledge and skills to a new situation, as illustrated in Case Study 12.3.

CASE STUDY 12.5

On a Biomedicine degree, students spend time in the lab to undertake a range of experiments to practice skills and understand consequences. The assessment for the module is to undertake an experiment presented to them on the day.

Their critical thinking across the semester has supported their ability to cope in an assessed experiment as they have greater knowledge and skills to enable them to undertake the experiment confidently in reacting to unexpected results. This enables them to manage the assessment challenges capably.

In order to assess your knowledge, the practical element of the assessment may be supplemented by an academic reflective task, which is illustrated using Case Study 12.6

CASE STUDY 12.6

On a Film Studies degree, students work together across six weeks to act, film, direct, produce and edit a short video.

The eventual short film is taken as the first element of the assessment.

This is a better finished product as collaborative experiential learning took place that developed ideas and skills. All students in the group benefit from the higher grade as a result.

A reflective assignment is the second element of the assessment.

Students have critically thought both independently and with their peers as the weeks have progressed. They therefore feel more confident in expressing their reflections on their knowledge and skill development as they have been tested against peers and enhanced by collaborative discussion.

This is the second benefit of practising critical thinking in practical learning activities that are assessed. The assessment will be easier for you, and you are likely to get a better grade. Whilst learning should not be so strategically considered, the reality is that teaching is structured to develop your knowledge and skills that will be assessed at the end of a module. Practical learning activities are structured to enable you to actively participate in a task, which teaches you skills. However, this must then be developed further by critical thinking to develop your knowledge around the task. Both knowledge and skills are developed, and this means that your practical learning assessment is more accessible for you as you have engaged with the learning through critical thinking.

Whilst we still see the benefit of increased performance and grade that has come from experiential learning (Kolb, 1984), here we also see that because students have undertaken critical thinking in the practice learning to develop their knowledge and skills, so too has their ability to critically think *within* the assessment. Schon (1983) argued that experiential learning is 'reflection on action' and is undertaken after a practice learning activity. In Case Study 12.3 we see the need for swift critical thinking to interpret the assessment dilemma and consider solutions for immediate application, which Schon (1983) labelled as 'reflection in action'.

Reflection in action is the use of the student's existing knowledge and skills applied in the moment to the practice assessment activity and is based upon learning from previous experiences, as discussed in Chapter three. In this case critically thinking about each previous experiment has provided a strong foundation of appropriate knowledge and skills to draw on in different situations with enhanced problem-solving skills. It is this transferability of knowledge and skills that is important here; it is not about responding to an exact replication of a practice learning activity but knowing how to draw upon the learnt knowledge and skills and apply them to a new, but similar, situation.

Like any skill, critical thinking comes with practice. It can be argued that it is the practice of critical thinking across the semester that enables critical thinking in reflection in action to be undertaken in the assessment of the biomedicine experiment.

Work-based assessment

In contrast, work-based assessment of knowledge and skill development may be carried out by the mentor over a longer period. As such assessment may be considered the 'sum of the parts' rather than the result of a final practical assessment task. This is important to be aware of as it means that you cannot just turn up at the end and pass a placement. Instead, you will need to be engaging with the learning opportunities throughout the work-based learning opportunity.

CASE STUDY 12.7

On a Social Work degree, students undertake two practice placements that they need to successfully complete to become a qualified social worker.

Across the length of a placement, they need to demonstrate development of a range of set knowledge and skills, which has defined nationally agreed minimum criteria.

Development to each of the knowledge and skills is monitored throughout the placement, with an interim assessment made to support students' understanding of progress towards final assessment.

Critical thinking here is vital as students need to engage with collaborative experiential learning and self-reflection on knowledge and skill development to identify and address areas for development. Furthermore, critical thinking demonstrates engagement and accountability by a student, often skills that work-based assessment considers. This includes how do you plan for work you will undertake (reflection for action), how do you respond to problems and analyse situations (reflection in action), how do you respond after positive events or difficult situations (reflection on action) (Schon, 1983, 1991) which can be evidenced using the CEL model (Beesley, 2024).

Individual learning needs

Students with a reasonable adjustment often look forward to practical learning elements on their course, as it can reduce the anxiety and pressures of written academic work. Nevertheless, it often comes with other challenges, which include the following complex verbal instructions or physical demands on students. It is important here to be aware of your learning needs, have strong coping strategies and be confident to express them constructively, but be aware that this can be challenging to do and that it is dependent on others to hear and respond to your needs (Beesley and Walkden, 2024).

For ethnically diverse students, practical learning can create further division where they may be expected to conform to Eurocentric norms whilst feeling isolated as a learner. In social work, for example, Tedam and Finch (2024) found that Black African students were more likely to fail practice placement than white British students, attributing this to (prejudiced) perceptions about cultural differences and expectations of failure. If less is expected of a student, they are less likely to be encouraged to participate in collaborative experiential learning and critical thinking skills are less likely to be developed. As such, the importance of preparation and critical thinking before collaborative discussion is emphasised here, so that you are able to prove these expectations wrong whilst absolutely acknowledging the self-awareness and criticality required by mentors.

More than anything, in practical learning you will need to be confident and value your knowledge, skills and contributions where you have individual learning needs.

Critical thinking action plan

Please reflect on your critical thinking skills in relation to practise learning opportunities and where you need to develop a skill develop your critical thinking action plan.

Worksheet 12.1 Critical thinking action plan

Critical thinking skill	Action to be taken	Review after six weeks
Ability to critically think independently before and after a practical learning activity		
Ability to be open and honest about your critical thinking with other people		
Ability to be open to hearing other people's ideas and queries		

Conclusion

Where you have a practical learning experience, learning is more than just *doing* the activity. It is important that you critically think about the learning from the experience to ensure that you learn the skill and underpin it with the knowledge to understand the skill. Experiential learning (Kolb, 1984) is premised on learning from your mistakes (and successes) so that you undertake an activity, reflect on how it went, understand why it went the way it went and make a plan to do it better next time.

However, where you have a peer or mentor available to talk through your practice learning activity, it is enhanced by collaborative experiential learning (Beesley, 2024). Here your initial thoughts are developed by another person asking you to think further and enhancing your ideas, so that you are supported to develop your knowledge and skills through stimulated critical thinking.

Finally, critical thinking can be seen to enhance practical assessment outcomes as it helps you to engage with the assessment task from an enhanced problem-solving perspective if you have developed the skill of approaching all practice learning opportunities from a critical thinking perspective.

Further reading

Beesley, P. (2020) *Making the Most of Your Social Work Placement*. London: Sage. Whilst this is directed at social work placement, the principles of engaging with your placement proactively are applicable to any placement setting. In particular, Chapter one on getting to know your self as a learner and Chapter six on enhancing your ability to critically reflect.

Helyer, R., Wall, T., Minton, A. and Lund, A. (eds) (2021) *The Work-Based Learning Student Handbook*. London: Bloomsbury. This book is an excellent guide for students who are undertaking work-based learning.

Kelly, R. (2023) *Prepping and Shooting Your Student Short Film: A brief guide to film production*. Abingdon: Routledge. This book provides a great overview on directing films. In particular, Chapter ten on collaboration and communication is helpful.

Reed, R., Holmes, D., Weyers, J. and Jones, A. (2022) *Practical Skills in Biomolecular Science*. Harlow: Pearson Education. This book is directed at any students studying biochemistry, biomedical sciences, biotechnology, genetics, microbiology and molecular biology, and offers clear support on how to maximise your learning in the lab and experiments. Similar books are available in other science fields.

13

Critical thinking and responding to feedback

CHAPTER OBJECTIVES

- Understand feedback and its purpose
- Develop critical thinking skills when accessing feedback, hearing feedback and implementing feedback

Introduction

This chapter considers where different feedback comes from: assignments, tutors, practice mentors and peers. It will support you in developing your approach as a critical learner accessing and hearing feedback, enabling you to critically reflect upon your strengths as well as areas for development, in order for you to respond to feedback. It will outline strategies to support you in hearing the feedback and using it to implement change within your educational journey to enhance your learning and develop your academic skills.

Feedback

Feedback tops the list of factors leading to good learning (Biggs and Tang, 2007), it is that important to engage with. However, learners often see written feedback on assessed work as the only feedback available (Naylor et al., 2014). It is important to recognise the breadth of feedback that is available to students.

> **WHICH STUDENT IS CRITICALLY THINKING?**

Fred and Lily are public health students eagerly waiting for the mark from their first essay on the course.

Fred is disappointed to see that whilst his work has achieved a pass grade, the mark is not as high as he hoped for. Fred quickly glances over the general comments that have been given, and then feels deflated.

He then emails his tutor asking for quality feedback to be provided. His tutor replies, requesting that he read what has been written, list any questions that he has and then book a time for a tutorial discussion.

Fred does not look at the feedback again, and does not arrange the suggested tutorial, instead he decides to concentrate on his next assessment task.

Lily passed and achieved an average mark. She reads the overall comments that have been provided and pays attention to the feedback comments including suggested areas for improvement.

One area identified as needing work is Lily's referencing. Her tutor has provided her with a link to guidelines for referencing, so she accesses that information and then books onto a library tutorial called Harvard referencing.

After attending she is confident that she understands her tutor's comments and that she can reference correctly in her next submission.

In its simplest form feedback can be considered to be the explanation provided to students on why the grade has been given or decision has been made, similar to the *show your working* that maths GCSE requires. It enables students to understand why the tutor came to the decision that they came to. However, we know that feedback is far more useful than that! Lily demonstrates that she applies a critically thoughtful approach to her feedback and applies it to understand the areas she needs to develop and, having addressed them, is able to implement her new academic skills and enhance her future grades, whilst Fred does not value and dismisses the feedback. It is likely he will make the same academic errors again in his next assessment submission.

Sadler et al. (2022) state that there is a difference between seeing feedback as a product (e.g. comments on your work) or as a process (e.g. where you look at how you can improve based on your tutor's guidance). Naylor et al. (2014: 3) state: 'In the university context, feedback assists students in developing mastery of their disciplines and more general graduate attributes. It helps them understand what is expected of them and how to reach that standard.'

Educational feedback is intended to support you as a learner to both develop and improve (Panadero and Lipnevich, 2022), therefore it is more than just information transition, but is student-centred in its intention to improve performance (Boud and Malloy, 2013). It is useful for you to know that any feedback provided to you as a learner is based upon a set of supportive principles:

Principles of Feedback

Feedback helps you to understand what good performance is.

Feedback helps you to develop your own self-assessment skills.

Feedback provides you with high-quality information about your performance.

Feedback should encourage discussion between tutors and you as a learner.

Feedback should motivate learners and develop their self-esteem.

Feedback should help to improve performance.

Feedback is also a useful tool for tutors.

(Adapted from Nicol and Macfarlane-Dick, 2006)

Top tip 13.1

As a new learner at university, do you feel that you understand the principles and processes of feedback? Use the principles above to reflect on your understanding.

It can be tempting to view feedback in very narrow terms; for example, seeing written feedback provided at the end of an assessment and the accompanying grades as the only source available to you. Learners therefore often request more feedback (Boud and Dawson, 2023), whilst dreading receiving it, and not being aware of all that is available. However, several types of feedback are provided to you as a student in university. To be able to use feedback you first need to understand and access all your feedback opportunities, so audit your own channels of feedback as a starting point (Race, 2007).

Examples of feedback channels

- A tutor provides model answers, or exemplars of work with accompanying feedback, which enables grading criteria exploration through discussion. The tutor also identifies common difficulties with these assessments.
- A tutor involves you in assessment practices. For example, you practise marking other students work as a seminar task.
- Tutors provide written comments on essays, reports and assignments. These will be both formative and summative, but all will identify areas in which you need to

take action. These sometimes include the application of marking criteria and rubrics, illustrating the areas in which you perform better against the module learning outcomes.
- Discussion of feedback can be held between peers, where students work together to identify areas for action.
- Summary reports issued by lecturers on the work of the whole group. These may include overall comments about common mistakes, and generic suggestions for where improvements should be made. They can be provided verbally in class, or electronically via email and virtual learning environments.
- Email comments sent directly to you from your tutor are another form of feedback. If you ask a question about an assignment task, the module content, relevant literature or referencing, you will be provided with a feedback response.
- Frequently asked questions. Some tutors may provide you with generic guidance in advance of assessment in the form of frequently asked questions about the task.
- Tutors may also provide classroom space and time to discuss assignments so verbal feedback and associated conversation about assessments will be provided within these sessions. A tutor may also discuss and explain what assessment criteria means and how it will be used.

(Adapted from Race, 2007 and Nicol and Macfarlane-Dick, 2006)

In considering these examples, reflect on some of the feedback channels you are already seeing on your course. As you begin to recognise the breadth of what is available to you, you can then consider how to best use this information.

Feedback is undeniably where tutors do most of the work; for example, they provide you with written comments on your draft work (formative feedback) as well as notes about why you have been awarded a specific mark (summative feedback). It is important here to note that despite the separation of feedback into these two categories, there is often overlap between them in reality. For example, the written comments provided with summative marks are often still intended to help you to improve in later assessments and so they have a formative element, as they may suggest areas in which you can develop your own skills and improve the standard of your work (Naylor et al., 2014).

Feedforwards

Feedback that is designed to help the development of future knowledge and skills is sometimes called *feedforward*, which involves you as a critical thinker, using feedback to develop your skills, knowledge and future practice to support improvements (Sadler, 2010). For example, comments on draft work, discussion of assignment criteria, critical questions about practice learning and suggestions for where you can improve are all feedforward strategies. Ideally you should engage with and reflect on feedforward comments and then develop action points going forwards (Beaumont, O'Doherty and Shannon, 2011). Feeding forward is therefore a strategy often utilised by tutors to ensure that you have clear guidance about the next steps that are required for you to work with in future tasks (Hine and Northeast, 2016). Indeed, we learn from our experiences, as

> learning is all around us, it shapes and helps create our lives – who we are, what we do ... it requires personal commitment. It utilizes interaction with others, it engages our emotions and feelings, all of which are inseparable from the influence of context and culture. (Boud et al., 1993: 1)

Similarly, Carless (2015) discusses how feedback needs to be seen as an ongoing process in which all parties have a role to play. In thinking about your own learning, you cannot bypass any of your previous experience, as you will bring these with you to education, and then form more learning through your course experiences.

Top tips 13.2

> Think about your past learning experiences, and how these are shaping your current course expectations.
>
> What are you bringing to your learning?
>
> What strengths has previous feedback identified?
>
> What areas for development has previous feedback identified?
>
> What might you need to reconsider based upon your course experiences so far?

Critical thinking and reflection can be used to enhance learning through experience, and Kolb's (1984) experiential learning cycle is important here in understanding that as a learner you need to take action to improve. The *concrete experience* can be varied including participation in lectures and seminars, formative academic work, assessments, practical learning activities and presentations, whilst feedback can provide stimulation for the *reflective observation* of your practice. As such feedback can enhance your critical thinking as it provides areas for improvement that you may not yet have thought about and reinforces the importance of critical thinking about those that you have already identified.

Accessing feedback

It is important to access all feedback, and to critically think about it as a learning opportunity. Indeed, for you to work with feedback in an optimal way you need to value it, discuss it if possible and learn to judge your own work (Boud, 2015).

Top tip 13.3

> Pay attention to all feedback opportunities and channels available to you and be open to listening to these.
>
> To be able to hear and action feedback and use it as part of your collaborative experiential learning you should focus on developing your own process of working with feedback.

Earlier chapters have discussed how you can be an active participant in your own learning, with engagement in feedback being part of such an approach (Boud and Molloy, 2013).

Race (2014) helpfully suggests a number of ways in which you as a learner can engage with feedback:

- Request feedback rather than waiting for it. For example, you can ask tutors questions, such as 'What do you think was the best thing I did?' and 'What would have been the most useful change I should make next time?'
- Before you submit your next assignment, look back at the feedback that you have already been given. Have you addressed all of the things that caused you to lose marks previously?
- Reflect on your grades and feedback irrespective of what you achieved. So, if your grade was low, why was this and what do you need to address? If your grade was high, do not be complacent, take some time to consider why you did well, to replicate this. Analyse your grade against the marking scheme to develop a focus on next steps for example, did you score lower in one particular area? Do you have enough knowledge about the standards that you are required to meet (Boud, 2015)?
- Seek clarification if you need it – you can contact your tutor with questions about any comments and grades. Send a polite request via email and make an appointment for further discussion.
- Develop your own action plan for next steps. Draw upon the experience of completing the work, as well as your feedback to note what you need to repeat (what you did well), and what you need to improve on. Reflect on your main priority as a starting point.

It is important to develop your own confidence because believing in our ability to act and so improve our learning is essential, otherwise as learners we will remain passive participants (Boud et al., 1993).

Hearing feedback

In the examples provided above, detailing different student responses to feedback, emotions are evident in Fred's response to his feedback. Emotions and feelings are important facilitators and barriers to our learning (Boud, 1995), and so need to be critically thought about by you as a learner.

Race (2007) suggests that you pay attention to the ways in which you react to feedback, including positive praise. In considering how you react, for example if you dismiss nice comments, then this is ignoring feedback and not hearing it. Research identifies that despite providing students with lots of comments and feedback in various forms, tutors have noticed that these are not always viewed, used or implemented by students (Boud and Molloy, 2013). It is important that you *hear* your feedback.

As an adult learner in a university setting, tutors expect you to orientate to your own learning (Knowles, 1973; Knowles et al., 2020) and to use feedback to facilitate this. Boud (1995) notes that when we learn, we question ourselves and in doing this we are judging our own learning so far, as well as thinking about how we can best learn in the future. Reflection on how you are doing, and how you can try to do better are important self-assessment strategies that support experiential learning.

Top tip 13.4

> To maximise your learning, you need to read any comments that are provided with your grades.
>
> If you feel emotional about your grade or any feedback comments about your work, take a break from thinking about them.
>
> Come back to the comments later, and think about it from the tutor's perspective – are you now more able to understand what they are saying to you? Can you emotionally 'park' your first and immediate reaction to be able to carefully look at the suggestions for how you can do better next time? It can be helpful to practise different strategies to help you to cope with your initial emotional response. Remember that feedback is intended to help you.

However, there are some barriers to hearing feedback, and as learners we all react differently to the feedback that we are provided with. Emotionally intelligent learners are better positioned to react to feedback and more able to use it effectively. As learners if we overrate our own abilities and performance, then we are less able to hear feedback messages and work with them (Sheldon et al., 2014). So, it is also important to work on developing your emotional intelligence, so that you do not feel defensive about any feedback that you receive and are able to remain open to constructively engaging with it (Carless and Boud, 2018).

It is important to hear feedback, by which we mean that you need to be able to understand what your tutors mean. You can develop your own understanding in this area by improving your own *feedback literacy*. Consider the examples provided in Table 13.1, which show you some common tutor comments, as well as offering you suggestions about what these mean (adapted from Cooke et al., 2014).

Table 13.1 Interpreting feedback comments

Feedback comment	This means ...
Evidence? Reference? Says who?	These comments are telling you to pay attention to academic integrity and be careful not to plagiarise in future assessment tasks.
Your own opinion? Conjecture? Quote?	In future work be sure to avoid unsupported statements. Do this by providing citations from the literature to back up what you say. Ensure that you know and adhere to the university required reference strategy.
Emotive language Style? Colloquialism Slang!	These types of comments are feeding back about your writing style, telling you to be more formal, and to write in a more academic manner – similar to the work that you are reading in your subject area.
Academic language? Avoid cliches Terminology	In future work, do not write in text speak or as if you were speaking. Use appropriate technical or subject specialist terms.
Insufficient critical evaluation Insufficient analysis	These comments indicate that you are describing more than analysing and evaluating. In future work, reflect on the complexity of your subject and evaluate the strength/weight/validity of data and arguments (your own as well as those from other people).

A number of strategies can help you with developing feedback literacy such as self-assessment, reflective practice in relation to feedback and discussion about the feedback received (Little et al., 2023), as outlined in the case study below.

CASE STUDY 13.1

First-year students on a BSc Public Health degree joined together in small groups at the suggestion of their tutor following on from their first assignment submission (a written essay).

They meet to discuss the comments that they had received to identify key themes and discuss how they feel, what they have learnt from the feedback, and hear and learn from other students' feedback.

Nijella is able to express her disappoint in the feedback, which she needed to do to move past it, but is also able to hear other students' perspectives on why enhancing her writing style is so important and starts to engage with the feedback now she has normalised it.

Floella is quiet within the peer discussion as she prefers a one-to-one discussion, but she listens to the ideas discussed. She contacts the tutor who provided the feedback and meets with him to hear the feedback and talk through her individual needs and ideas from the peer discussion. This suits her well as she is able to engage with the tutor and feedback positively. She leaves the tutorial with a clear plan of what she will do next.

Tino does not attend the peer discussion. However, she reads the feedback and reflects on it. She is able to critically think about her areas for development and develop a plan on what to do next to enhance her referencing skills.

The case study demonstrates that there are a variety of ways to engage with feedback from an assignment, and whilst no one way will be right for all students, the common theme here is to ensure active critical thinking in response to the feedback.

Finally, it is important in hearing feedback to develop your understanding about:

1. what good performance looks like in your own subject area in relation to the assessment tasks that you are expected to undertake;
2. what tutor comments mean; academic language will be new to you, so familiarise yourself with it, and seek clarification if you need it;
3. identifying feedback priorities that are personal to you to ensure that you focus your efforts on implementing feedback to improve your own educational journey.

Implementing feedback

Thinking about feedback as part of a learning cycle (Kolb, 1984) is important in feeding forwards. As a learner it is important to interact with feedback, and to make effective use of it. Implementing feedback means that you are responding to it by using it to take action, to work towards future improvements. Implementing feedback is about developing strategies in response to it. A feedback loop should be created in which you use the information provided by your tutors to facilitate reflection (Murtagh and Baker, 2009), to develop changes in your own strategy (Boud, 2015). Carless and Boud (2018) suggest that you need to:

1. *Appreciate the feedback process* – to see it as more than just telling and to avoid being passive in response to it. So as a learner you need to develop feedback literacy so that you are better able to understand and interpret feedback.
2. *Make judgements* – to be able to work with feedback as a learner you need to develop your own evaluative capabilities, working with peers, and using assessment criteria to work towards improved performance.
3. *Manage affect* – as mentioned earlier, emotional responses to feedback need to be managed, to enable learners to respond to the challenges outlined to them.
4. *Take action* – this is where implementation occurs, as learners we need to take action in response to feedback provided to us, using comments to inform future work.

Hattie and Timperley (2007) provide a model of feedback identifying four levels of feedback for learners to pay attention to:

1. Tasks – how well do we perform tasks?
2. Process – the main process needed to understand and complete tasks.
3. Self-regulation – monitoring ourselves, and regulating our actions.
4. Self-level – personal evaluations and positive emotions.

Hattie and Timperley (2007) argue that students who implement feedback well to improve their performance don't simply do more, but rather respond to and engage with more challenging tasks, improve their error detection skills and own self-feedback to strategize in response to assessments. They suggest that as a learner you should consider the question: 'Where to go next in terms of the types of activities that you need to undertake to make better progress?'

The development of a critical thinking action plan to support you in targeting your approach for implementing feedback is a useful starting point (Duncan, 2007). Your plan can be developed with support from your course team, or it can be entirely created by you as a learner.

CASE STUDY 13.2

Marlo is on a BSc Public Health degree and after he has engaged in peer discussion about feedback on the first submitted assignment on the course and undertaken some individual reflection on the feedback, he is ready to implement the feedback.

First, he creates an action plan to implement the feedback:

1. Book onto the university library workshop session on referencing, to support me to develop my understanding of how to reference correctly.
2. Access study skills books.
3. Engage with university specific guidance on required referencing style.
4. Practise by going through an assessed assignment and correcting all referencing and citations.
5. Apply referencing skills to my next academic submission.

When he receives his next feedback, he can see clear enhancement on his referencing skills. Nevertheless, he accesses, hears and implements the feedback from this latest assignment to develop new academic skills.

Individual learning needs

Here, it is useful to think about cultural similarities and differences in both past and present learning experiences; home-based students may see learning differently compared to international learners. Try to critically analyse how previous experiences and personal characteristics (such as gender and ethnicity) are influencing you, especially in relation to your views about feedback, and your ability to understand it.

Many institutions are now working to offer a more inclusive curriculum, considering equality and diversity within learning experiences. As an active learner and critical thinker, you can work with your course team to understand how to access, interpret and use feedback. If you have a reasonable adjustment plan, arrange to meet your tutors to ensure that you can access your feedback in a suitable form, for example, is audio feedback more suitable for you rather than written comments? If you are an international student, or a global majority student, consider the ways in which you can open up a learning dialogue with tutors to enable you to engage in feedback discourse (Burns and Foo, 2012) to increase your understanding.

Top tip 13.5

> Learners have diverse needs, which need to be considered in relation to the principles of feedback.
>
> Consider your own learning needs and learning style in relation to feedback and then think about how you can develop your own strategies to enable you to hear feedback.
>
> How can you review feedback and generate action points that will work for you?

Critical thinking action plan

Please reflect on your critical thinking in relation to how you will implement actions related to feedback.

Worksheet 13.1   Critical thinking action plan

Critical thinking skill	Action to be taken	Review after six weeks
Feedback: making sure that you are aware of all of the feedback opportunities available		
Accessing feedback: ensuring that you are accessing all of the feedback that is provided		
Hearing feedback: developing your own understanding about what the feedback is telling you and undertaking self-reflection		
Implementing feedback: identifying areas where you can maintain good performance. Developing yourself in areas that have been identified as needing more work and creating a feedback loop		

Conclusion

This chapter has considered how you can access feedback, hear it and implement it to develop your approach as a critical learner. The chapter also considers where different feedback comes from, for example assignments, tutors and peers, and illustrates a range of feedback channels for you to consider. The chapter also offers suggestions and strategies to support you in implementing changes related to feedback as part of your educational journey. Finally, it is good to remember that feedback is not linear (Murtagh and Baker, 2009).

Race (2007) argues that feedback can tell you about what is going well and support you to build on those areas. More importantly, feedback is also a useful tool, if heard, to signpost you to the issues that will prevent you from doing as well as you might want to. Hence, working with feedback is an essential part of your educational journey enhancing your learning and develop your academic skills.

Further reading

- Higher Education Academy (2012) 10 feedback resources for your students. www.advance-he.ac.uk/knowledge-hub/feedback-toolkit-10-feedback-resources-your-students. This resource details links to a range of tools and advice to assist you with understanding and building on feedback that you receive from your tutor.
- Professor Phil Race has a website with tips and advice about both feedback and feedforward called Assessment, Learning and Teaching in Higher Education: https://phil-race.co.uk/2018/02/feedback-feedforward-just-tips-including-students/ – see the section tips for students.
- Stone, D. and Heen, S. (2015) *Thanks for the Feedback: The science and art of receiving feedback well*. Penguin. This book tells us how to accept and work with feedback in all areas of life, with key points being relevant to higher education contexts.

Conclusion

This book has focused on critical thinking in university. Part I introduced students to the concepts of critical thinking, critical thinking in university, models of critical thinking and consideration of individual learning needs in relation to critical thinking. Part II supported students through the experiential learning loop, which included critical thinking in preparation for, engagement within, and embedding learning after lectures and seminars. Part III addressed critical thinking in assessed work, which presented critical thinking in written assessed work, particularly academic essays, assignments, presentations and exams, before turning to critical thinking in practical learning opportunities and accessing, hearing and actioning feedback.

The book concludes with consideration of graduate attributes, the critical thinking skills that you will develop during your time at university to apply to post-education employment opportunities.

Graduate attributes

Graduate attributes are skills, strengths and characteristics that employers look for in graduate employees. Often, graduate attributes form part of the person specifications of the job description, and you will be asked to demonstrate them in job application form and interview. Indeed, a benefit of having developed critical thinking skills at university is that you will be able apply critical thinking to a job application process to enhance your answers and set yourself in a more competitive position to be successful in getting the dream job.

Wong et al. (2021) found that UK student graduate attributes generally included:

- self-awareness and lifelong learning;
- employability and professional development;
- global citizenship and engagement;
- and academic and research literacy.

It can be seen that each of these graduate attributes requires critical thinking. Firstly, self-awareness and emotional intelligence require critical thinking on self, strengths, areas for development and impact on others, key to being an effective graduate employee who interacts effectively with colleagues, management and, where appropriate, customers to maximise organisational efficiency and profitability. Similarly, professional development requires critical thinking to be able to able to hear, access and action feedback to be able to take action to address areas for development and enhance your productivity as an employee. Global citizenship and engagement comes from an awareness and interrogation of the world around you and how it presents so that you can advocate not only for the organisation you work within but also the needs of the wider community. Finally, academic and research literacy comes from critical thinking when reading materials so that you understand bias and perspective but also have the ability to make informed decisions in a graduate role.

Critical thinking is therefore not just for university but for life. Indeed, Indrašienė et al. (2023) found that both employers and employees saw critical thinking as an invaluable skill in employment that is associated with creative thinking, innovation and competitive organisations.

Finally

Develop your critical thinking skills as you would any other academic skill, with practice, reflection on strengths and areas for development, accessing support and asking for more when required, and more practice. We very much hope that critical thinking enhances your life as you see more and value that broader understanding of life – it's what university education and life beyond it is all about, so enjoy.

References

Alexander, R.J. (2001) *Culture and Pedagogy: International comparisons in primary education*. Oxford: Blackwell.

Álvarez-Huerta, P., Muela, A. and Larrea, I. (2022) Disposition toward critical thinking and creative confidence beliefs in higher education students: The mediating role of openness to diversity and challenge. *Thinking Skills and Creativity*, 43, 101003, pp.1–9

Anderson, L., Krathwohl, D. and Bloom, B. (2001) *A taxonomy for learning, teaching, and assessing: A revision of Bloom's taxonomy of educational objectives*. Harlow: Pearson.

Ashokka, B., Lee, T.L. and Verstegen, D.M. (2021) 'Exam preparedness': Exploring non-academic predictors of postgraduate exam success. *The Asia Pacific Scholar*, 6(4), pp. 80–91.

Bancroft, A. and Ferve, R. (2016) *Dead White Men and Other Important People: Sociology's big ideas*. London: Palgrave.

Baron, J. (2019) Actively open-minded thinking in politics. *Cognition*, 188, pp. 8–18.

Beaumont, C., O'Doherty, M. and Shannon, L. (2011) Reconceptualising assessment feedback: A key to improving student learning? *Studies in Higher Education*, 3, pp. 671–687.

Beck, S. (2022). Evaluating the use of reasonable adjustment plans for students with a specific learning difficulty. *British Journal of Special Education*, 49(3): pp. 399–419.

Beckett, S. (1983) *Worstward Ho*. London: Calder.

Beesley, P. (2024) Collaborative experiential learning in social work practice placements. *Social Work Education*, 43(8), pp. 2154–2169. DOI: 10.1080/02615479.2023.2245837

Beesley, P. and Walkden, A. (2024) Supporting a social work student with a complex reasonable adjustment plan. In R. Baikady (ed.) *Routledge International Handbook of Social Work Teaching* (pp. 548–555). Abingdon: Routledge.

Beesley, P., McGurn, G. and Walkden, A. (with journal) Ensuring effective transitions for social work students with a reasonable adjustment plan. *Journal for Disability Studies in Education*.

Belbin, R.M. (1981) *Management Teams*. London: Heinemann.

Bellaera, L., Weinstein-Jones, Y., Ilie, S. and Baker, S.T., (2021) Critical thinking in practice: The priorities and practices of instructors teaching in higher education. *Thinking Skills and Creativity*, 41, 100856, pp. 1–16.

Bennion, J., Cannon, B., Hill, B., Nelson, R. and Ricks, M. (2020) Asking the right questions: Using reflective essays for experiential assessment. *Journal of Experiential Education*, 43(1), pp. 37–54.

Biggs, J. & Tang, C. (2007) *Teaching for Quality Learning at University: What the student does* (3rd edn). Maidenhead: Open University Press.

Bloom, B. (ed.), Engelhart, M., Furst, E., Hill, W. and Krathwohl, D. (1956) *The Taxonomy of Educational Objectives*. New York: David McKay. Available at: https://eclass.uoa.gr/modules/document/file.php/PPP242/Benjamin%20S.%20Bloom%20-%20

Taxonomy%20of%20Educational%20Objectives%2C%20Handbook%201_%20Cognitive%20Domain-Addison%20Wesley%20Publishing%20Company%20%281956%29.pdf

Borton, T. (1970) *Reach, Touch and Teach*. London: Hutchinson.

Boud, D. (1995) *Enhancing Learning through Self-Assessment*. London: RoutledgeFalmer.

Boud, D. (2015) Feedback: Ensuring that it leads to enhanced learning. *The Clinical Teacher*, 12, pp. 3–7.

Boud, D., Cohen, R. and Sampson, J. (2001) *Peer Learning in Higher Education*. London: Kogan Page.

Boud, D. and Molloy, E. (2013) Rethinking models of feedback for learning: The challenge of design. *Assessment & Evaluation in Higher Education*, 38(6), pp. 698–712.

Boud, D., Cohen, R. and Walker, D. (1993) *Using Experience for Learning*. Buckingham: Open University Press.

Boud, D. and Dawson, P. (2023) What feedback literate teachers do: An empirically-derived competency framework Assessment and Evaluation. *Higher Education*, 48(2), pp. 158–171.

Britton, J., Walker, I., Waltmann, B. and Zhu, Y. (2022) *How Much Does It Pay to Get Good Grades at University? Research Report*. London: Department for Education and Institute for Fiscal Studies.

Bunce, L., King, N., Saran, S. and Talib, N. (2021) Experiences of black and minority ethnic (BME) students in higher education: Applying self-determination theory to understand the BME attainment gap. *Studies in Higher Education*, 46(3), pp. 534–547.

Burns, C. and Foo, M. (2012) Evaluating a formative feedback intervention for international students *Practitioner Research in Higher Education*, 5(1), pp. 40–49.

Burns, T. and Sinfield, S. (2022) *Essential Study Skills: The complete guide to success at university*. Los Angeles: SAGE.

Carless, D. (2015) *Excellence in University Assessment: Learning from award winning practice*. London: Routledge.

Carless, D. and Boud, D. (2018) The development of student feedback literacy: Enabling uptake of feedback. *Assessment and Evaluation in Higher Education*, 43(8), pp. 1315–1325.

Chen, P.H. (2021) In-class and after-class lecture note-taking strategies. *Active Learning in Higher Education*, 22(3), pp. 245–260.

Cerbin, W. (2018) Improving student learning from lectures. *Scholarship of Teaching and Learning in Psychology*, 4(3), pp. 151–163.

Chatfield, T. (2022) *Critical Thinking: Your essential guide*. London: Sage.

Chivers, B. and Shoolbred, M. (2007) *A Student's Guide to Presentations*. London: Sage.

Cooke, B. with O'Donnell, T. and Jarrett, K. (2014) *Interpreting Feedback on Your Writing: Feedforward*. Leeds: Leeds Beckett University.

Cottrell, S. (2012) *The Exam Skills Handbook: Achieving Peak Performance*. Basingstoke: Palgrave Macmillan.

Cottrell, S. (2019) *The Study Skills Handbook*. London: Red Globe Press.

Cottrell, S. (2023) *Critical Thinking Skills*. London: Bloomsbury.

Craik, F. and Lockhart, R. (1972) Levels of processing: A framework for memory research. *Journal of Verbal Learning and Verbal Behavior*, 11, pp. 671–684.

Day, T. (2023) *Success in Academic Writing*. London: Bloomsbury Academic.

De Bono, E. (1985) *Six Thinking Hats*. Boston: Little, Brown and Company.

Dekker, T.J. (2020) Teaching critical thinking through engagement with multiplicity. *Thinking Skills and Creativity*, 37, 100701, pp. 1–9.

Driscoll, J. (ed.) (2007) *Practising Clinical Supervision: A reflective approach for healthcare professionals*. Edinburgh: Balliere Tindall

Duncan, N. (2007) 'Feed-forward': Improving students' use of tutors' comments. *Assessment and Evaluation in Higher Education*, 32, pp. 271–283.

Elhinnawy, H. (2022) Decolonising the curriculum: The students perspective in criminology. *Race Ethnicity and Education*, 26(5), pp. 663–679.

Ennis R.H. (1996) *Critical Thinking*. Upper Saddle River, NJ: Prentice Hall.

Fan, M., Tran, N., Nguyen, L. and Huang, C. (2024) Effects of outdoor education on elementary school students' perception of scientific literacy and learning motivation. *European Journal of Educational Research*, 13(3), pp. 1353–1363.

Feeley, A.M. and Biggerstaff, D.L. (2015) Exam success at undergraduate and graduate-entry medical schools: Is learning style or learning approach more important? A critical review exploring links between academic success, learning styles, and learning approaches among school-leaver entry ('traditional') and graduate-entry ('nontraditional') medical students. *Teaching and Learning in Medicine*, 27(3), pp. 237–244.

Fiennes, C., Oliver, E., Dickson, K., Escobar, D., Romans, A. and Oliver, S. (2015) The Existing Evidence-base About the Effectiveness of Outdoor Learning. *UCL Institute of Education, Giving Evidence, Institute for Outdoor Learning and The Blagrave Trust*. Available at: www.blagravetrust.org/wp-content/uploads/2015/11/The-Existing-Evidence-base-about-the-Effectiveness-of-Outdoor-Learning-Executive-Summary-Nov-2015.pdf

Fink, L. (2013) *Creating Significant Learning Experiences: An integrated approach to designing college courses*. San Francisco, CA: Jossey-Bass.

Fleming, N. (1987) *VARK: A Guide to Learning Styles*. Available at: http://vark-learn.com

Franco-Tantuico, M.A. (2022) Active learning: A concept analysis with implications for nursing education. *Nursing Education Perspectives*, 43(4), pp. 233–237.

Gergen, K. (2023) *An Invitation to Social Construction: Co-creating the future*. London: Sage.

Gibbs, G. (1988) *Learning by Doing: A guide to teaching and learning methods*. Oxford: Further Education Unit, Oxford Polytechnic.

Godfrey, J. (2018) *How to Use Your Reading in Your Essays* (3rd edn). London: Palgrave.

Godfrey, J. (2023) *Reading and Making Notes*. London: Bloomsbury.

Godwin, J. (2012) *Studying with Dyslexia*. (Pocket Study Skills.) London: Bloomsbury.

Greenaway, R. (2014) Doing reviewing. Available at: www.academia.edu/27674568/Doing_Reviewing

Greetham, B. (2016) *Smart Thinking: How to think conceptually, design solutions and make decisions*. London: Palgrave.

Hattie, J. and Timperley, H. (2007) The power of feedback. *Review of Educational Research*, 77(1), pp. 81–112.

Hauck, A.A., Ward, C., Persutte-Manning, S.L. and Vaughan, A.L. (2020) Assessing first-year seminar performance with college engagement, academic self-efficacy, and student achievement. *Journal of Higher Education Theory and Practice*, 20(4), pp. 88–101.

Higher Education Statistics Agency (HESA) (2023) Table 15 – UK domiciled student enrolments by disability and sex 2014/15 to 2021/22. Available at: www.hesa.ac.uk/data-and-analysis/students/table-15

Hine, B. and Northeast, T. (2016) Using feed-forward strategies in higher education. *New Vistas*, 2(1), pp. 28–33.

Honey, P. and Mumford, A. (1982) *Manual of Learning Styles*. London: P. Honey.

Hopkins, D. and Reid, T. (2018) *The Academic Skills Handbook*. London: Sage.

Humphrey, L. (1970) Tearoom Trade. Impersonal Sex in Public Places USA: Aldine Transaction.

Indrašienė, V., Jegelevičienė, V., Merfeldaitė, O., Penkauskienė, D., Pivorienė, J., Railienė, A. and Sadauskas, J. (2023) Value of critical thinking in the labour market: Variations in employers' and employees' views. *Social Sciences*, 12(221), pp. 1–15.

Jasper, M. (2013) *Beginning Reflective Practice*. Cheltenham: Nelson Thornes.

Jensen, J.L., McDaniel, M.A., Woodard, S.M. and Kummer, T.A. (2014) Teaching to the test … or testing to teach: Exams requiring higher order thinking skills encourage greater conceptual understanding. *Educational Psychology Review*, 26, pp. 307–329.

Joseph Rowntree Trust (JRT) (2024) UK Poverty 2024. The essential guide to understanding poverty in the UK. Available at: www.jrf.org.uk/uk-poverty-2024-the-essential-guide-to-understanding-poverty-in-the-uk#:~:text=In%20October%202023%2C%20around%3A,having%20enough%20money%20for%20food.

Jung, C. (1921) *Psychological Types*.

Karpacheva, T. (2023) Critical Thinking Skills of Students of Diverse Backgrounds. *International Journal of Education and Social Science*, 11(1), pp. 2410–5171.

Kelly, R. (2023) *Prepping and Shooting Your Student Short Film: A Brief Guide to Film Production*. Abingdon: Routledge.

Kirton, B. (2012) *Brilliant Academic Writing*. Harlow: Pearson.

Klausner, E., Pitchford, K., Schmidhammer, J. and Phillips, B. (2021) Pharmacy, nursing, and physician assistant studies student self-report and perceptions regarding classroom etiquette. *Pharmacy Education*, 21, pp. 194–202.

Kneale, P. (2019) *Study Skills for Geography, Earth and Environmental Science Students*. Abingdon: Routledge.

Knowles, M. (1973) *The Adult Learner: A Neglected Species*. Houston, TX: Gulf Publishing.

Knowles, M., Holton, E., Swanson, R. and Robinson, P. (2020) *The Adult Learner: The definitive classic in adult education and human resource development*. Abingdon: Routledge.

Kolb, D. (1976). *The Learning Style Inventory: Technical Manual*. Boston, MA: McBer.

Kolb, D. (1984) *Experiential Learning*. Englewood Cliffs, NJ: Prentice Hall.

Leberman, S.I. and Martin, A.J. (2002) Does pushing comfort zones produce peak learning performance? *Journal of Outdoor and Environmental Education*. Vol 7, pp. 10–19.

Lee, S. and Oliver, L. (2023) *Social Work Practice with Adults: Learning from lived experience*. London: Learning Matters.

Lewin, K. (1936) *Principles of Topological Psychology*. London: McGraw-Hill.

Lim, H. (2022) Case study: Enhancing the learning experiences of BAME students at a university: The university role. *Social Policy and Society*, 21(1), pp. 134–141.

Little, T., Dawson, P., Boud, D. and Tai, J. (2023) Can students' feedback literacy be improved? A scoping review of interventions. *Assessment & Evaluation in Higher Education*, 49(1), pp. 39–52.

Mann, J., Gray, T., Truong, S., Brymer, E., Passy, R., Ho, S., Sahlberg, P., Ward, K., Bentsen, P., Curry, C. and Cowper, R. (2022) Getting Out of the Classroom and Into Nature: A Systematic Review of Nature-Specific Outdoor Learning on School Children's Learning and Development. Front Public Health. doi: 10.3389/fpubh.2022.877058.

Mason-Bish, M. (2019) The elite delusion: reflexivity, identity and positionality in qualitative research. *Qualitative Research*, 19(3), pp. 263–276.

May, C.A. and May, G.S. (2011) *Effective Writing: A handbook for accountants* (9th edn, International edn). Boston: Prentice Hall.

McIlroy, D. (2005) *Exam Success*. London: SAGE.

McMillan, K. (2021) *The Study Skills Book*. London: Pearson.

McNicholas, A.M. (2020) The Dyslexia, ADHD and DCD-friendly Study Skills Guide: Tips and strategies for exam success. London: Jessica Kingsley.

Meyer, J. and Land, R. (2003) *Threshold Concepts and Troublesome Knowledge: Linkages to ways of thinking and practising within the disciplines ETL project*. Occasional Report 4: Edinburgh: Teaching and Learning Research Project (TLRP).

Minton, A. and Hadfield, P. (2021) Making the most of your learning opportunities at work. In R. Helyer, T. Wall, A. Minton and A. Lund (eds) *The Work-Based Learning Student Handbook* (pp. 93–114). London: Bloosbury.

Modood, T. (2004) Capitals, ethnic identity and educational qualifications. *Cultural Trends*, 13(2), pp. 87–105.

Molyneux, T., Zeni, M. and Oberle, E. (2023) Choose Your Own Adventure: Promoting Social and Emotional Development Through Outdoor Learning. *Early Childhood Education Journal*, 51, pp. 1525–1539.

Moon, J. (2009) *Achieving Success through Academic Assertiveness*. London: Routledge.

Murtagh, L. and Baker, N. (2009) Feedback to feed forward: Student response to tutor's written comments on assignments. *Practitioner Research in Higher Education*, 3, pp. 20–28.

Nardi, P.M. (1995) 'The breastplate of righteousness': Twenty-five years after Laud Humphreys' tearoom trade: Impersonal sex in public places. *Journal of Homosexuality*, 30(2), pp. 1–10.

National Grid (2023) How does solar power work? Available at: www.nationalgrid.com/stories/energy-explained/how-does-solar-power-work

Naylor, R., Baik, C., Asmar, C. and Watty, K. (2014) *Good Feedback Practices: Prompts and guidelines for reviewing and enhancing feedback for students*. Centre for the Study of Higher Education, University of Melbourne.

Nicol, D. and Macfarlane-Dick, D. (2006) Formative assessment and self-regulated learning: A model and seven principles of good feedback practice. *Studies in Higher Education*, 31(2), pp. 199–218. https://doi.org/10.1080/03075070600572090.

Nosich, G. (2009) *Learning to Think Things Through: A guide to critical thinking across the curriculum*. Upper Saddle River, NJ: Pearson Prentice Hall.

O'Brien, S. (2009) Classes – preparation and participation. In M. Abbott (ed.), *History Skills: A student's handbook* (pp. 51–72). Abingdon: Routledge.

The Office for Students (OfS) (2024) The Office for Students annual review. Available at: https://officeforstudents.org.uk/publications/annual-review-2023/a-statistical-overview-of-higher-education-in-england

O'Hare, L. and McGuinness, C. (2015) The validity of critical thinking tests for predicting degree performance: A longitudinal study. *International Journal of Educational Research*, 72, pp. 162–172.

Oliver, M. (1983) *Social Work with Disabled People*. Basingstoke: Macmillan.

Osbourne, L., Barnett, J. and Blackwood, L. (2021) 'You never feel so Black as when you're contrasted against a White background': Black students' experiences at a predominantly White institution in the UK. *Journal of Community & Applied Social Psychology*, 31(4), pp. 383–395.

Panadero, E. and Lipnevich, A.A. (2022) A review of feedback models and typologies: Towards an integrative model of feedback elements. *Educational Research Review*, 35, 100416, pp. 1–22. https://doi.org/10.1016/j.edurev.2021.100416.

Pascarella, E. and Terenzini, P. (1991) *How College Affects Students: Findings and insights from twenty years of research*. CA: Jossey-Bass.

Patton, M. (2015) *Qualitative Research and Evaluation Methods*. London: Sage.

Pearson Education and Talentlens (2021) How to use the RED model to develop critical thinking skills. Available at: www.talentlens.com/Insights/blog/2021/09/the-red-model-for-developing-critical-thinking.html

Plummer, K. (2021) *Sociology: The basics*. Abingdon: Routledge.

Pollard, C. (2019) Explainer: The ideas of Foucault. *The Conversation*, 26 August. Available at: https://theconversation.com/explainer-the-ideas-of-foucault-99758

Price, B. (2024) *Critical Thinking and Writing in Nursing*. London: Sage.

Prince, H. and MacGregor, L. (2022) Outdoor learning. In H. Cooper and S. Elton-Chalcraft (eds) *Professional Studies in Primary Education* (pp. 348–368). London: Sage.

Quibell, T., Charlton, J. and Law, J. (2017) Wilderness Schooling: A controlled trial of the impact of an outdoor education programme on attainment outcomes in primary school pupils. *British Educational Research Journal*, 43(3), pp. 572–587.

Race, P. (2007) *How to Get a Good Degree*. Maidenhead: Open University Press.

Race, P. (2014) *Making Learning Happen: A guide for post-compulsory education*. London: Sage.

Race, P. and Pickford, R. (2007) *Making Teaching Work*. London: Sage.

Ramsden, P. (2003) *Learning to Teach in Higher Education*. London: RoutledgeFalmer.

Redman, P. and Maples, W. (2017) *Good Essay Writing*. London: Sage.

Roberts, J.Q. (2017) *Essentials of Essay Writing: What markers look for*. London: Palgrave.

Sadler, D. R. (2010) Beyond Feedback: Developing student capability in complex appraisal. *Assessment and Evaluation in Higher Education*, 35, pp. 535–550.

Sadler, I., Reimann, N. and Sambell, K. (2022) Feedforward practices: A systematic review of the literature. *Assessment & Evaluation in Higher Education*, 48(3), pp. 305–320.

Sareen, S. (2022) Legitimating power: Solar energy rollout, sustainability metrics and transition politics. *Environment and Planning E: Nature and Space*, 5(3), pp. 1014–1034. https://journals.sagepub.com/doi/full/10.1177/25148486211024903

Schon, D. (1983) *The Reflective Practitioner*. London: Maurice Temple Smith.

Schon, D. (1991) *The Reflective Practitioner*. London: Ashgate.

Seibert, S.A. (2023) Scaffolding questions to foster higher order thinking. *Teaching and Learning in Nursing*, 18, pp. 185–187.

Sennett, R. (2008) *The Craftsman*. London: Allen Lane, Penguin.

Sheldon, O.J., Dunning, D. and Ames, D.R. (2014) Emotionally unskilled, unaware, and uninterested in learning more: Reactions to feedback about deficits in emotional intelligence. *Journal of Applied Psychology*, 99(1), pp. 125–137.

Singer, P. (2018) *Marx: A very short introduction* (2nd edn). Oxford: Oxford Academic Press.

Sirazova, L. (2019) The perceived influence of self-efficacy concerning oral presentations. *Revista San Gregorio*, 36, pp. 81–84.

Smith, A. (2018) Cognitive fatigue and the wellbeing and academic attainment of university students. *Journal of Education, Society and Behavioural Science*, 24(2), pp. 1–12.

Snead, W.R., Joseph, M., Capriotiti, M., Saminatahn, S., Parewa, A., Thao, C. and Belogortsev, A. (2023) *The Effects of Pre-Reading Assignments on Academic Performance*. Available at: https://files.eric.ed.gov/fulltext/ED629606.pdf

Somerset Maugham. W. (1915) Of Human Bondage . New Hampshire: Heinemann.

Tedam, P. and Finch, J. (2024) 'I do not know if I will have the energy to come to placement tomorrow': Fast-tracking racially minoritised students to failure in social work education. *The British Journal of Social Work*, bcae138, https://doi.org/10.1093/bjsw/bcae138

Toulmin, S.E. (1958). *The Uses of Argument*. Cambridge: Cambridge University Press.

Thompson, S. and Thompson, N. (2008) *The Critically Reflective Practitioner*. London: Bloomsbury.

Tracy, E. (2006) *The Student's Guide to Exam Success*. Maidenhead: Open University Press.

Tripp, D. (1993) *Critical Incidents in Teaching: Developing professional judgement*. London: Routledge.

Umejima, K., Ibaraki, T., Yamazaki, T. and Sakai, K. (2021) Paper notebooks vs. mobile devices: Brain Activation differences during memory retrieval. *Frontiers in Behavioral Neuroscience*, 15, pp. 1–11.

University of Reading (2014) Studying with dyslexia and other specific learning difficulties. Available at: https://libguides.reading.ac.uk/dyslexia/lectures

University of Reading (2024) Study Advice, Available at: www.reading.ac.uk/library/study-advice

Vygotsky, L. (1978) *Mind and Society: The development of higher psychological processes*. Cambridge, MA: Harvard University Press.

Wallace, M. and Wray, A. (2021) *Critical Reading and Writing for Postgraduates*. London: Sage.

Williams, K. (2022) *Getting Critical*. Basingstoke: Red Globe Press.

Wingate, U. (2012) 'Argument!' Helping students understand what essay writing is about. *Journal of English for Academic Purposes*, 11(2), pp. 145–154.

Wong, B., Copsey-Blake, M. and ElMorally, R. (2022) Silent or Silenced? Minority ethnic students and the battle against racism. *Cambridge Journal of Education*, 52(5), pp. 651–666.

Wong, B., Chiu, Y.L.T., Copsey-Blake, M. and Nikolopoulou, M. (2021) A mapping of graduate attributes: What can we expect from UK university students? *Higher Education Research and Development*, 41(4), pp. 1340–1355.

Xuwei, L. and Feipeng, L. (2021) Corpus-based move analysis of TED Talks about education. *Creative Education*, 12(1), pp. 166–175.

Yorke, M. (2006) *Employability in Higher Education: What It Is – What Is It Not*. York: HEA.

Index

Note: Page numbers in *italic* type refer to figures and tables.

abstract conceptualisation, 36, 184, 185
academic assertiveness, 23, 92
academic integrity, 124
academic literacy, 212
academic voice, 24
acceptance, in CIA model, 101
'accommodating' learning style, 26
accuracy of sources, 62–3
active experimentation, 36, 184, 185
active listening, 77–9
active participation
  in lectures, 81–3
  in seminars, 86–91, 95
active preparation, 56–8
activist learners, 183
activities, 68, 82
  see also practical learning activities
adult learning principles, 24–5, 57
AI (artificial intelligence), 123–5
alternative perspectives, 12, 120
analysis, 27–8
analysis section of discussion, 141, 142
Anderson, L., 115
andrological principles, 24–5, 57
application, 27
apprenticeships, 183
artificial intelligence (AI), 123–5
assessment criteria, 29, 117–18, 150, 157–9
assessment instructions, 117–18
assessments
  core principles for writing, 119–20
  and individual learning needs, 125–6
  learning outcomes, 113–16, 119–20
  proofreading, 122–3, 142, 174
  technological assistance, 123–5
  types *see* assignments; essays; exams; practical assessments; presentations
  using sources, 121–3
  see also feedback
assignments
  critical discussions in, 140–3
  critical reading for, 139–40
  essay planning, 134–9, 143–4
  and individual learning needs, 143–5

  structure, 131–4
  types, 130, 133–4
'assimilating' learning style, 26
assumed knowledge, 66
attendance, 75
auditory learners, 77, 80, 103
authority of sources, 62, 141

Baron, J., 12–13
Beckett, Samuel, 180
Beesley, P., 46, 186
Belbin's Team Roles model, 87
bias, 11, 13, 44, 63
Biggerstaff, D.L., 166
Bloom, B., 27–8, 115
Boud, D., 201, 203, 206
breaks, in exams, 169
breathing techniques, 173, 174

Carless, D., 206
case study assessments, 191
CEL (collaborative experiential learning), 186–91, 195
Cerbin, W., 56
Chatfield, T., 39
Chen, P.H., 102
chronological notes, 64–5
CIA (critical incident analysis), 40
CIA model of reflection, 100–1
citations, 124–5, 204
close reading, 66–7
closed book exams, 168
closed-minded students, 16
cognitive fatigue, 16
collaborative experiential learning (CEL), 186–91, 195
communication in presentations, 160
communication styles, 95
comprehension, 27
conclusion of essay, 133
conclusions (informed), 12–13
concrete experience, 36, 184, 185, 201
confidence, 149–50, 155–7, 203
control, in CIA model, 100

Index

'converging' learning style, 26
coping strategies, 46, 173, 174
Cornell template, 64–5, 80–1
Cottrell, S., 9, 15, 66
counter-arguments, 12, 120
CRAAP method, 60–1, 62, 140–1
Craik, F., 29
creative production skills, 180, 184–5, 188–9, 191
critical incident analysis (CIA), 40
Critical Race Theory, 46
critical thinking
   actions to support, 16–17
   in assessed work *see* assessments; essays; exams; feedback; practical learning activities; presentations
   barriers to, 15–18
   benefits, 6, 14–15
   compared with reflective thinking, 38
   concept of, 8–14
   as continual, 18
   as employment skill, 211–12
   importance, 1, 7, 21–3
   in learning loop *see* lectures; seminars
   models, 40–4
   skills related to, 15
   synonyms, 11
   ten commandments of, *39*
cultural differences, 47–8, 95, 207
   see also ethnically diverse students
curiosity, 11–12, 13
currency of sources, 62, 141

deep learning, 29–31, 103
deep reading, 66–7
deeper thinking, 27–8, 153
disability-related learning needs, 45–6, 68–9, 83, 108, 143–4, 175
discussion
   in essays, 140–3
   following presentations, 159–60
   with mentors, 186, *187*, 189–91
   peer discussion, 82, 186–9, 205
   to develop position, 119
'diverging' learning style, 26
Driscoll, J., 37, 190

educational objectives, 27–9, 115–16
Elhinnawy, H., 47
emotional intelligence, 16, 82, 204, 211–12
emotional responses to feedback, 203
emotional wellbeing, 165
   see also health-related learning needs; stress
employment, 14–15, 211–12
engagement in lectures, 77–9
ERA model, 37

essay exam questions, 169
essays
   critical discussions in, 140–3
   critical reading for, 139–40
   definition, 130
   and individual learning needs, 143–5
   planning, 134–9, 143–4
   structure, 131–3
ethics, 9, 123–4
ethnic capital, 109
ethnically diverse students, 46–8
   and essay writing, 144
   and exams, 176
   and feedback, 207
   and language needs, 70, 83, 95, 144, 176
   and lectures, 83, 108–9
   and practical learning activities, 195
   and seminars, 95–6, 108–9
   student networks, 109
etiquette in lectures, 75
evaluation, 28
evidence, 119, 121–3
   see also sources
evidence section of discussion, 141
exam location, 168
exam questions, 169, 173
exams
   content, 166–8
   format, 168–9
   and individual learning needs, 175–6
   oral *see* presentations
   preparation for, 166–72
   reflection on past experiences, 164–5
   technique in, 172–4
excursive approaches, 31
experiential learning, 183–6
   collaborative, 186–91, 195
experiential learning cycle (Kolb), 35–6, 184, 185, 201
experiential learning loop, *28*, 51–2, 111–12
   stages of *see* lectures; seminars
experiment-based assessments, 191, 192
experiments, 180–1
extroverts, 81

fatigue, 16
feedback
   accessing, 202–3
   channels, 199–200
   hearing, 203–5
   implementing, 206–7
   and individual learning needs, 207–8
   principles, 199
   purpose, 198–9
feedback literacy, 204–5

feedforwards, 200–1, 206
Feeley, A.M., 166
Feipeng, L., 151
field trips, 180–1
Finch, J., 195
Fink, L., 88
five whys model, 42
Fleming, N., 77, 102–3
formative feedback, 200
4Fs model, 188–9
FRISCO model, 41, 106–7

Gergen, K., 7, 9
Gibbs, G., 37–8, 40
global citizenship, 212
Godfrey, J., 56
graduate attributes, 211–12
Greenaway, R., 188
group presentations, 148–9, 150, 151–3, 157, 160
group tutorials, 89
group working, 87–8
  see also peer discussion; seminars
group-based assessments, 192

Hadfield, P., 189
hats see six thinking hats model
Hattie, J., 206
health-related learning needs, 45–6, 83, 108, 175
Hopkins, D., 58–9, 64, 86, 95, 151

imposter syndrome, 89
inclusive curriculum, 47, 207
inclusive teaching, 83
individual learning needs, 44–8
  before lectures/seminars, 68–70
  during lectures, 83
  during seminars, 95–6
  for essay writing, 143–5
  for exams, 175–6
  and feedback, 207–8
  following lectures/seminars, 108–9
  for practical learning activities, 195
  for presentations, 160
  reflecting on, 125–6
  use of AI tools, 124
Indrašienė, V., 212
influence, in CIA model, 101
instructions for assessments, 117–18
international students, 46, 144, 207
  see also ethnically diverse students
interrogation, in critical discussions, 142
introduction of essay, 131–2, 136, 137
introduction of presentation, 151
introverts, 81, 82

Jasper, M., 37
'joining the dots', 119–20

kinaesthetic learners, 77, 103
Kipling Rudyard, 142–3
Klausner, E., 75
knowledge development, 27
Kolb, D., 26, 35–6, 184, 185, 201

language
  academic, 24
  in critical discussions, 142
  in exams, 174
  and individual learning needs, 70, 83, 95, 144, 176
  in presentations, 155–6
'learning by doing' model, 37–8, 40
learning categories (Fink), 88
learning disabilities, 45, 68–9, 83, 143–4, 175
learning needs see individual learning needs
learning objectives, 58
  of lectures/seminars, 67, 76–7
  taxonomy, 27–9, 115–16
learning outcomes, of modules, 113–16, 119, 138, 166–7
learning principles, 24–5, 57
learning styles, 26–7, 77, 102–3, 166, 183
lecture preparation, *101–2*
  active preparation, 56–8
  activities, 68
  and individual learning needs, 68–70
  learning objectives, 58, 67
  PowerPoint presentations, 67
  reading materials, 58–67
lecture recordings, 83
lectures
  active listening in, 77–9
  active participation in, 81–3
  characteristics of, 74–5
  critical thinking before, 58–67
  critical thinking during, 78–9, 80–3, *101–2*
  critical thinking following, 100–3, 106–9
  etiquette in, 75
  individual learning needs, 68–70, 83, 108–9
  learning objectives, 76–7
  note making in, 79–81, 83
  student engagement in, 77–83
Lim, H., 109
listening, 77–9
literature reviews, 134
location of exams, 168
Lockhart, R., 29

McNicholas, A.M., 46
main body of essay, 132, 137

marking *see* assessment criteria; feedback
May, C.A., 138
May, G.S., 138
mental health, 165
   see also health-related learning needs; stress
mentors, 186, *187*, 189–91, 194
mind maps, 65
Minton, A., 189
module learning outcomes, 113–16, 119–20, 138, 166–7
Moon, J., 23
motivation to learn, 25, 57
multiple choice exam questions, 169

Naylor, R., 198
norms, 9–10
Nosich, G., 41
note making
   after lectures, 102
   from reading materials, 64–6
   in lectures, 79–81, 83

objective structured clinical examination (OSCE), 192
objectivity, 12
observation-based assessment, 191
online exams, 169
open book exams, 168
open-minded thinking, 12–13, 23
oral language assessments, 192
orientation to learning, 25
OSCE (objective structured clinical examination), 192
over-scepticism, 120

paragraph structure, 141
participation
   active participation in lectures, 81–3
   active participation in seminars, 86–91, 95
   barriers to, 89–90, 95
   over-active, 82, 90
pattern notes, 65
PEAL method, 134, 141, 151
peer assessments, 192
peer discussion, 82, 186–9, 205
peer support, 107, 109
performance-based assessment, 191
phrasebanks, 142, 156
phrases, use in presentations, 155–6
placements, 181, 185, 190–1, 194, 195
planning
   of answers in exams, 173–4
   compared with preparation, 57
   of essays, 134–9, 143–4
   of presentations, 151–2, 154–5

plenary, 159–60
PowerPoint presentations, 67, 151
practical assessments, 191–4
practical learning activities
   collaborative experiential learning, 186–91, 195
   experiential learning, 183–6
   individual learning needs, 195
   skills practice, 180–1, 184–5, 188–9
   work-based learning, 181–3, 185–6, 189–91, 195
practice sessions, 180–1
pragmatist learners, 183
preparation
   before exams, 166–72
   compared with planning, 57
   during exams, 173
   for essay writing, 139–40
   for lectures *see* lecture preparation
   for seminars *see* seminar preparation
presentation-based assessments, 192
presentations
   advantages, 148–9
   assessment criteria, 150, 157–9
   characteristics, 147–8
   confidence in, 155–7
   content, 152–5
   and individual learning needs, 160
   method, 150
   plenary following, 159–60
   preparation, 157–9
   structure, 150–2
production-based assessments, 192, 193
productions *see* creative production skills
professional benefits of critical thinking, 14–15, 211–12
professional development, 212
proofreading, 122–3, 142, 174
purpose of sources, 63

questioning approach, 41–2
questions
   in exams, 169, 173
   following presentations, 159–60
   in lectures, 81–2

Race, P., 202, 203, 209
readiness to learn, 24, 57
reading (preparatory), 58–67, 119, 139–40
reading/writing learners, 77, 80, 103
Reasonable Adjustment Plan (RAP), 45, 46, 69, 143, 175
recordings of lectures, 83
recursive approaches, 31
RED model, 40–1

Index

referencing, 124–5, 159, 204
reflection
  on exam experiences, 164–5
  models, 35–8, 100–1, 186
  role of feedback, 203
  tips, 16–17
  as written assignment, 133
reflection-for-action, 18, 35, 36, 52
reflection-in-action, 18, 35, 36, 52, 85, 86, 193–4
reflection-on-action, 18, 35, 36, 52, 193
Reflective Cycle (Gibbs), 37–8, 40
reflective observation, 36, 184, 185, 201
reflective practitioner model, 35
reflector learners, 183
Reid, T., 58–9, 64, 86, 95, 151
relevancy of sources, 62, 141
reliability of sources, 60–3
reports, 133
research bias, 63
research literacy, 212
REVIEW method, 61
revision plans, 167
revision structuring, 170–2
role plays, 180–1

Sadler, D.R., 198
scaffolding of learning, 25, 51
scepticism, 12, 120
scheduling, of revision, 170, 171
Schon, D., 18, 35, 193
selective reading, 59
self-assessment, 125–6, 203
  see also reflection
self-awareness, 211–12
self-concept, 24
self-support see coping strategies
seminar preparation, *104–5*
  active preparation, 56–8
  activities, 68
  and individual learning needs, 68–70
  learning objectives, 58, 67
  PowerPoint presentations, 67
  reading materials, 58–67
seminars
  active participation in, 86–9, 95
  barriers to participation, 89–90, 95
  critical thinking before, 58–67
  critical thinking during, 91–4, *104–5*
  critical thinking following, 100–1, 104–9
  group working, 87–8
  individual learning needs, 68–70, 95–6, 108–9
  nature and benefits, 86, 96
  tips for participation in, 91
short exam questions, 169

'showing your working out', 119, 121
Sirazova, L., 149–50, 152, 157
six thinking hats model, 43–4
skills-based assessments, 191–4
skills practice, 180–1, 184–5, 188–9
Snead, W.R., 56
Socrates, 8–9
sources
  citations, 124–5, 204
  preparatory reading, 58–67, 139–40
  reliability, 60–3
  using, 121–3
spider diagrams, 65
stigma, 46
strategic reading, 58–9
strengths and skills, 87–8, 90
stress, in exams, 173, 174
success attitude, 46
summative feedback, 200
support
  in group work, 149
  peer support, 107, 109
  scaffolded learning, 25, 51
  self-support in exams, 173, 174
  see also individual learning needs
surface learning, 29
synthesis, 28
systematic reading, 59–67

task-based assessment, 191
teams see group working
technological assistance, 123–5
Tedam, P., 195
theorist learners, 183
theory, in presentations, 153, 158
thinking hats model, 43–4
Thompson, N., 100–1
Thompson, S., 100–1
threshold concepts, 30–1
Timperley, H., 206
topic choice, for presentations, 152–3
Toulmin model, 41
transferable learning, 15
translation, of reading materials, 70
Tripp, D., 40
troublesome ideas, 30
tutorials see group tutorials; seminars

understanding, 27

VARK learning styles, 77, 102–3
visual learners, 77, 80, 103
voice (academic), 24
volunteering hours, 181–2
Vygotsky, L., 23

Walkden, A., 46
wellbeing, 165
   see also health-related learning needs; stress
What? Model, 37, 190
Wingate, U., 132
Wong, B., 211
work-based assessments, 194
work-based learning, 181–3, 185–6, 189–91, 195
'working out' (showing), 119, 121
writing
   in exams, 169
   reading/writing learners, 77, 80, 103
writing style, 204
written assessments
   core principles, 119–20
   and individual learning needs, 125–6
   instructions, 117–18
   learning outcomes, 113–16, 119–20
   proofreading, 122–3, 142, 174
   technological assistance, 123–5
   types see assignments; essays; exams; presentations
   using sources, 121–3
   see also feedback

Xuwei, L., 151

zone of proximal development, 23

www.ingramcontent.com/pod-product-compliance
Lightning Source LLC
Chambersburg PA
CBHW051351070526
44584CB00025B/3715